# EUGENE A. SLOANE'S

A FIRESIDE BOOK
*Published by Simon & Schuster, Inc.*
NEW YORK

# COMPLETE
# GUIDE
# TO
# ALL-TERRAIN
# BICYCLES

A Fireside Book

Published by Simon & Schuster, Inc.
Simon & Schuster Building
Rockefeller Center
1230 Avenue of the Americas
New York, New York 10020

FIRESIDE and colophon are registered trademarks of Simon & Schuster, Inc.

Designed by Stanley S. Drate/Folio Graphics Co., Inc.

Manufactured in the United States of America

Printed and bound by Fairfield Graphics

10 9 8 7 6 5 4 3 2 1

Library of Congress Cataloging in Publication Data

Sloane, Eugene A.
    Eugene A. Sloane's complete guide to all-terrain bicycles.

    "A Fireside book."
    Includes index.
    1. All terrain bicycles.   2. All terrain cycling.
I. Title.
TL410.S55   1985       629.2′272       85-11877
ISBN: 0-671-53233-2

# Contents

# 6

# Introduction

There's a new breed of bicycle on the market that is fast capturing the interest of the American bicycling public. It's the all-terrain bicycle. Industry data spells out in hard facts that the ATB is the fastest growing segment of the bicycle industry.

The all-terrain bicycle, also called a mountain bicycle, is being purchased in record numbers by all types of riders. The outstanding comfort of this longer wheelbase, fatter-tire machine explains at least in part why it's fast becoming the favorite bike for just going around town, for commuting, for off-road cycling in the country, and even for distance touring on paved roads.

When I began research on my first of four books on bicycling, *The Complete Book of Bicycling*, back in 1967, bicycling was mostly an activity of youngsters. Relatively few adults were to be seen on bikes, and they often suffered abuse from motorists as they rode on city streets and country lanes. Bikes of that era were mostly single or three speed, heavy coaster-brake models. By 1971 the scene had changed drastically. Thousands of adults were riding higher performance 10-speed bikes. By the mid-1970s millions of adults were riding bikes, most of which were good quality 10-speed bicycles, and the bike boom was off and running.

Today I see another type of bike boom in the making. In a way it may even seem to be a reverse boom so far as the bicycle itself is concerned. I see adults as well as youngsters changing back to the fat tire bicycle so popular in the 1930s, but with a major difference. The all-terrain bicycle that millions are just beginning to enjoy is a far cry from the 60-pound ballooner of that era. Today's ATB is a precision machine that offers the exceptional comfort of the 60-pounder, with the high performance and lightness only today's high technology can offer.

## Many Helped with This Book

During the many months of research that preceded this book, I interviewed ATB authorities, went on mountain rides with them and was advised by them on every aspect of all-terrain bicycling. In particular I am grateful for the many hours they gave me from their busy schedules, and for this I wish to thank:

Joe Breeze, of Mill Valley, California, who reviewed and critiqued chapters 1 through 4, and to whom I am very greatly indebted for his insights and expert advice. Joe is one of America's top authorities on ATBs and one of the originators of today's ATB design.

I am particularly grateful to Glenn Odell, president of the National Off-Road Bicycling Association, Solvang, California, for his cooperation and assistance on off-road riding and racing.

To Gary Fisher (Fisher MountainBikes, San Anselmo, California), Tom Ritchey (Ritchey, U.S.A., La Honda, California), Charlie Cunningham (Cunningham Wilderness Trail Bikes, San Anselmo, California), Jeff Lindsey (MountainGoat Bikes, Chico, California), Scott Nicol (Ibis Bikes, Sebastopol, California), Steve Potts (Steve Potts Cycles, Mill Valley, California), and to Bob Wilson (Sweetheart Sports, Inc., Long Beach, California), who all make very fine hand-built all-terrain bicycles, go my thanks for the many hours they so graciously gave me in interviews on riding techniques and the mechanics and design aspects of ATBs, as well as for the photographs of riding and racing scenes they furnished.

Charlie Kelly deserves a "thank you" paragraph all to himself for his willingness to provide his expertise on ATB riding. Charlie is another of those pioneers of off-road riding who knows so much about the art and science of this new form of recreational cycling. He's the editor of *Fat Tire Flyer* (see Appendix).

My thanks also to Eric Koski of Tiburon, California, who provided much of the data on which of the many patterns and treads of fat tires are best to ride on which kind of terrain. John Olsen of Issaquah, Washington, and Glenn Erickson, Seattle, Washington, ran an observed trials event just for me, and provided the information on observed trials events in chapters 3 and 6.

Jeff Fleming of Modesto, California, wrote the section on making your own ATB from old bikes, my son Todd Sloane wrote chapter 6, on racing, and John Rankin, who runs a bike shop called The Greasy Wheel, in Plymouth, New Hampshire, was most helpful in providing data on the ATB scene in the East. And finally, John Ross of Berkeley, California, was my guide on mountain riding in the hills behind Berkeley and in northern California.

I also received much help from the Mantey brothers; John contributed his expertise in engineering and Paul his encouragement.

I thank them all.

# 1

# The Joys of All-Terrain Bicycling!

Welcome to the new world of all-terrain bicycling! Not since the 1930s has the bicycle seen such a radical change toward far greater versatility and increased riding comfort. This new breed of machine (Fig. 1) is fast becoming the new-wave bike of the 1980s. Although ATBs were born in California (where they are called mountain bikes; in Louisiana, they're called bayou bikes; on the beaches, beach bikes; and by commuters, city bikes), they are most definitely not a fad, like the hoola hoop and the pet rock. Almost every bicycle company in the United States, Europe, Japan, and Taiwan is busy churning them out. Bike stores around the country tell me they are selling like hot cakes. Buyers include kids who want an unbreakable bike (Fig. 2); parents who want to ride in comfort with a child on the back (Fig. 3); policemen for use on patrol duty; off-road riders in mountain (Fig. 4), desert, and seashore areas; commuters; hunting guides; fishermen who want to get out to remote trout streams; and park rangers who patrol their trails on them.

Just what is an all-terrain bicycle? It's a 10- to 18-speed machine with heavy-duty frame and components, and fat tires that will float you over terrain that would totally destroy a skinny-tired road bike.

Today's ATB has flat handlebars that give you an upright stance for greater visibility on the road and trail (Fig. 5). Motorcycle-style brake levers, contoured to your hand, are right there on the handlebars, easier to reach. Cantilever brakes (Fig. 6) are more powerful. The frame is of stronger tubing and has a geometry that is designed for comfort and safe traction, stability and steering control, uphill and down.

9

*Fig. 1:* This is a top grade ATB, for riding on the trail, paved roads, just about anywhere you want to go. The fat, knobby tires absorb road shock and grip the terrain firmly. The cantilever brakes are needed to clear the fat, 2.125-inch tires and give greater stopping power and control on steep descents. The flat bars permit an upright stance. This machine has 18 speeds, including a super-low gear that lets you climb mountains while sitting down.

*Fig. 2:* Youngsters like ATBs because these bikes are virtually unbreakable. Note the handy location of brakes and shift levers. Frame tubing is stronger than regular road bikes, as are other components.

*Fig. 3:* Parents can carry children in greater safety on an ATB thanks to its better brakes and stronger frame and, above all, because of the superior stability of this type of bicycle. This photo was taken in Carissa Plains, California. Note that parent and child are both wearing helmets!

**Fig. 4:** Climbing mountain trails is duck soup for an ATB, even when you have to go through snow. This photo, taken by Jeff Lindsey, who builds MountainGoat ATBs (see chapter 2), is near the peak of California's 10,435 foot high Mt. Lassen. Jeff and friends actually made it all the way to the top, totally astounding a pair of mountain climbers who had scaled the mountain to reach the summit.

**Fig. 5:** ATBs have flat handlebars that let you sit up straight for a better view of what's ahead. Note handy location of brake and shift levers.

*Fig. 6:* One side of a pair of cantilever brakes that give great stopping power on ATBs, and so safer control on fast, bumpy mountain descents.

## An Old Sport, and a New One!

The sport of bicycling goes back well over 100 years, yet the popularity of bicycle riding off the paved highways is a new one, at least in the United States. In England, however, the sport of "rough-stuff" riding on country lanes, mountain trails, and other unpaved terrain has been popular at least since the 1930s. "Rough-stuff" riders used conventional, skinny-tired road bikes for this sport, and a jolting one it is because these bikes do not absorb bumpy trail shock nearly as well as a good ATB.

All-terrain bicycling in the United States started in the early 1970s when a group of young people in Marin County, California, across the Bay from San Francisco, discovered the fun of "bombing" full tilt down the trails and fire roads of Mt. Tamalpais. The bikes they rode were not conventional road racing bikes, although many of them were bicycle racers and had good 10-speed road bikes. The preferred bike for riding down the 2,500-foot drop of Mt. Tam was the same 60-pound balloon-tire bicycle that was so popular in the early 1930s (Fig. 7). In fact, these bicycles became so popular that riders scoured bike shops in the area and picked them up for $5.00 or so. The most sought after ballooner was the old Schwinn *Excelsior* (Fig. 8). This bike had one

*Fig. 7:* Here's the granddaddy of today's ATBs. It's a 1930s bike with single-speed hub. Its owner has added a front centerpull brake and lighter rims and tires. Nevertheless, this clunker weighs in at around 50 pounds.

*Fig. 8:* The famous Schwinn *Excelsior,* another 1930s ancestor of modern ATBs. This bike was prized for its strength by early mountain-trail riders in California's Marin County.

speed, a coaster brake, wide, flat handlebars, balloon tires that imitated those that were so popular on cars of that era, and an imitation gas tank complete with working horn, which also gave the bike overtones of a motorcycle. Kids loved this bike. As a bomber for tearing down the mountain the bike was amazingly quick, had good steering response, comfort, and stability. Even its frame, although made of mild carbon steel, held up well.

Eventually the supply of these oldies but goodies ran dry, and those that were left began to break beyond the ability of frame repairers to patch. At about the same time, the mountain riders, who had to bum rides up to the top in pick-up trucks, began trying to ride their heavy one-speed steeds to the peak of Mt. Tam. But only the strongest could make it; even though stripped of the imitation gas tank and the heavy steel rack, the bikes still weighed around 50 pounds. Finally, around 1975, Gary Fisher (see chapter 2), a veteran road racer, got the idea of adding a multi-speed derailleur transmission to the clunkers, similar to the bike shown in Fig. 9. Now the clunkers could be ridden up to the top by everybody.

*Fig. 9:* This ballooner was upscaled a bit by its owner, who added derailleur gears, caliper brakes, and better rims and tires. The frame is basically a 1930s ballooner design, except for the fork, which is adapted from today's ATB designs. This clunker still weighs around 40 pounds, at least.

As these old frames wore out and fell by the wayside, premier frame builder and bicycle racer Joe Breeze built the first batch of some dozen true ATBs, using high quality steel but borrowing frame geometry from the Schwinn *Excelsior*. The bikes were quickly snapped up and the mountain bikees asked for more. This was in 1977, and the all-terrain bicycle, much as we know it today, was off and running. These early bikes weighed between 35 and 40 pounds.

Now that the frames were hi-tech and strong, the problem was what to do about the wheels and tires. It took awhile, but Joe Breeze and others, such as Tom Ritchey (see chapter 2) who began to make ATBs in volume, persuaded Japanese manufacturers to make aluminum rims, cutting about four more pounds off the ATB. By 1979, the heavy, dead, unresponsive balloon tires of the *Excelsior* era were replaced by today's light, responsive, skinwall 26-inch tires that cut two more pounds off the ATB. Now these bikes were down to around 30 pounds, and racing versions were refined down to around 28 pounds. By 1979 Tom Ritchey was in large volume production of high-quality ATBs, and by 1980 just about every major bicycle manufacturer, in this country and abroad, either began making them domestically or importing them under their own label from Japan and Taiwan. The rest is history.

## ATBs Are Versatile

What I like most about an ATB is its versatility. For me, this type of bicycle is ideal for riding over the serpentine twists of remote, narrow trails (Fig. 10), fast down mountain fire roads (Fig. 11), up steep trails (Fig. 12), as well as over bumpy city streets or smoothly paved highways. Compared to an ATB, a road bike is quite limiting. True, you *can* ride a road bike on gravel or on sandy, washboard country lanes. But you will be fighting to stay upright all the time because the narrow road-tire profile, with its smooth tread, has very poor traction and ground hugging qualities. And the shorter wheelbase road bike, with its hard-pumped skinny tires, translates every tiny bump right up your spine.

The versatility of an ATB is, however, only a means to an end. That end is to get you off the beaten path, the well-trodden trail, out and off into the wilderness and quiet. Hikers can only walk 2.5 to 3 mph, backpackers a bit less. But an ATB can go 3 to 8 mph, depending on the trail. On a five-hour trip, an ATB, even loaded with camping gear, can get you 25 to 30 miles out into the wild, whereas a hiker or backpacker can only get half as far, at best. These speeds and distances can, of course, vary considerably, depending on terrain. In the East, mountain trail growth is much more dense, trails are narrower

*Fig. 10:* This trail spells disaster for a conventional skinny-tired road bike, but an ATB picks its way surefootedly over this rocky path on the way to the summit of Mt. Lassen. (Photo courtesy MountainGoat Cycles.)

*Fig. 13:* Off-road trails are more open in the West, as this California trail scene shows. Trails are narrower and more overgrown in the East.

*Fig. 11* (opposite, top): The inherent stability of an ATB lets this rider, who is in an ATB race in California's Sierra Mountains, maintain control on this fast descent. Note rider's position, with weight on the pedals, which are parallel to the ground, so his center of gravity is as low as possible. He's actually off the saddle, weight on the pedals, which is the safest way to go down steep hills.

*Fig. 12* (opposite, bottom): Nearing the crest of Mt. Lassen, California, the rider is pushing hard up a slope on this pebble-and-rock-strewn trail. Much of the debris you see came from seven years of volcanic eruptions (from 1914 to 1921). (Photo courtesy MountainGoat Cycles.)

and more winding generally than in the West, so daily mileage is going to be less. In the West, where trails are often more open, you can get away from it all quicker (Fig. 13), which isn't to compare hiking and backpacking adversely with ATBs. Both have their place and I enjoy both. For me, though, the joy of trail riding on an ATB is the ability to challenge the wilderness, to get into the back country quickly and enjoy the scenery and the challenge of maneuvering my bike on the trail as I go. On day rides, particularly, you can travel the equivalent of two or three days hiking, and reach views and scenery impossible to get to any other way, except perhaps by helicopter.

I would also like to point out that an ATB, ridden with care on the trail, is no more harmful to the ecology of the trail itself than a hiker (Fig. 14) and certainly far less than a 1,500-pound horse and rider. On some clay soils in the West, I've ridden over trails after a rain and after horses had ridden on the trail. Those horses' hooves left deep imprints in the trail, like 3-inch-deep empty flower pots embedded in

*Fig. 14:* **Rounding a switchback on the road to the top of Mt. Lassen, California. Note that riders respect the switchback and do not shortcut across it, indicating good off-road consideration for mountain ecology. (Photo courtesy MountainGoat Cycles.)**

the soil. The ATB handled the trail O.K. and it left nothing but the faint impression of its tire tread behind. Now, to give you a feeling for the fun of off-trail cycling on an ATB, here is a brief description of a typical day ride.

## A Typical Day's Fun on an ATB

We started early in the morning from a staging area at Briones Reservoir trails region in northern California. The sunny blue waters of this 15-mile-long reservoir are surrounded by jagged, steeply rising, tree-covered hills. Mounting our ATBs, we pedaled off down a narrow, winding, twisting trail through pine, madrone, and buckeye trees. The trail, shared by hikers and equestrians, dipped sharply downward to the sparkling blue waters of the reservoir, then began to climb steeply. Compared to the road bikes we were used to, the 4 or 5 mph we traveled seemed at first like a snail's pace. But within thirty minutes we had left the hikers far behind. For the rest of the day, except for a pair of equestrians, we had the trail to ourselves. We were quickly deep in the wilderness, alone with the solitude of the mountains, the sun and the sky, and the animals.

There were no cars, no trucks, no motorcycles, no Yuckabagoes on the trail. We caught up to the two people on horseback, and as we came near them, one of us tinkled a bike bell to let them know we were approaching. The horsemen were cooperative about our mechanized form of travel and pulled over to the side of the trail so we could pass. A wave of the hand, a thank you, and the horses quickly faded to the rear.

In two hours we were nearly 10 miles into the park, and had climbed 1,500 feet high above Briones Reservoir (Fig. 15). We stopped several times to watch a bald eagle soar majestically overhead, riding the thermals, looking for food. Down toward the water we spotted a blue heron. A herd of deer watched us from a nearby ridge. As we bicycled, there was no sound except for the wind through the trees, the soft squish of fat tires on the trail, the occasional chatter of a chipmunk, suddenly aware of our presence as we pedaled soundlessly along the trail.

Climbing the steep slopes to the ridge top was slower, but made possible by the super-low gears of our 18-speed ATBs. Going down the sometimes steep incline of the mountain trail was much faster, but we had great cantilever brakes that kept our speed well under control. The knobby, waffle tread of our balloon tires seemed glued to the ground as we sped down the sandy trail, and the fat tires and resilient frame of our bikes absorbed the shock of riding over bumps and

*Fig. 15:* **Overlooking scenic Briones Reservoir in northern California, this rider takes a rest break after climbing to this overlook at 1,500 feet.**

stones. A safety feature we appreciated was the extra high 12-inch ground clearance of our ATBs which cleared ground obstacles. Best of all, the steering geometry (see chapter 2) allowed us to steer accurately and quickly around obstacles and over narrow, twisting trails.

## ATBs—Great for Commuting

Back home the next day, I mounted my ATB and commuted to work over rough city streets. I found very little difference in rolling resistance between my fat-tire ATB and my expensive, hand-built, narrow high-pressure tire road bike. Over a 10 mile ride I spent perhaps five minutes longer, at the most, to get to work on my ATB. But the way that bike literally floated over bumps, ignoring holes and junk in the road, turned what had been a jolting ride into a real pleasure. The ATB really, literally, turned those badly maintained city streets into as smooth a ride as you could expect from the surface of a newly paved road. I rode over stuff in the road that would have penetrated and punctured the thin tread of my high-pressure tires on my road bike. I liked the go-anywhere, gung ho attitude I experienced on my ATB. It was great to know that I could get away from a careless driver by riding over toward the curb without worrying about getting a puncture in this junk-strewn area. If necessary, I could easily jump a curb to avoid being hit, without damage to my ATB, and remain under complete control of the bike at all times. I would have bottomed out on my skinny road-tires and most likely have dented a costly rim beyond repair had I tried to pull a wheelie and leap a curb with my road bike.

## At Last, a Great Way to Ride in the Winter!

If you've ever tried to ride a road bike in the snow or on the ice you know how slippery and even downright hazardous such riding can be. Now, thanks to the ATB, all is changed. All you do is mount waffle tread tires (see chapter 3) on your ATB and take off. The fat-tire waffle tread, 2⅛ inches wide, takes you, as sure footed as a llama, over snow up to 3 or 4 inches deep (Fig. 16). There's more on winter riding in chapter 3, including information on studded tires and how to stud your own, for winter fun on hard packed snow and even on ice. Ever try racing on a lake! It can be fun!

**Fig. 16:** The fat, knobby tread of ATB tires gives traction in snow.

### Touring on an ATB Is the Way to Go!

I am simply entranced by the freedom, comfort, and the go-anywhere options that I get on most any kind of road or trail surface with an ATB. I have a wide choice of tire treads for mud, sand, hard packed dirt, or city streets. There are even combination tires with a high ridge for hard roads and an open pattern for the wilderness. (More on tires in chapter 2.)

The ATB for me is my ticket to absolute freedom. It's great to be able to load up my panniers with camping gear, strap on tent and sleeping bag, take off on city streets and wind up going over remote mountain trails or sandy, rutted side roads, far from the madding throng. And do it all in far greater comfort than on a skinny-tired bike that jars the back of your teeth on every bump, on roads that would rupture my road bike's frame.

It's not *just* that the ATB is so shock resistant and less fatiguing on any kind of trip. The ATB cuts its path true and clear through sand and mud, is able to ford rivers, bounce down hills that would send me spilling over the bars a hundred times over on a bike designed for smooth, shiny road surfaces. Traction is the name of the game for an ATB, and to try climbing a steep mountain trail with any other kind of bike is to me sheer lunacy. I am afraid that I have become addicted to my ATB, "fer shure," as they say in California.

You may know I have written four other books on bicycling. The first was published way back in 1970 *(The Complete Book of Bicycling)*. Two subsequent editions followed and the current version is *The All New Complete Book of Bicycling*, published in 1981. *Eugene A. Sloane's Book of Bicycle Maintenance*, 1982, is the most recent. All of these books were published by Simon & Schuster. They reflect some twenty years of adult riding experience, all, of course, on high quality, lightweight road bikes. I say this because I do believe there is a place for road bikes. If you just want to take long distance tours on smooth pavement, and promise never to ride on sand, or dirt, or in mud or water, won't miss the excitement of trail riding in the wilderness, don't mind the occasional flat, bent frame or dented rim, then road bikes are for you.

### Who Buys ATBs? Everybody!

In surveys of over 100 bicycle dealers, I found no pattern, no set rule as to who buys these fat-tired bundles of fun. Just about everybody seems to fall in love with them. A few trends did pop up, though. For example, women like the flat handlebars and the easier handling of these bikes. Parents like them because they can hang a child carrier on the back and carry youngsters (see Fig. 3 on page 11) and groceries in much greater safety because of the ATB's greater stability.

Youngsters I queried say ATBs are great because they are so much stronger. The 2.125-inch tires on the ATB coupled with the wider rims and stronger frames, they say, don't "break" as easily as those on road bikes. Kids can hop an ATB up and down curbs, over ruts and bumps, flop them on the ground and still not hurt them. ATBs are, literally, child proof, and that says a lot for their sturdiness.

One young man said he bought his because he's moving to Vermont (he was in Berkeley, California, when I met him on his ATB) and he will live on a farm accessible only by a rutted dirt road. He wanted a bike he could safely take on both the pavement and the dirt road.

Other adults tell me they like the ATB because it's the one bike they have in the garage that they ride most frequently. It's more comfortable, they say, and the brakes and shift levers are right up there on the handlebars, easy to reach. They like the upright position from which traffic can be viewed more readily.

Experienced bikees buy ATBs too. They use it as a second bike for the special joys of off-road riding, in places where riding a fine road bike would bring anguish to the rider when that skinny-tired bike bumped, slid, and jounced over the rough trail.

Sportsmen are riding them too. For example, it's becoming almost a common sight to see trout fishermen, fly rods and equipment strapped to their back or top tube, pedaling an ATB through the woods to remote mountain streams it would take a half day to walk to. Bird watchers are getting out on ATBs, to where the winged creatures are, and you can see the occasional hunter, weapon on back, cycling to meet his quarry. (One can only hope that the hunter is not mistaken for meat on the table by other hunters on foot.)

Newsboys and city messengers are out there doing battle with urban traffic on ATBs. Rangers in state and national parks make their rounds on them, and police are beginning to patrol on ATBs in a few cities.

Finally, with sales of ATBs zooming and dozens of new manufacturers adding them to their line, we should see more and more Americans riding these comfortable machines on the road, on the trail, and just around town.

## About Rolling Resistance

One look at the most aggressive of the tires on an ATB (Fig. 17) may lead you to assume that it has high rolling resistance, that an ATB would be a lot harder to pedal than a skinny-tired road bike. If

*Fig. 17:* **This is today's all-terrain bicycle. The knobby, waffle tread tires are designed for ground gripping on loose terrain. (Photo courtesy MountainGoat Cycles.)**

you confined that observation to the tire in Fig. 17, you'd be right only as it concerns city streets or smooth off-road trails. But if you compared the same road bike to an ATB with that kind of tire in mud or sand, you'd leave the road bike far behind, stuck in the mud or skewing wildly around in the sand.

Furthermore, if you took that same ATB, removed the knobbies and installed a combination trail and road tread (see chapter 2) *you'd be wrong!* With the combination tire, a good ATB is only slightly slower than a good road bike. For example, Joe Breeze, a gonzo downhill racer of the past decade, and one of the originators of today's ATB, did a comparison rolling resistance test. Every day for a full year, Joe rode both his road bike and his ATB over the same paved course of some 17 miles. His ATB was equipped with fat 2.125-inch tires, inflated to 70 psi, and also equipped with toe clips and straps. He saved only three minutes over this course on his road bike. Joe figures that the difference, on flat terrain, is about three minutes every hour. On a century run (100 miles) he finds little difference in the elapsed time on either bike, but a world of difference in fatigue from shock on the road bike vs. little shock on the ATB. Joe also notes that riding an ATB is less fatiguing than riding a road bike because on an ATB you can pretty much ignore irregularities in the road. On a road bike you have to keep a sharp lookout for anything that would puncture a tire or dent a rim. In addition, you will find that you almost never get a flat, if you use the right tire for the surface you're on and keep it properly inflated. Joe makes hand-built ATBs in his shop at 28 Country Club Drive, Mill Valley, California 94941.

### Bicycling Makes You Healthier and Happier (Maybe Even Wealthier and Wiser)

If you engage in regular, daily exercise, you can live a healthier, less stressful life. Bicycling is just such exercise. What's great about bicycling is that you can exercise as easily or as hard as you wish. Cycling does not put nearly the strain on leg muscles and ligaments as does jogging or running, for example. Yet you can get just as much aerobic fitness exercise by riding your bike as you can any other way. Here's what bicycling can do for you.

Cycling an hour a day can substantially decrease risk of heart attack, reduce hypertension (high blood pressure) caused by stress, and give you more energy all day long. This enjoyable exercise can help reduce or control your weight and control or end osteoporosis (calcium loss from bones that so often accompanies the aging process and that makes bones more brittle and more prone to fractures). Regular cycling exercise will make you stronger and help you feel better. For that matter, a healthier you will be more mentally alert as well as physically active. You'll be able to perform better on the job and with your significant other. A more alive you will have a greater attention span, better blood circulation. Cycling *can* make you healthier and happier. Here's how bicycling improves your health.

#### BICYCLING AND YOUR HEART

Heart disease due to build-up to fatty substances on the lining of blood vessels (atherosclerosis) can be prevented by bicycling, in six ways.

1. As you ride your bike, your heart beats faster to supply blood to your muscles. The increased pulse rate thus pumps more blood through the arteries, a blood flow that helps prevent the deposit of fats on the artery linings. If arteries become plugged the heart has to work harder to force blood through the narrower channels, thus raising the blood pressure to potentially dangerous levels.

2. There is good evidence that exercise reduces blood cholesterol levels, so there is less fat to deposit in the first place.

**3.** Bicycling helps delay the progress of hardening of the arteries, a process which begins at birth. Calcified arteries cannot carry as much blood as healthy arteries. If arteries are coated with calcium deposits, the heart has to work against greater resistance and the blood pressure can build up to dangerous levels. The danger is that high blood pressure can burst arteries in the brain (cerebral hemorrhage) and cause strokes or even death.

**4.** Bicycling helps create auxiliary networks of arteries and veins which supply blood to heart muscles, so in the healthy person, should one artery be blocked, the auxiliary arteries can take over to prevent damage to the heart (coronary heart failure).

**5.** One of the great stress relievers in this hectic age is exercise, particularly bicycling. Yet stress can cause situational high blood pressure. If stress is relieved, blood pressure drops back to normal levels. I have found that an hour's bike ride after a tough day at work is a great mood changer. Pedaling through the park, along a lake or a river, calms me down considerably, so that by the time I get home, I am ready to speak sweetly to people. I like to think that bicycling has helped reduce the number of people suffering from hypertension. The U.S. National Center for Health Statistics data does show that the number of people suffering from high blood pressure (160 stystolic/95 diastolic mm/Hg) dropped about 16 percent between 1971 and 1980, thanks to the nationwide emphasis on diet and exercise.

**6.** About 40 percent of the cardiac reserve is in the leg muscles. Cardiac reserve is the use of muscle tissue that helps push blood through arteries. As a pulse of blood flows through an artery, surrounding muscles expand. If these muscles are strong, they push back down on the arteries and help push the pulse of blood along. Cycling is a great way to build muscles in the legs and also in the upper torso, arms, and chest.

The emphasis on health that started back in the 1960s has done wonders for the American heart. For example, between 1970 and 1980 the death rate for all U.S. males dropped 21 percent, from 422 to 333.1 per 100,000, according to the U.S. National Center for Health Statistics. The drop for ages 25–44 was dramatic, down 37% from 57.3 per 100,000 in 1970 to 36.1 per 100,000 in 1980. And for males 65 and over, the drop was fantastic, down 15.5%, from 3,258 to 2,751.7 per 100,000. Women have always had a lower death rate from heart disease than men, but the drop in the death rate from heart disease for them was also impressive during this same period. For example, for women over 65, the rate dropped 12.3%, from 2,268.2 to 1,989.5 per 100,000. Did bicycling have anything to do with this major drop in deaths from heart disease? I like to think so. There's no direct evidence, but the fact is that the sale of bicycles jumped from 6.8 million in 1970 to a whopping 10.8 million in 1980, an increase of 59 percent! In fact, bikes outsold cars in 1980, since 8.9 million passenger cars were sold in that year.

Aside from heart-related illness, cycling just plain makes you feel better. You'll have an afterglow of well-being after a bike ride that carries you through the day. You'll be able to do a lot more physically, too. You'll be much more immune to heart attacks while shoveling snow or doing other unusually stressful work than a deskbound sedentary worker, for example.

Business has found that the cost of executive fitness programs (health club fees and the like) is cost effective in two ways. First, it keeps management healthier, so they live longer. Business has a major investment in the people who manage it, so fitness programs to protect that investment make a lot of sense. Second, the physically fit executive can work harder and longer. Since the physically fit person is more immune to the afternoon blahs, decisions are less likely to be made in a cloud of fatigue.

By encouraging executives to ride a comfortable mountain bike to work, the company saves in two ways. The company saves the high cost of health club fees, and they save the time the executive has to take off from work to go to the health club. It's a lot less expensive to provide bike lock-up, showers, and lockers than to pay health club fees. Executives have to get to work anyway. So why waste time on the train or limo, or in a health club, when both transportation and exercise can be accomplished at the same time? Makes a lot of sense to me.

I found, for example, that after I started to bike to work, I could carry a full head of steam all day. I saved time and money, too, because it took about the same time to bike the 10 miles to work as it did to take the train. Sure, the train got there in thirty minutes. But it also took fifteen minutes to walk to the train station from home, and another fifteen minutes to walk to the office from the station in the city. On the way, on my bike, I planned my day's work, and on the way home, thought about what I wanted to do that evening. I also saved the $2.50 train fare, which on a 48-week per year basis totaled $600. I amortized my commuter bike in one year that way.

### BICYCLING MAKES YOUR BODY TRIM AND LEAN

If you bike an hour a day, and do it vigorously, you will burn between 350 to 500 calories. If you eat your normal good diet (lots of veggies, easy on the red meats and fats) of between 1,800 and 2,100 calories a day, you should find yourself leaner and trimmer in a few months. It worked for me. After a couple of months of biking to work, I could take in my belt an inch and a half, and my nether extremities had melted away to a most satisfactory extent. I weighed about the same, though. What had happened was that the lard around my waist was replaced by muscle tissue in my legs, abdomen, upper torso, and arms. Biking is sure a lot more fun and an easier way to lose weight than dieting. Just eat sensibly, that's all.

## A MEDICAL CHECK FIRST

Before you start any bicycling exercise program, I urge you to get a thorough physical checkup. That way you'll have some assurance that your body can take the physical stresses of cycling.

After the physical check-up, start out slowly. Begin by cycling 3 or 4 miles daily, and avoid steep hills. Add a mile a day until you can cycle 10 miles without strain or pain. Go on longer rides, up to 25 miles and see how it goes for you. Work up to 50 and 75 miles a day. But don't sit around all week and expect to keep up with your bike club buddies on that 75-miler on Sunday.

## BICYCLING BRINGS VIGOR DURING THE AGING PROCESS

No matter how old you are, it's never too late to get in shape for your golden years. Although the younger you start laying up health credits in your body for old age the better, you *can* start at any age. The credits you get from bicycling add up to vim and vigor in your later years in addition to the immediate benefits. Many, many cases have been documented about the active life even octogenarians can lead if they ride a bike frequently. I know of people in their late seventies who have crossed the United States on their bicycles in recent years, at a pace that would put unfit younger persons to shame. There's at least one case on record of an 85-year-old man who did the century (100 miles). It took him a while longer than the record of well under four hours, but he did it inside of eight hours.

## CYCLING AND YOUR BONES

As you get older, your bones tend to demineralize. Calcium, instead of being deposited in bones to keep them strong, flows the other way. Bones lose calcium. The result is osteoporosis, porous bones that are brittle and break easily. The kind of exercise you get on a bicycle can prevent osteoporosis, or at least delay it until a very, very ripe old age. Also the stronger muscles attached to your skeletal framework help prevent damage to ligaments and cartilages of the knees and other joints.

## BALANCED MUSCLES AND BIKING

When you bicycle, you'll develop stronger muscles that will be better balanced, so one set won't pull against and harm the other. An analogy would be putting a jet engine in a light car. The jet's muscle would tear the little car's body apart. You want a balance, so one set of muscles will not be stronger than the others. That balance is what bicycling gives you. For example, adductor muscles of the leg, which help twist or turn your leg, will be balanced against equally strong muscles that pull the leg up or push it down. Unbalanced muscles can lead to extremely painful muscle tears of the weaker muscles.

## A WORD ABOUT CONDITIONING

Those of us who live in what is laughably called the "Temperate Zone" can't ride our bikes much in winter. To keep in shape during these inclement periods, you can ride a bicycle exerciser. This is a very boring operation. You can watch TV, braze a book holder to the handlebars and read, as I do, or clamp on a pair of headphones and listen to your favorite music. The problem, dullness aside, in indoor exercise, even on a bike trainer, is that the tendency (at least for me) is to goof off and not pedal hard enough to get much aerobic benefit.

The best way to discipline yourself to an aerobically meaningful workout on a trainer is to gradually work out until you have reached about 25 percent of your maximum pulse rate. You can find your maximum pulse rate by subtracting your age from 220, and determine your workout or exercise pulse rate by taking 75 percent of that rate. For example, say you are thirty years of age. Take $220 - 30 = 190$ as your maximum pulse rate. Your workout pulse-rate goal would be to reach $190 \times .75$ or 142.5 pulse beats a minute. If you work to get your pulse rate up to your exercise pulse, you'll be bathed in sweat at the end of a half hour, believe me. If your brow is cool, dry, and collected, you've been loafing along and not getting the aerobic exercise you need (assuming your doctor has said you can do it with impunity). You can buy a gadget that gives you your pulse rate while you pedal and, at the same time, alleviates some of the boredom by telling you how fast, how far, and how long you've been pedaling. Or, you can stop periodically and check your own pulse rate. Just put a finger on your pulse, start counting when the second hand hits a fifteen second interval, count the number of pulses for fifteen seconds and multiply by four. It takes real effort to boost your pulse rate to the exercise maximum, but it's worth doing.

Bicycling can truly be a major contributor to a longer, happier, healthier, and more active life.

In the next chapter, I will give you a capsule summary of the bikes I have tested, and review the pros and cons of the many fat tire treads on the market.

# 2

## How to Select the All-Terrain Bicycle That's Right for You

In this chapter I will discuss price considerations, how to fit the bike to your body, technical selection criteria, and ride test reports of the all-terrain bicycles that I have personally tested. Selecting the ATB that's best for you is not a simple decision to make. If you went according to price alone, you could regret the choice later on. If you ignored price and stuck to quality alone, or what seemed to be quality under the paint job, you could wind up with a bike that might be fine for commuting but terrible for climbing mountains. A combination of price, your intended use, and an analysis of the quality and design of the ATB should lead you to the right machine.

### Some Riding Experience Vital to Choice

Actual off-road riding experience is an important prerequisite in the selection of an all-terrain bicycle, even before you consider price, quality, or design. For example, before my very first off-road ride on an ATB I really almost scorned them. To me they were overweight, over-engineered adult versions of a kid's BMX bike. Boy, was I wrong! My first ride into the wilderness, some years ago, pointed up all the joys of off-road riding (and even on-road riding) noted in chapter 1. But until I had had actual riding experience, all my years of paved road riding across country, commuting, city riding, you name it, were almost useless when it came to selecting the right all-terrain bicycle.

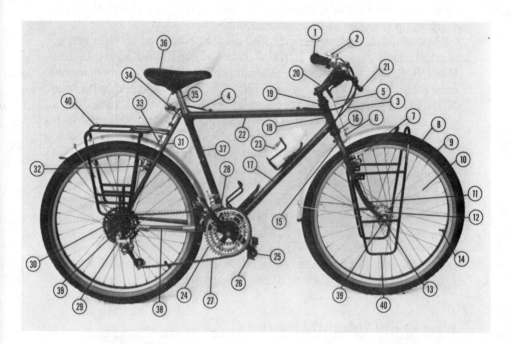

*Fig. 18:* Anatomy of an All-Terrain Bicycle: 1: Handlebars. 2: Gear shift lever. 3: Derailleur cables. 4: Rear brake cable. 5: Front brake cable. 6: Front brake crossover cable. 7: Front cantilever brake. 8: Knobby fat tire for comfort and good ground gripping. 9: Extra sturdy 2.125 × 26 inch rim. 10: Heavy gage steel spokes. 11: Fork blade. 12: Wheel hub. 13: Front wheel dropout (in fork blades). 14: Tire valve. 15: Fork crown. 16: Bottom fork bearings (inside steering head tube). 17: Downtube. 18: Steering head tube. 19: Top fork bearings (inside steering head tube), washer and locknut. 20: Stem. 21: Rear brake lever. 22: Top tube. 23: Water bottles in bottle cages, mounted in brazed-on fittings in downtube. 24: Triple chainwheel. 25: Crank. 26: Pedal. 27: Chain. 28: Front derailleur, specially designed for wide gear ratios and triple chainwheel. 29: Rear derailleur with extra long cage to handle wide gear ratios. 30: Freewheel. Many ATBs have a 6-cog freewheel which, with triple chainwheel, gives 18 speeds. 31: Seat stay. 32: Rear cantilever brake. 33: Rear brake crossover cable. 34: Quick release to adjust saddle height without tools. 35: Seat post. 36: Saddle. 37: Downtube. 38: Chainstay. 39: Front and rear wheel axle nuts, which lock hubs to dropouts. 40: Front and rear carriers.

I urge you to borrow an ATB and go with an experienced ATB biker before you make even a preliminary decision about what kind of all-terrain biking you think you want to do. If you put in even a few hours on an off-road bike trip, your ultimate ATB purchase is much more likely to match projected use and budget. Sloane's law of hobby purchases says that one's budget is infinitely stretchable to fit the perceived "need." I started out with a $25.00 Brownie camera and finished with a $1,500 Hasselblad. I began adult cycling twenty-five years ago with an el cheapo coaster-brake bike, and over the years worked up to bikes costing over $2,000.

How can you find an experienced all-terrain cyclist to help you get started? That's easy. Just join the National Off-Road Bicycle Association (NORBA). With your membership comes a list of experts in your area and names of bicycle shops that specialize in all-terrain bicycles. NORBA's monthly newsletter also offers lots of sound advice on all aspects of all-terrain biking. There's more about NORBA in chapter 4 and in the Appendix, including information about the membership fee and where to send your application. There is a magazine devoted (I use the word deliberately) to all-terrain bicycles. It's called the *Fat Tire Flyer*. It has a lot of good information both technical and on racing and safe riding techniques, and I also urge you to subscribe to it. The address is in the Appendix. Before you embark on your first trip, I advise you to review the basic off-road riding techniques given in chapter 3. You will need to know how to ride safely on bumpy descents, how to negotiate trails, how to use "body English" for accurate steering, to name a few of the riding techniques covered.

### What Kind of Riding Will You Do?

Quality and price aside, the first thing you want to decide when you look for an all-terrain bicycle is what kind of riding you expect to do. I know it's not always possible to predict the use to which you will put an ATB, in the long run. What you do need to decide is whether or not you will be riding on the flats, in the mountains, whether or not you will race ATBs, or if you just want a really super-comfortable bike for commuting to work and biking around town.

### Commuting

For commuting and biking about town, mostly on the flats but assuming the presence of some hills, you can scarcely buy a more comfortable, ideal bicycle than even the least expensive ATB. An

ATB for commuting and for short trips around town doesn't need really wide-range gearing, unless you live in a hilly terrain. Basically, so far as gearing is concerned, a low gear of say from 28 to 38 inches and a high gear of 85 should get you over the hills and through the woods very nicely, if you are riding in relatively flat country. (For an explanation of gear "inches," see the Gear Table and discussion on gearing on page 55). If you live in up and down country, like Pittsburgh or San Francisco, a low gear of 28 should get you up most hills.

## The Importance of Sizing

Before you buy an ATB make sure it fits you. You should know that ATB frame sizes are different from conventional road-bike frame sizes. For example, say you now ride a 22-inch road bike. When you straddle your road bike in your stocking feet, you should have at least a comfortable one inch or so clearance between you and the top tube. You may think you can order the same 22-inch frame-size ATB and it will fit you. *Wrong!* If a 22-inch road bike fits you, a 22-inch ATB will be from 1½ to 2 inches *too big* for you, because the top tube will be higher than your crotch. If you had to come down hard on the top tube to control your ride as shown in Fig. 19, you could be hurt.

The reason an ATB is sized differently from a road bike is that the ATB's bottom bracket (where the seat tube and the down tube meet as shown in Fig. 20) is from 1½ to 2 inches higher up off the ground than road-bike bottom brackets, for two reasons. First, on a rough trail you need the extra bottom bracket clearance. Second, ATB pedals need to be higher than road-bike pedals so they won't scrape the ground as you lean the bike into sharp turns on twisty trails.

Frame size, whether it be an ATB or a standard road bike, is given as the length of the seat tube, in Fig. 20. But since the ATB's frame has a higher ground clearance, the seat tube for the equivalent same-size road bike has to be shorter. The best way to select the ATB that fits you is simply to straddle the top tube (leave your shoes on) with both feet on the floor. Then lift the bike up and down to make sure you have at least a 1½-inch clearance between you and the top tube.

Another reason for having more top-tube clearance is that a lot of off-road riding, in narrow trails, on slow uphill climbs, involves shifting your body to correct for steering around obstacles. Of course if you have no intention of doing battle with the trail but will be mostly street riding on the flats, then you can get by with less top-tube clearance. Here's what to look for in an ATB once you have narrowed your search down to a few specific models in a price bracket.

*Fig. 19:* **This rider does not have his saddle down low enough, so he can't reach the ground with his feet. The proper position would be to have his saddle lower, with his center of gravity more over the rear wheel, and his body-weight on pedals positioned parallel to the ground.**

## About Seat Posts

By the way, ATBs need a longer than normal seat post that leaves more of the post in the seat tube, Fig. 20, for safety. As you will see in chapter 3, you need to raise the saddle to maximum comfortable height for riding on the flats and uphill. But for descents, you should

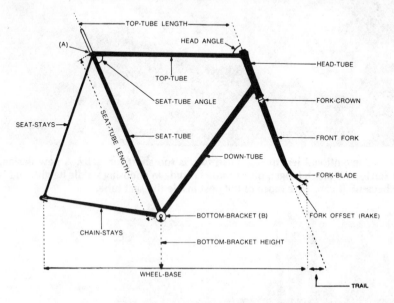

*Fig. 20:* Basic frame geometry. *Trail* is the distance between where an imaginary line drawn through the center of the fork touches the ground, and where a line from the wheel dropout touches the ground. It's called trail because the front wheel actually trails behind the line drawn down the middle of the fork. Fork *rake* is the extension of the fork where it bends.

lower the saddle so you can lower your center of gravity, for safe, accurate steering. This way you can smooth out the bumps by letting your knees bend, putting body weight on the pedals. If necessary you can also get a foot on the ground, to keep from going over the handlebars on a steep descent.

A new 273 mm seat post (Fig. 21) is now available as an aftermarket item from Sun Tour so you can get your saddle up as high as you like without danger of too little seat post inside the frame. You must have at least *3 inches* of seat post *inside* the seat tube for safety. Standard seat posts are only 160 to 185 mm long, (6.25 to 7.25 inches). They require that at least 2.5 inches be *inside* the seat tube (Fig. 22). So you really need a longer seat post on an ATB.

*Fig. 21:* Conventional length seat post, top, is too short for ATBs. A new design, from SunTour, is much longer, offers more latitude in choosing saddle height, and is safer because it can leave more of the post inside the seat tube.

*Fig. 22:* As shown, you should leave at least 2.5 inches of the seat post inside the seat tube for safety, particularly on an ATB.

## Handlebar Fit Is Important

Few of us have the same-length arms, torso, or legs. Now that you have selected the right-size frame for your leg length, you'll need to make sure that the width and height of the handlebars match your arm and torso lengths. If the bars are too far away or too low, you will have to position your body at an uncomfortable angle to reach the handlebars. If the handlebars are at the wrong angle for you, you will have wrist strain. There are a few minor adjustments you can make for a more comfortable handlebar fit.

You could raise the handlebars if they are too low for you, but not by much. You must leave 2 inches of the stem inside the fork tube (Fig. 22). Otherwise the stem may break off under the stress of riding. Chapter 5 has more details, including the necessity of readjusting front brake clearance if you raise or lower the handlebars. I urge you to read the brake section in chapter 5, should you move handlebars up or down.

You could move the saddle forward or backward by about 2 inches either way. But if you move the saddle forward, your center of gravity also moves forward. As you will see in chapter 3 under riding techniques, it's important to keep your center of gravity as far to the rear of the ATB as possible on downhill runs and for traction on uphill climbs, so moving the saddle forward is not always the best solution to getting your arms closer to the handlebars.

The best way to arrive at a comfortable handlebar fit is first to ride the bike. If you have to lean forward at an uncomfortable angle, the bars are too low. If you can't raise the handlebars, you need bars that have a greater degree of rise. If your wrists are strained as you hold the bars, you need handlebars with a more or less extreme angle. Fig. 23 shows three different handlebars. They have different lengths, different turns, and different heights. It's easy to change handlebars for ones that fit you. This procedure is explained in chapter 5.

One problem in changing handlebars involves the stem. There are two types of stems. One is called a *slingshot* design, because that's what it resembles (Fig. 24). This stem has a removable section that permits removal of the handlebar alone, and also lets you try out the fit of different handlebar configurations.

Another type of stem is called a *bullmoose* design, because the stem and handlebars are all one piece (Fig. 25). To change handlebars with this type of stem would involve changing both the stem and the handlebars, a more expensive proposition. Furthermore, as of this writing, bullmoose handlebars and stem are not available in a variety of configurations, as are the handlebars in Fig. 23.

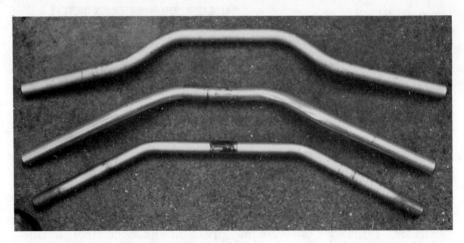

*Fig. 23:* Here are three handlebar bends, from Specialized. Different bends are useful to fit the dimensions of various riders.

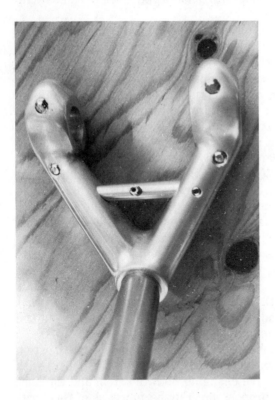

*Fig. 24:* Slingshot stem from Specialized lets you change handlebar angles or change entire bar.

*Fig. 25:* One-piece Bullmoose stem and handlebar is fixed in terms of bar angle.

## About Rear Dropouts

The rear dropout on a bicycle is where the wheel axle fits into the frame. Some ATBs have vertical dropouts (Fig. 26), some have horizontal dropouts (Fig. 27). Vertical dropouts hold the rear wheel in place, correctly aligned in the bicycle frame, under the extreme stress of uphill pedaling. But they do not permit the rear wheel to be moved horizontally. If you should break a derailleur on the trail, you will most likely have to manually put the chain on an intermediate cog on the freewheel (chapter 5 explains about freewheels). If the derailleur spring is broken, however, correct chain tension cannot be maintained on the chain, and the chain will jump off the freewheel cog, especially when you ride over bumpy terrain. With a horizontal dropout, you can

*Fig. 26:* Vertical rear wheel dropout gets a plus in keeping wheel aligned, a minus in terms of moving rear wheel to take out chain slack, should derailleur break.

*Fig. 27:* This is a horizontal rear wheel dropout. Advantage is that wheelbase can be adjusted to remove chain slack should derailleur break on the trail.

*Fig. 28:* Quick release lever used on road bikes. *Not* used on most ATBs because of possibility of lever striking an object such as a protruding tree branch on a trail, causing lever to open and wheel to fall out as bike bounces up over a bump or jump. ATB wheels are bolted into dropouts.

move the entire wheel further backward in the dropout to increase chain tension and help keep the chain from jumping off the cog. Horizontal rear dropouts do not hold the wheel axle as firmly as vertical dropouts. However, if you do a good job of tightening the axle bolts, the wheel should stay put and not move out of alignment and rub on the frame tubing. This is not as much of a problem with bolted axles as it is with the quick release mechanism (Fig. 28) used on road bike axles, because such bolts hold the axle in place much tighter than the quick release unit.

Here's a tip about chains falling off a rear or a front cog. Let's say you have just climbed a steep hill and are about to go down the other side. At this point, the chain will most likely be on the biggest rear freewheel cog and on the smallest chainwheel up front. This is a combination that gives you more chain slack than in other gear combinations. If you leave the chain in this position, you may find that the chain will jump off the chainwheel as you bounce down the trail at high speed, over rocks and other bumps. If the chain does bounce off, you will have to stop and put it back manually on the chain. To prevent chain bounce-off, shift to a higher gear as you begin your descent, to put more tension on the chain.

## Quick Check for Flex

A frame that's overly flexible will move from side to side at the bottom bracket when you pedal hard. You want a laterally (sidewise) rigid frame that will not waste your energy in flex. You want to be able to efficiently convert your muscle power into forward go-power. There is one quick check for flex you can make right in the bike shop. Put the pedals at the six o'clock position. Without mounting the bike, but standing next to it, push down hard on the lower pedal with your foot. Watch the bottom bracket (Fig. 20) area as you do so. If the frame shows much more than ⅛-inch sidewise deflection, the frame is going to waste your muscle power on hard climbs or racing on any terrain. Of course, there will be some sidewise deflection due to the softer balloon tires. I recommend you pump the tires up to 90 pounds to minimize deflection from that source, and take into consideration any flattening or bulging of the tire as you stomp on the pedal.

Another check for lateral flex is when you're powering your way up a hill. As you do so, look down and see if the chainwheel shows side to side movement. Watch the chain inside the front derailleur cage. If it moves laterally inside the cage, this could be another sign of excessive frame flex (unless, of course, you have a bent chainwheel). It's also possible to have chainwheel movement if the bottom bracket bearings are loose. Check for looseness by grasping both cranks, or the pedals, and wiggling from side to side.

## Stability Check

Ride the bike down a quiet, flat, smoothly paved street with little or no traffic, at around 8 mph. Remove your hands from the handlebar. The bike should not immediately weave from side to side, or head for the gutter. Steering should be self-correcting with a little balance assist from you. If not, you have a bike with super-sensitive steering that may be fine for quick, sharp turns on narrow trails, but bad for downhill runs. Here's why.

If you ride the bike at about 10 or 12 mph on a bumpy, flat road you will find that as the front wheel hits a bump, it tends to move one way or the other. But the bike was going straight ahead. How is this conflict of motions resolved? Ideally, you should get an assist from the steering geometry and be able to steer the bike straight. If the handlebar tends to twist away from your hands when the front wheel strikes a bump, and you have to fight to keep upright, you could face a problem on downhill runs.

On a fast descent you could easily get up to 30 mph or more. At that speed, if you hit a bump, an ATB with "quick" steering geometry can twist the handlebar from your grasp. The wheel will turn sharply, the bike will fall and you will too (Fig. 29).

*Fig. 29:* **This rider is skilled or lucky. In this picture, taken by your author, the rider did land on his feet, more or less, got up immediately and kept going in a race.**

What you need to look for is an ATB that gives you good stability under all conditions. The only quick way I know of to check stability is a road test. A reliable road test is the experience of others. Questions I'd ask riders about their all-terrain bikes, or their knowledge of what other riders have said, would involve handling, braking, steering stability, comfort, quality, durability, performance, and ease and frequency of maintenance of components such as derailleurs, hubs, headset, and pedals. I'd do this before deciding on a specific ATB machine. Remember, all-terrain bicycling is relatively new, and components are not at all necessarily equal to the job.

## Longer Wheelbase

The wheelbase of an ATB (Fig. 30) is 3 to 4 inches longer than on a road bike. The longer wheelbase not only gives you a more comfortable and stable ride, but it also gives you more options as to where you can place your body for maximum advantage. On steep descents you can place your weight back over the rear wheel. On hill climbs you can stand on the pedals and still get traction.

*Fig. 30:* ATBs have a two to three inch longer wheelbase than conventional road bikes. The longer frame absorbs more road shock so is more comfortable to ride. The longer frame also offers greater steering stability than shorter wheelbase frames on bumpy downhill descents. Wheelbase is measured from front wheel axle to rear wheel axle.

### More Road Tests You Can Do

Take the bike on a steep road, such as a fire trail. As you climb the hill, push hard on the pedals in the lowest gear. You should have traction; wheels should not skid. With your weight as far back as possible over the rear wheels on a steep downhill run, steer carefully from one side of the road to the other. The rear wheel should not slide out from under you. The front wheel should track where you put it. On the climb up, you should be able to climb in the lowest gear.

### Frame Materials

In a given price range, as noted earlier, you get pretty much what you pay for. Less expensive bikes have weaker, heavier, less expensive tubing of low-carbon steel. More expensive bikes use higher carbon steels. The best bikes use chrome-molybdenum double-butted steel tubing (Fig. 31), with higher fatigue resistance. Double-butted chrome-moly tubing, such as Reynolds 555mt tubing, is thicker at joints, where a greater wall thickness is required for strength, and thinner in the center to eliminate weight. There is an exception, and that's the heat-treated oversize aluminum tubing of Klein, Cunningham and Cannondale frames. These makers offer convincing metallurgical evidence that their frames are at least equal to or even stronger than frames of the highest quality steel tubing. Either builder will be happy to send you data on their metallurgical conclusions, based on stress tests.

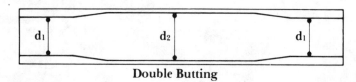

Double Butting

*Fig. 31:* Double-butted Reynolds 555mt tubing, used on fine ATBs, has double thickness at stress points where tubing is joined.

### The Heart of the Bicycle

The frame is the heart of a bicycle. You need a very strong frame if you intend to use the all-terrain bicycle on extended trips over rough terrain. Strength in a bike frame can be achieved two ways; with high-quality, high-strength steels, or with tubing that's weaker but thicker, so as to achieve the needed strength. Basically, there are four steel alloys used in making frames (aluminum and plastics are discussed elsewhere in this chapter). The frame can be made of very high-quality chrome-molybdenum steel (chrome-moly), which is an alloy containing carbon, silicon, manganese, phosphorus, sulfur, chromium, and molybdenum. The next strongest tubing is manganese steel, containing carbon, manganese, phosphorus, sulfur, and aluminum. Next lower in strength is high-tensile steel, containing carbon, silicon, manganese, phosphorus, copper, and titanium. Low-carbon steels are also used in bikes, but only for the least expensive models, where the tubing is made thicker and much heavier, in order to approach the required strength. This is one reason why low-cost bikes are so heavy and "dead" feeling.

## COMPARISON OF TENSILE STRENGTHS

(**Note:** Strengths are in $kg/mm^2$. If you wish to convert, 907 kg = 1 ton; 1 inch = 25.4 mm.)

| Steel | Before brazing | After brazing | % Strength retained during brazing |
|---|---|---|---|
| Chrome-moly double-butted | 82 | 75 | 91 |
| Chrome-moly straight-gage | 79 | 72 | 91 |
| Manganese double-butted | 72 | 70 | 97 |
| Manganese straight gage | 67 | 65 | 97 |
| High-tensile double-butted | 60 | 50 | 83 |
| High-tensile straight gage | 52 | 43 | 83 |

## TIG vs. Lugged vs. Lugless Welded Frames

How bike frames are joined together so no person can rend them asunder is a controversial issue among frame builders. I am going to try to step gingerly here and give the facts as I see them. There are three methods of joining bicycle-frame tubes. Properly done, any of the three methods make strong tube joints. Improperly done, any of the three methods can result in a weak frame. The three methods are: TIG welding (tungsten inert gas); brass brazing with lugs; and brass brazing without lugs (fillet brazing). Each method has its advantages and disadvantages.

A TIG welded frame (Fig. 32) is electrically welded in an inert gas (argon) environment. The tubing can be high-quality, chrome-moly steel or weaker, low-carbon steel. Done wrong, a TIG welded joint can have a substantially reduced life. This is because a poor TIG weld can undercut the tubing and cause a weak spot at the weld. Undercutting occurs when the tube is overheated to the point where tube steel actually vaporizes. You can usually spot an undercut TIG weld by looking closely at it. If the tubing next to the weld looks smaller in diameter than the tubing farther away, then the weld is undercut and the tube will be weaker by the amount of metal vaporized away from the tube. Obviously, with less metal, the tube is thinner and thus weaker. A severely undercut TIG weld can so weaken the tube as to

*Fig. 32:* **Example of a well-made TIG-welded frame. This is on a Ross ATB.**

cause frame failure, particularly on rough terrain. If the frame buckles, you can be hurt if you are going fast on a steep slope. At best you can have a long walk home. In my opinion, a properly TIG welded frame can be every bit as strong as a frame made any other way, but just a few ounces heavier. The result can be a high-quality bike at substantially less cost. Quality of tubing and components being equal, you are likely to save at least 30 percent of the cost of a good ATB if the frame is TIG welded.

A lugged and brass brazed frame can, if done right, be very strong. Done wrong, the lug can hide a poorly mitered tube. (A miter is where the tube end is cut to fit precisely against the contours of the tube to which it is being joined.) The lug can also hide a poor brazing job. A good lugged frame is shown in Fig. 33.

*Fig. 33:* **Example of a well-made lugged frame. This is a Trek ATB.**

*Fig. 34:* **Here is an excellent example of a fine lugless hand-brazed frameset. Note the fillets of brazing metal at the joints, where seat stays and top tube join the seat tube. This type of frame is very strong, at least as strong as the best lugged frame. It's also usually more costly because it takes more hand work to build up the fillets, and to file them to a smooth radius, as shown here. Such a frame can truly be a work of art, a fine example of the framebuilder's craftmanship.**

A lugless, filleted brass joint (Fig. 34) is right out there in the open. It's hard to hide a poor brazing job in this kind of joint, although it's possible under the brazing and paint. The main advantage of a lugless joint is that the fillet of brass is spread out over a wide area, thus distributing riding stress over a wider area. Lugless frames are very strong, when done right. In fact they are used on tandems as well as on single ATBs.

## Don't Scratch That Paint!

All-terrain bicycles, by their very nature, are much more prone to getting their paint scratched, chipped, and otherwise assaulted. These bikes kick up gravel and mud, pass through tree-lined narrow trails, fall, drop, somersault, and perform various other acrobatics in off-road biking. I think Ross has the right idea, chrome plate the frame and it'll stay that way. Well, of course, the chrome can be scratched through to the base metal. Then rust starts. But that's even more true of the best paint job. In two hours on a muddy trail, any ATB will look like a mud-caked beast anyway. These bikes were meant to be ridden hard, not babied for fear of a scratch. Well, I guess the fancy paint job does sell bikes in the store, at that.

## The Final Touch

Better ATBs have fittings brazed on to the frame. These fittings eliminate clamps that mar paint finish, let you hang water bottle cages, carriers, cable stops, and the like on your beautiful frame. These fittings, except of course cable stops, are threaded to receive an Allen bolt. (My gripe about Allen bolts is that bike manufacturers have yet to agree to a standard size, and they can be 4 to 6 mm.) Braze-ons can be added later, but you'd have to refinish the frame. An aluminum frame would have to be sent back to the manufacturer to have braze-ons attached by welding.

## What You Should Know about Warranties

There is one negative aspect of custom builders, or makers of ATBs that cost over $600. Some of the components, such as handlebars and even, in one case, hubs, and certainly the frames, are unique to the builder. As such, if anything breaks, you may have to go back to that builder for parts replacement or frame repairs. On the plus side, these builders, like many of the manufacturers of stock ATBs, usually offer a lifetime warranty on the frame. If the frame or any part of what's brazed or welded on the frame, such as the fork, should fail, the builder will fix it free. All the builders of over $600, high-quality, hand-built machines also say they put a high priority on getting repairs made and parts shipped back to the customer as quickly as possible. But the warranty, except Cannondale's, does not cover the frame's being run over by a car or other such accident. Nor does the lifetime warranty on the frame cover components such as hubs, bearings, pedals, or headset. These parts have the normal manufacturer's warranty of six months.

Some manufacturers of stock bikes, particularly in the over-$300 range, also offer a lifetime warranty on the frame. Cannondale offers to replace the frame even if it breaks through your own negligence, such as running over it in the driveway. You will have to pay Cannondale $150 for the frame, but considering the $400 cost of a new frame, that's a pretty good deal. To sum up, make sure you get a warranty in writing, understand what it covers, and keep a record of the purchase date, such as the dealer's receipt or your cancelled check.

## All About Gears (See Fig. 35)

In a number of places in this chapter I've talked about gears. It may seem to you that when an all-terrain bicycle specification mentions specific gears that you are stuck with those gears. That's not true. It's easy to make simple modifications to the gear train to obtain a lower or a higher gear. If the gears aren't low enough, you can have trouble climbing steep hills. If they are not high enough, you won't be able to get up the speed you are capable of sustaining with the superior muscular development you've gone to such trouble to obtain. I am here to tell you that the gears that come with the bike are not what you have to put up with.

*Fig. 35:* **Typical wide gear range transmission system for an ATB. (A) Rear derailleur; has long cage to handle as many as 38 teeth on big freewheel cog and as few as 24 teeth on small chainwheel. (B) Freewheel (may have 5 or 6 cogs). (C) Chain. (D) Front derailleur. (E) Triple chainwheel. (F) Crank. (G) Pedal. A 5-cog freewheel combined with a triple chainwheel gives you a 15-speed ATB. A 6-cog freewheel plus a triple chainwheel gives you 18 speeds.**

To change to a lower gear, all you need do is exchange a freewheel cog (Fig. 36) for one with more teeth. For example, say your ATB, or the one you want to buy, has a low gear of only 26 inches and you want to climb short, steep grades, and plan to be carrying around 30 pounds of camping gear. You would be quite right in changing to a 21-inch gear. Chapter 5 will show you how to change freewheel cogs and chainwheels. First, however, you need to know how to figure gears so you can select the freewheel cog or chainwheel with the number of teeth that will give you the gear you need. For an explanation of gear inches, see page 55.

*Fig. 36:* **The easiest way to get a lower gear is to add a freewheel cog with more teeth. Chapter 5 gives details.**

## HOW TO FIGURE GEARS

How many teeth must the freewheel cog have in order to get a 21-inch gear, if the small cog on the chainwheel has 28 teeth? To find the answer, just look at the Gear Table on page 55. First find the chainwheel column with the 28-tooth heading. Scan down this column until you come to 21. Look to the left, in the freewheel column, and you'll see you need a freewheel cog with 34 teeth. **Note:** Freewheel cogs made by different manufacturers are unlikely to be compatible. Check with the dealer. The same may also be true for chainwheels, if you go that route to changing gears.

## DERAILLEUR CAPACITY EXPLAINED

One final point. If you change to a lower gear, make sure the rear derailleur you now have will handle the extra number of teeth. You may have to change the derailleur. Derailleurs are rated by "total gear capacity." Total gear capacity is arrived at by subtracting the number of teeth on the smallest freewheel cog from the number of teeth on the biggest freewheel cog. Wait, there's more. Then you do the same for the smallest and biggest chainwheels. For example, say your freewheel has a small cog of 14 teeth and a big cog with 30 teeth. That's a difference of 30 − 14 = 16 teeth. Say your smallest chainwheel has 26 teeth and the biggest one has 48 teeth. That's a difference of 48 − 26 = 22 teeth. Adding both differences, 16 + 22 = 38 teeth. That's within the capacity of wide-range derailleurs, such as the SunTour *Le Tech* or the Shimano *DeOre XT.* However, total gear capacity ratings are conservative. I have successfully used much larger total gear differences. One of my ATBs has a freewheel with teeth from 14 to 38, and the chainwheel has 26 to 48 teeth. That's a total gear of (38 − 14) + (48 − 26) = 46. I had to add a few links to the chain to get good wraparound. That is, if I put the chain on the big front chainwheel, the one with the most teeth, and on the big rear cog, also the one with the most teeth, I would not stress the derailleur. Gear shifting works fine and I enjoy the advantage of a super-low 18-inch gear. Sure I could probably walk up a hill just about as fast with my bike in that low a gear, but I find it's a lot easier to ride up, particularly when I can sit down doing it and when I am carrying 30 pounds or so of camping gear on the bike. See chapter 5 for details on changing freewheel cogs and chainrings, chain links, and adjusting derailleurs, which you will probably need to do if you go to lower (or higher) gears. If you want to add extra links, it's a good idea to check chain wear first. Adding new links to a worn chain is not a good idea. Even using a worn chain is bad; it wears out the expensive chainring teeth faster because they are made of a softer alloy. You can up the total gear capacity from 34 to 40 of a SunTour *Tech, Moun Tech,* or *AG Tech* by adding a *SunTour Tech* extra-long cage. All you need is the extra-long inner cage plate. This is SunTour part no. 27909007 for all but the *AG Tech,* and for that the part number is 24149008. Use your old derailleur wheels, or take this opportunity to change to the new sealed derailleur wheels (that should be available at your bike shop).

## CRANK LENGTH AND GEARING

Another way to achieve a lower gear is to change the length of the crank arm. ATBs come with crank lengths of 170 to 185 mm. The larger the frame, the longer the crank. It's assumed that the bigger frames will be used by riders with longer legs. I have tried various lengths of cranks, leaving everything else unchanged, and I have two subjective, empirical observations on the results. First, the principle: Think of a crank as a lever, which it is. The longer the lever, the greater the force you can apply. Archimedes said, "Give me a long enough lever, and I will move the world." He didn't say where he would stand, but you get the point. My own tests showed that for every 5 mm of greater crank length, I got the equivalent of about five inches of lower gear. Say my chain is on the 34-tooth freewheel cog and on the 26-tooth chainwheel. From the Gear Table below you can see that this gives me a 20-inch gear. Changing cranks from 170 to 175 mm added another 5 inches to my gear, in terms of leverage. I could climb hills more easily with the longer cranks. I tried a 180 mm crank and found that my legs weren't long enough to use them efficiently for hill climbing or pedaling on the flats, with the saddle at maximum height. My second empirical observation is that changing crank lengths is an expensive way to add low gearing. You have to buy a complete new set—spindle, bearings, cranks, chainwheel, the works—and that's around $70. If you want to go this route, I'd wait at least until these parts need replacing.

## GEAR TABLE FOR ALL-TERRAIN BICYCLES WITH 26-INCH WHEELS*

| Number of Freewheel Teeth | Number of Chainwheel Teeth | | | | | | |
|---|---|---|---|---|---|---|---|
| | 26 | 28 | 36 | 38 | 40 | 46 | 48 |
| 13 | 52 | 56 | 72 | 76 | 80 | 92 | 96 |
| 14 | 48 | 52 | 67 | 71 | 74 | 85 | 89 |
| 15 | 45 | 49 | 62 | 66 | 69 | 80 | 83 |
| 16 | 42 | 46 | 59 | 62 | 65 | 75 | 78 |
| 17 | 40 | 43 | 55 | 58 | 61 | 70 | 73 |
| 18 | 38 | 40 | 52 | 55 | 58 | 66 | 69 |
| 19 | 36 | 38 | 49 | 52 | 55 | 63 | 66 |
| 21 | 32 | 35 | 45 | 47 | 50 | 57 | 59 |
| 22 | 31 | 33 | 43 | 45 | 47 | 54 | 57 |
| 23 | 30 | 32 | 41 | 43 | 45 | 52 | 54 |
| 24 | 28 | 30 | 39 | 41 | 43 | 50 | 52 |
| 28 | 24 | 26 | 33 | 35 | 37 | 43 | 45 |
| 30 | 23 | 24 | 31 | 33 | 35 | 40 | 42 |
| 32 | 21 | 23 | 29 | 31 | 33 | 37 | 39 |
| 34 | 20 | 21 | 28 | 29 | 31 | 35 | 37 |
| 38 | 18 | 19 | 25 | 26 | 27 | 31 | 33 |

*Gear tabulations are rounded off to the nearest whole number. Differences in the diameters of 1.50, 1.75 and 2.125 tires have not been calculated for this table because they are so small.

Using the above table you can calculate your own gear by multiplying the wheel diameter (26) by the number of teeth in the chainwheel and dividing that result by the number of teeth in the freewheel. If you have a 30-tooth chainwheel, and a 40-tooth freewheel, your gear would be $(26 \times 30) \div 40 = 19.5$ inches of gear. Let's call it 20 inches.

### NOW ABOUT THOSE INCHES

When referring to gearing, the word "inches" is a reference that comes from the high-wheeler, or Penny Farthing of the 1880s. It had a tiny rear wheel and a huge front wheel (or vice versa, as in Fig. 37). Pedals were attached to the big wheel. No chains, no gears, just direct drive. The bigger the front wheel diameter, the faster the bike would go, if the rider had the strength. The smaller the wheel, the easier the bike would go uphill. The bikes were built so a person could use the biggest wheel (i.e. the highest gear) that could be straddled. The backbone frame that curved around next to this large wheel, and the saddle too, was as close as possible to this wheel, to permit the rider to utilize the highest gear possible. Joe Breeze, a pioneer in the

*Fig. 37:* The concept of gears in "inches" used today comes from the High Wheeler of yesteryear, when the bigger the wheel diameter, the faster you could pedal, but the smaller the wheel diameter, the easier you could pedal uphill. High Wheeler wheel size was usually selected as the biggest the rider could manage, a function of his leg length.

sport of off-road bicycling, points out that this is where the term "high gear" originated, and certainly it preceded the automobile by at least a decade. On a 60-inch Columbia high-wheeler, the rider would be quite far from the ground, and literally astride the high gear, the big wheel. So Penny Farthings were sized by the diameter of the front wheel. This out-moded, archaic concept of figuring gears in "inches" has stuck, and we are all stuck with it. But now you know that if someone says he's riding a 26-inch gear, you know he's geared down to go up hills.

One further point about gears. You will note that in the Gear Table on page 55 there are some repetitions. For example, the gear "52" appears in various places. Obviously a number of different combinations of chainwheel and freewheel teeth will give you the same gear. In selecting your gear, try to avoid duplications, or even close relationships. You don't want too big a jump, either, at least not in the three higher freewheel gears, or four if you have a 6-cog freewheel.

Workable gear combinations are, for a 15-speed ATB (triple chainwheel, 5 freewheel cogs): 26-, 38-, and 42-tooth chainwheels and 13-, 16-, 20-, 26-, and 32-tooth freewheel cogs. This combination gives a low gear of 22 and a high gear of 88. For an 18-speed ATB (triple chainwheel, 6 freewheel cogs), good combinations are: 28-, 36-, and 46-tooth chainwheels and 14-, 17-, 20-, 24-, 28-, and 34-tooth freewheel cogs. This combination gives a low gear of 22 and a high gear of 89.

## Biopace Chainwheels

Shimano has recently introduced a triple chainwheel set they call the *Biopace*. It's computer designed to even out your pedaling stroke. To quickly sum up the jillion words about this product in the literature, what it does is let you apply muscle power more evenly around the pedal stroke. Next time you're out on the bike, feel how your legs apply power as the cranks rotate. You will notice that there's a sort of dead spot at the 12:00 o'clock and 6:00 o'clock positions, where your legs seem just to drag around for a few degrees. The computer designed shape of the Biopace lets you pedal more efficiently, in my experience. Here's why.

On ride tests, I found the Biopace a help on hill climbs because it gives me power around the clock and because, by smoothing out my pedal stroke, I could keep slow-speed balance easier. On the flats and on downhill runs the outer, bigger ring also gave smoother pedaling. The only drawback I have found to the Biopace (it's a minor one) is that the inner ring is only available with 28 teeth. Shimano people say there's no plan now to make it with 26 teeth because the mounting bolt would come too close to the chainwheel. A word of caution: Don't mix round and Biopace chainwheels on the same chainset (you can buy individual Biopace chainwheels). Biopace chainwheels will fit Shimano, Specialized, and Sugino triple cranksets.

## Sealed vs. Conventional Bearings

Some ATBs offer sealed bearings as a feature. I certainly would not let that sway me as a final buy decision. First of all, there's no such thing as a sealed bearing. The concept is nice, I'll admit, particularly on an ATB that you'll be running through mud, sand, water, and assorted grit. Sealed-bearing people tell you that the bearing won't need lubrication for years, or for some figure like 5,000 miles. That's not even true for road bikes, let alone all-terrain bicycles. First, let's look at what a sealed bearing is.

A sealed bearing is nothing more or less than a small bearing in a self-contained shell (Fig. 38). This is the type of bearing in, for example, a residential warm-air furnace-blower motor, or a bench grinder. It has conventional, round, ball bearings, in a retainer, inside a round

*Fig. 38:* **Some ATBs come with sealed bearing wheel hubs. This photo shows the sealed bearings of one such hub, made by Phil Wood.**

race. It also has neoprene seals pressed into place on one or both sides, which constitutes the "seal." Obviously fine particles of dust, grit, and water can penetrate around the edges of the seal where it fits into the bearing, and also around the axle. These bearings can be relubricated, up to a point, as I will discuss in detail in chapter 5. The major drawback to some of these bearings is that they are not all user friendly. Some sealed bearing hubs and bottom-bracket bearings, for example, cannot be replaced by the average bike owner, without an arbor press (a machine shop tool) or special tools, or both. Some bearings are user removeable, but not easily. And unless you are careful, it's easy to overtighten bearing retainer bolts and exert excessive side loading on the bearings, which they are not designed to carry. Fortunately, sealed bearings seldom fail suddenly. The failure is more like a long, lingering illness. Sealed bearings are used in wheel hubs, bottom brackets, headsets, and rear derailleur jockey wheels. You should check all sealed bearings on your ATB before every ride. If you feel grating or grittiness, the bearing should be cleaned, relubricated or changed, if possible. Check also for sideplay, which cannot be adjusted out of a sealed bearing. The bearing should turn smoothly and easily, without binding. It's pretty unlikely a sealed bearing will fail you on the trail, far from a bike shop. But it pays to check them often just in case.

Conventional cone, cup, and loose bearings, however, are easy to maintain and can be worked on in the field. The better of such bearing systems, when correctly adjusted (chapter 5), offer at least as low a rolling resistance as sealed bearings. The newer crop of conventional cup and ball bearings also have excellent labyrinth seals, which approach sealed-bearing protection against the elements, without the hassles of sealed-bearing maintenance.

## Primer on Fat Tire Selection

There are four basic fat-tire tread patterns in each of the three tire widths on the market, and there is some overlap between them. Which of these treads you use depends on the road or trail surface you ride on. Remember, too, that these tires are much easier to change than skinny high-pressure tires on road bikes. While you're still in the store, it can save you time if, at least, you buy a pair of the dual-purpose tires that are suitable for both road and trail (if the bike you want doesn't have them on already).

The fat tire widths are 1.50, 1.75, and 2.125 inches. The 2.125-inch size is best for road and trail shock absorbance. For paved road use, you can cut rolling resistance by pumping these tires up to between 60 and 90 pounds of pressure. For maximum traction in off road use, stay with the lower limit of 30 to 40 pounds of pressure, as printed on the tire side wall. You can even go down to 20 psi if you are not going to be hitting big rocks or other such obstacles. The two smaller-width tires offer a stiffer, harsher ride than the 2.125 tire. I simply don't like the 1.50-inch tire at all for any kind of ATB riding, but they are useful for racing.

### Tires to Use on Specific Surfaces

A skinside tire is not a skinside design. It's one without the tread coming all the way down the side. The ancestor to today's skinside tires is the Carlisle TRA shown in Fig. 39. This is a heavy, very dead, very slow tire you'd only want to use if you were faced with riding over a lot of shale and rock, such as around a quarry. This tire has sidewalls covered with a thick layer of rubber that cuts its resiliency way down. It's the toughest tire on the market, but it has weak sidewalls. Its maximum safe pressure is 40 psi. Note that none of the

*Fig. 39:* **This Carlisle TRA is the ancestor of today's light, more flexible fat tires used on ATBs. This tire is very tough, but gives a "dead" ride due primarily to the heavy layer of rubber extending down sidewalls.**

*Fig. 40:* IRC Racer X-1 has an open pattern, ideal for snow and mud.

tread extends to the side of the tire, so it would not be a good one to use for high speed cornering on loose soil.

The IRC Racer X-I (Fig. 40) has the most open tread of all ATB tires. This waffle, knobby design is the most aggressive made. It has the largest and tallest knobs on the market. It is preferred for use mainly on the front tire to insure that the front wheel does not break loose (see chapter 3) and cause you to lose control. This is an excellent mud and snow tire. Its main drawbacks are lots of noise and high rolling resistance on paved roads.

A somewhat similar tire is the Competition III (Fig. 41), from Specialized Bicycle Imports. This tire has a uniform row of knobs on the top so it can be used on paved surfaces as well as off-road. However, the rubber compound is very soft, so it won't last long on the pavement.

Another excellent tire in loose soil and mud is Specialized's Tri-Cross (Fig. 42). That tire has a specially designed knob to throw off dried mud which would otherwise reduce road adhesion and traction. These are the tires I ride in the snow. For more snow or ice traction you could do what the men of Crested Butte, Colorado, do. Screw sheet metal screws into the tread knobs, and protect the inside of the tire where screws come through with a layer of Mr. Tuffy tire liner, available from your bike shop. You can use this liner to protect against flats in thorn country, too. Commuters use this tire liner in city riding, where they sometimes can't avoid glass and other sharp objects, but simply don't have time to fix a flat on the way to work. The trade-off

*Fig. 41:* Specialized Competition III is made for use on both paved and trail surfaces.

*Fig. 42:* A Tri-Cross ATB tire from Specialized Bicycle Imports. Excellent for muddy trail riding. Tread is designed to throw off dried mud that might cut road adhesion.

here is that the thick lining gives you a deadened ride, with less shock absorption by the fat fires.

The Cycle Pro Snakebelly (Fig. 43) is the first skinside, lightweight tire on the market, circa 1978. It saddens me to hear from bike shops around the country that this trendsetter may be discontinued. It's an excellent all-purpose tire with good road adherence qualities in loose dirt. Its closely spaced knobs cut rolling resistance on the highway. If you have to ride in the dirt and on the paved road consistently, this would be a good tire to use. Specialized's Crossroads (Fig. 44) is also an excellent combination tire. It has a more closely spaced top ridge that gives less rolling resistance than the Snakebelly, yet has knob-

*Fig. 43:* Cycle Pro's Snakebelly is an excellent all-purpose tire.

*Fig. 44:* Specialized's Crossroads is another good all-around tire.

*Fig. 45:* This Streetstomper tire from Specialized is ideal for city street riding. Its smoother tread cuts rolling resistance. The fatter tire soaks up road shock for a more comfortable, smoother ride.

bies on the side for good traction in loose soil, even on sharp, fast turns. Another excellent combination tire is the IRC Mountain Trek. This tire has a wider top ridge than any of the above tires, and more closely spaced knobs on the sides. The trade-off here is that the center ridge, as in all such tires, gives relatively poor traction, especially while climbing on loose soil trails. Specialized's Streetstomper (Fig. 45) is an excellent tire for paved-road riding. It gives you fat tire comfort plus low rolling resistance. It's not designed for off-road trail use.

### Accessories to Buy While in the Shop, and Why

Eventually you'll want to go on a long trip in the wilds, I hope. For such a trip you will at least want to carry food, rain gear, and perhaps a stove. For longer trips you'll need to bring along a tent, sleeping bag, more food and cooking gear, tools and spare parts, to name a few of the basics. To carry all this stuff you will need a rack which is mounted on the bike frame (Fig. 46) and bike packs which are mounted on the rack (Fig. 47).

*Fig. 46:* A close-up of typical brazed-on fittings for mounting a bike rack. Fittings are brazed onto seat stays.

*Fig. 47:* This multipocket bike pack is strapped securely to a hand-made Bruce Gordon rack, which is bolted to fittings brazed on the seat stays.

While the bike is still in the shop and your checkbook is at the ready, that is the best time to buy a rack and set of packs. This is because ATBs are still fairly new to the bicycling scene, and not every rack will fit every ATB frame. You should make sure the rack you buy fits the bike you buy, and the dealer should demonstrate this fit. Furthermore, some bike packs interfere with cantilever brakes. I suggest you have the dealer mount a rack on both front and rear of the bike. Then you can mount a set of front and rear packs and check that they clear all bike moving parts including brakes, wheels, and the pedals. The better ATBs have brazed on fittings for mounting a rear bike rack (Fig. 48) and sometimes a front rack as well.

You will need tools for routine maintenance as well as for on-the-trail emergency repairs. Some parts, such as hubs, headsets, and bottom brackets, may also need special tools, and it will save you a trip back to the shop to get them all at the same time. See chapter 4 for a list of recommended tools.

You should not go out without a patch kit and I would also take along at least one spare tube. A frame mounted pump is also necessary, of course. You may need special brackets from your dealer for mounting the pump. You can get by without a pump if you use a carbon-dioxide-cartridge inflator. It is possible to obtain an adapter for Presta valves. The drawback to using $CO_2$ cartridges is that if you

*Fig. 48:* Front fork of an ATB showing how front rack and fender can be mounted. Fender struts are fastened to brazed-on fitting on rack. Top of fender is fastened to fork crown. Rack is mounted on fork blades by clamp-on fittings. (Some ATBs have brazed-on fittings so clamps aren't needed. Such fittings can be ordered when buying more costly frames.)

use them to find a puncture, you will consume an entire cartridge each time, and that's expensive. Once the cartridge is punctured, it can't be resealed. They will work to pump up a spare tube, though. If you go this route, I recommend the SpAir inflator. It has a special fixture that you screw down tight on the valve, allowing you to insert the cartridge, pull a cord, and inflate the tire. You will have to use two cartridges to fill a fat tire, though. The SpAir is made by Code Mfg., Inc.

A bell is a wise and inexpensive investment in good will on the trail. It can be mounted on the handlebars. Its gentle tinkle tells the hiker or other person ahead that a bicycle is coming up.

Fenders are available for fat-tire bikes (Fig. 49). You *can* ride in rain, snow, and loose mud without them, but who wants a streak of water or mud up the back and in the face? They're great for snow, too. I use the aluminum fenders from Specialized, which fit perfectly, with plenty of clearance to prevent mud or snow build-up.

## Price Considerations

All-terrain bicycles cost anywhere from $150 for a utility version, to $1,500 or more for a machine of expedition quality. Within this price stretch I have arbitrarily broken down ATB's into three price

*Fig. 49:* **Fenders are a good idea if you ride in the rain and mud. They keep most of the greasy, clothes-staining, street rainwater off your clothes. Fenders also help protect bottom bracket and headset bearings from water and mud. Note: ATBs require special wide fenders that fit over their fat tires.**

brackets: less than $300, from $301 to $600, and over $600. Below is a general discussion of what you will find in each category. After that I will give you results of ride tests and information about models I can recommend.

### UNDER $300 ATBs

Generally, the bikes in the lower range of the "under $300" price bracket have weaker frames, poorer components, and are heavier (34 to 44 pounds) than the bikes in the upper range of this bracket. Yet even the heaviest, clunkiest ATB is stronger than comparably priced road bikes. They're great for teenagers. For the past year, every time I saw a teenage boy on an ATB I asked him why. Always the answer was "This is the first bike I've ever owned that doesn't break on me." These inexpensive tanks are also fine for delivering newspapers and for urban messenger services.

At the upper end of this price spectrum, ATBs under $300 can offer surprisingly good performance, even with somewhat heavier frames and components. Not all bikes in this price bracket are alike, either. Far from it. For example, some of them, even in the $250 range, have heavily chromed steel wheel rims that add upwards of five to eight pounds to the bike. Chromed steel rims also have considerably less stopping power when wet. Finally, some of the frames are made of weaker low- or mild-carbon steel. For example, I noticed that after a rough race in the Sierra, a few of the less expensive bikes had hairline cracks in the seat tube. The cracks were evidence of metal fatigue that occurred as the seat tubes were stressed by frequent use of the seat post binder quick-release bolt (Fig. 50). The upper end of the seat tube should, ideally, be reinforced to prevent such metal fatigue. Most ATBs have (and should have) a quick release seat post binder bolt, so the rider can quickly move the saddle up or down while on the trail. *Up* for hill climbing and flat terrain, *down* to get the rider's center of gravity lower over the rear wheel for better control.

### ATBs IN THE $301 TO $600 RANGE

All-terrain bicycles in the $301 to $600 range offer excellent value and performance for the money. Differences between them are basically in the quality of components, frame material quality, and strength. There are some differences in frame geometry that affect stability, quickness, and accuracy of steering and, to some extent, frame stiffness, which I will review later on in this chapter.

### OVER $600 ATBs

Some machines in the $600 plus range are made by low volume producers. Like a few of the better bikes in the $500 to $600 range,

*Fig. 50:* Seat post quick release lets you position saddle correctly for descents and climbs.

they usually have hand-made frames. They carry the very best components and are well worth the money. You can pay as much as $1,500 or more for the very highest quality ATB. These are the kind of expedition quality, super-tough, high-performance, incredibly reliable machines I would choose to take over the Sahara, up the Alcan Highway in Alaska, up (and down) the highest peaks of the Rockies, through the jungles of the Amazon. These are also the bikes I would choose to go on day trips. They are beautifully built, have paint jobs that are truly works of art, and are truly precision machines. Some of these are specialty ATBs built for racing, observed trials, or high-speed downhill events.

The differences between the top-of-the-line bikes in the $500 to $600 range and the bikes over $600 are, however, minor in terms of componentry. It's important to remember, in considering the more expensive bikes, that the small producers of these hand-made bikes are not locked into a design dictated by the economies of mass production. The low-volume producers (less than 800 ATBs a year) can and do change frame geometry and adopt the latest improved components and materials. Many of these makers, most of them in western states, although a few are in East Coast states, are themselves ATB riders. As such, they are right out there on the trails and can make improvements as the need arises. These small producers are at the leading edge of the state of the art. Their products are the ultimate in hi-tech design and construction.

## Here Are All-Terrain Bicycles I Have Road Tested

There are a great many manufacturers of ATBs. Everybody is getting into the act, and with good reason—there's a great demand for them. It was, regrettably, impossible for me to spend the five years it would take to ride each and every model of every manufacturer. In some cases it was not possible to obtain a test bike from the manufacturer in time for my publishing deadline. Therefore, just because a particular make or model of ATB is not given here by no means implies anything about it. All this list does show is that I have tested the bikes shown under both off-road and on-road conditions and that they met with my approval. (Please note also that prices and components are subject to change without notice, and that goes for *all* the bikes listed in this book.)

### BIANCHI ATBs
Bianchi makes two ATBs, the *Grizzly* and the *Alaska*. Both Bianchi models offer good value for the money, although I would prefer a bit

lower gear. Both models have a low gear of 26 and a high gear of 89. (See Gear Table on page 55 for an explanation of gearing terminology.) But at the price, you could afford to change the 28-tooth freewheel cog it comes with at the low end to a 32- or 34-tooth cog, and get a much lower gear that way. The *Grizzly* is light for an ATB at 28 pounds, due mostly to the use of chrome-moly straight-gage steel. The *Grizzly* comes in 19-, 21-, and 23-inch frame sizes, so if you're under five feet six even the 19-inch model may be too big for you. The *Grizzly* retails for $431. The Bianchi *Alaska* (Fig. 51) weighs in at 30 pounds, comes in 18-, 20-, and 23-inch frame sizes. The frame is manganese straight-gage steel. Components aren't quite as high-quality as the *Grizzly*, but they work fine. This model is quite reasonably priced at $289. Both models gave good performance on the trail and on the road, with good stability and comfort. Braze-ons include cable guides and stops and, on the *Grizzly*, one water-bottle cage fitting.

*Fig. 51:* The Bianchi *Alaska* ATB is a good example of a good quality, moderately priced machine.

## CANNONDALE ATBs

Cannondale makes the only production aluminum-frame ATB (Fig. 52) available in bike stores in the U.S. It's unique in that it has a sloping top tube and a 24-inch rear wheel, with a 26-inch front wheel. The sloping top tube and small rear wheel give a frame size as low as 16 inches to fit the smaller rider under five and one-half feet in height. In riding this bike on steep slopes in the Sierra of northern California, I found the frame to be surprisingly stiff. Yet it absorbed road shock

*Fig. 52:* Cannondale's ATB features heat-treated aluminum frame, sloping top tube, 24-inch tire rear, 26-inch front.

well, which means that it translates pedal power into go-power and comfort combined. The high gear of 81 inches is a bit low for pedaling at speed on smooth roads. That's a disadvantage of the 24-inch rear wheel. On the other hand, the smaller wheel gives you a really low 19-inch gear that should all but let you climb a wall. You could change the high gear easily enough by swapping the 44-tooth big chainwheel for a 48 or 50, to get an 89- or 92-inch gear, respectively. The frame is TIG welded and heat treated, with large diameter aluminum tubing. Price of the complete bike is $595. The frame alone is $395. Frame sizes are 16, 18, 20, and 22 inches. Braze-ons include fittings for two water-bottle cages and cable guides and stops. Model SM-600 has better components; it costs $695.00.

### FUJI ATBs

The first time I saw Fuji's *Mt. Fuji* model ATB, it looked like a two-wheel tank (Fig. 53). I think it was the oak-green color that helped. Certainly this bike is a toughie. It performed well uphill and down, gave good traction, comfort, and steering. It weighs in at 30 pounds. The chrome-moly double-butted frame comes in 18-, 20.5-, and 22.5-inch sizes, an adequate spread that should fit most people. The high gear is a bit low for the flats, but you could push it up to 88 inches by simply changing the 14-tooth freewheel cog to a 13-tooth cog. The low gear is 23 inches, more than adequate for most hills. This bike comes with braze-ons for two water-bottle cages and a carrier on the seat

**Fig. 53:** The *Mt. Fuji* is one of the strongest stock ATBs on the market.

stays. After a hard ride down rocky and sandy roads, I found the right chainstay paint to be pitted, like very rough sandblasting. That's not unique to the Fuji bike, though; all ATBs suffer this fate. You can avoid it by sticking a plastic half-tube on that chainstay, available in any bike store. The *Mt. Fuji* sells for $585.

The Fuji *Sundance* is very similar to the *Mt. Fuji*, including frame sizes and gearing. Its tubing is lighter (chrome-moly straight gage), which accounts in large measure for its 27.5-pound weight. It has frame braze-ons for cable carriers and stops and for one water-bottle cage. Handling on the trail is quick. I liked its steering on narrow trails. With a 72 degree steering-head and seat-tube angles, a 21.8-inch top tube, and a 41-inch wheelbase, this bike handled more like a road bike. It was a bit less forgiving on bumpy descents. This would be an excellent combination bike for all-trail and street riding. Frame sizes are 19, 20.5, 22.5, and 24 inches, and in the "women's" mixte frame (no top tube, instead, double down tubes) 19 inches. It's a tough bike, and at $380 it's an excellent buy.

**LOTUS ATBs**

Here are two excellent ATBs, the Lotus *Pegasus* and the Lotus *Viking*. Both have frames of high-quality tubing and top grade components, at a reasonable price. The *Pegasus* frame is double-butted chrome-moly throughout (Fig. 54). It has brazed-on cable guides, two

*Fig. 54:* **The top-of-the-line Lotus *Pegasus,* another excellent stock ATB.**

sets of water-bottle cage bosses, rack hangars, and fender bosses, all using Allen hardware. The *Pegasus* has a high gear of 89, a low of 23. Frame sizes are 17.5, 19, 21, 23, and 24 inches. It retails for a reasonable $479.

The Lotus *Viking* is essentially a TIG welded version of the lugged frame *Pegasus*, with virtually the same high-quality components and ride performance. The frame is double-butted manganese steel throughout. Frame sizes are the same as for the *Pegasus*. Its price is $321; an excellent buy. Both models weigh 29 pounds.

### MARUKIN ATBs

Marukin has come up with a pair of ATBs with a front-end geometry that makes for stable steering on bumpy descents. After ride testing both the *Viking* (Fig. 55) and the *Northstar*, I would describe the ride as "neutral." On narrow trails, steering was quick and accurate. On the descents, steering was "forgiving" in that on bumps and jumps steering control was good. Dropouts (where wheel axles fit into frame) are vertical, which keeps the rear wheel from cocking under pedal pressure and rubbing on the chainstays. Both models come with braze-ons for two water-bottle cages and seat stay rack. Both have a high gear of 89 and a low of 21, a good combination. Both also have lugged frames. The *Viking* frame is chrome-moly double-butted tubing throughout. The *Northstar* frame is manganese double-butted steel throughout. The *Viking* weighs 28.5 pounds and sells for $500. The Northstar weighs 30 pounds and costs $380.

*Fig. 55:* This Marukin ATB has lugged frame, wide-ratio gearing.

## MIYATA ATBs

Miyata makes three ATB models. The top-of-the-line model, the *Ridge Runner* (Fig. 56), has a laid back 68 degree head angle and a 70 degree seat-tube angle, which made for accurate and stable steering

*Fig. 56:* The Miyata *Ridge Runner* ATB showed good stability on bumpy trails.

on bumpy, downhill runs. On uphill climbs I found excellent traction. Steering was quick, which made sharp turns on narrow trails easy to do. The *Ridge Runner* has a frame of chrome-moly double-butted TIG welded tubes. High gear is 93, low is 23. Quite a spread, more than adequate for paved road riding on the flats and the steep off-road hills. Braze-ons are present for cable guides and hangars, carrier bracket and fender bosses, and for two water-bottle cages. Retail price is $555. Frame sizes are 17.5, 19.5, 21, and 23 inches. The *Terra Runner* has a straight-gage chrome-moly frame, comes in 19.5-, 21-, and 23-inch sizes. Price: $415. A scaled down model, quality-wise, the *Street Runner*, is more suitable for commuting and around town use, it comes in 17.5-, 19.5-, 21-, and 23-inch sizes. Cost: $335.

## PANASONIC ATB

There's just the one true ATB in Panasonic's line, though they do have a model called the *City Bike* which is more of a special purpose bike. First, the ATB, which is appropriately called the *All-Terrain Bike* (Fig. 57). Sizes are 20 and 22 inches, not a wide selection, and one that will fit only persons roughly between 5'9" and 6'2". There's no size for the short person or the very tall rider. This is a really good buy, though, at $350. It has a frame with main tubes of single gage chrome-moly, with fork blades of high-tensile steel. Components are high class. This is a well performing, median quality ATB. It has braze-on fittings for one water-bottle cage. High gear is 84, low is

*Fig. 57:* Here's the only true ATB made by Panasonic, a well-performing medium cost bike.

24—a wide range selection. The Panasonic *City Bike* is really a compromise between a street bike and an ATB. It's designed with the commuter in mind, with a shorter wheelbase and quicker steering than a true ATB. But the price is right, at $250, and you can take it on the trail. It has a low gear of 28, and a high of 93 for city streets. Frame sizes are 20 and 22 inches.

### PEUGEOT ATBs

From somewhere in the Orient come these three ATBs (two are shown in Fig. 58) carrying a French name. The top-of-the-line model, the *Canyon Express*, has chrome-moly double-butted main tubes and a manganese steel fork. Braze-ons include two water-bottle cage fittings, cable guides and stops, and carrier braze-ons on the seat stays. Frame sizes are 19.5, 21, and 23 inches. Weight is 29.9 pounds in the 19.5-inch size. Price: $470. The *Urban Express* leans more toward a commuter bike than an ATB, but it will do for either. Braze-ons include two water-bottle cages, cable guides and stops, and seat-stay carrier fittings. Main tubes are straight-gage manganese steel, fork is manganese steel. Weight is 30.5 pounds, price is $370. The *Orient Express* has 4130 chrome-moly single-gage main tubes, TIG welded frame. Braze-ons include cable guides and stops and double water-bottle cage fittings. Weight is 31.8 pounds in the 23-inch size. Sizes are 19.5, 21, and 23 inches. Price is $300.

*Fig. 58:* A pair of Peugeot ATBs meet at an off-road rally in Carissa Plains, California.

## RALEIGH

Raleigh makes three ATBs. They also make a commuter bike that's great for city riding, but without the wide-ratio gearing needed for off-road cycling. Of these four models, I road tested the *Elkhorn*, next to the top of the Raleigh line. All Raleigh ATBs are TIG welded. They differ mostly in quality of frame tubing and components and, of course, price.

I liked the *Elkhorn* (Fig. 59); it tracked well on descents, and on most hills. The 26-inch low gear let me climb hills sitting down, without losing traction. On really steep hills I did have to stand up on the pedals, but that's normal in hill climbing. The *Elkhorn*'s main tubes are Raleigh 502 chrome-moly single-gage tubing, with stays of high-tensile steel. This model comes with 26 × 2.125 tires. The *Elkhorn* comes in just two sizes, 19 and 22 inches, so there really isn't a size for people over 6 feet tall. It sells for $420.

The *Crested Butte* top-of-the-line model is basically an *Elkhorn* with better tubing of Raleigh 555 double-butted chrome-moly steel main tubes. Sizes are rather limited, in 17 and 19 inches, and the tires are 26 × 2.125 inches. This model sells for $550. The *Tamarack* and *Yukon* models both come in 19- and 22-inch sizes and have frame tubing of single-gage chrome-moly steel. They also both have 650 cm × 35 cm tires, a popular size in Europe but which may be hard to find in the U.S.

The *Tamarack*, like the *Crested Butte* and *Elkhorn*, is an 18-speed model. It sells for $350. The *Yukon* is a 12-speed model, sells for $280.

*Fig. 59:* A Raleigh *Elkhorn* ATB is an excellent stock machine.

If you're looking for a commuter bike and aren't interested in off-road riding, the 10-speed *Grand Mesa* should get you to work or around town in comfort. It sells for $230.

### ROSS ATBs

You're going to hear a lot more about Ross in coming years. They are making some darned good bikes these days, with great attention to detail, frame construction, and all-around quality. I can't speak about all of their ATB line because they only delivered one model for test, but if the rest of the line is anything like the one I rode, you can't go wrong on a Ross.

The model I tested, the *Mt. Whitney* (Fig. 60), gleams with heavy chrome plating on the entire frame, which is a great idea, considering the beating ATBs take on the trail. This model has a TIG welded frame of chrome-moly steel, all top grade components, and excellent steering and traction capability. It has a low gear of 20, a high of 85, ample for off-road and street use. The only drawback to this handsome machine is its limited frame sizes of 21 and 23 inches, which means you have to be around 5'10" to fit the 21-inch size, and 6 feet or over for the 23-inch size. The *Mt. Whitney* weighs 30.2 pounds, comes with braze-ons for two water-bottle cages and cable guides. It sells for $543.

I did not test the Ross models below, but if they match the *Mt. Whitney* in quality, you can't go wrong. Top-of-the-line *Mt. McKinley* is similar in most respects to the *Mt. Whitney*, except that it has a

*Fig. 60:* This is the Ross *Mt. Whitney* ATB, a great handling, well-made ATB, which offers excellent value in a high-grade bike.

lugged frame, which probably accounts for its price of $850 as compared with $543 for the *Mt. Whitney.* But the *Mt. McKinley* comes in a much wider choice of frame sizes, which are 18, 19, 20.5, 22, 23.5, and 25 inches. Both models have reinforced seat tubes and sealed bottom brackets.

Ross' *Mt. Rainier* is a less expensive version of the *Mt. Whitney,* without the chrome plating. It too is TIG welded, with a sealed bottom bracket. It sells for $433. Other bikes in this ATB line include the *Mt. St. Helens* at $253, and the *Mt. Washington,* at $193. Both of these models have 10-speeds and frames of 1020 carbon steel. The *Mt. Washington* has a one-piece steel crank and steel rims.

### SPECIALIZED BICYCLE COMPONENTS

The four bikes in Specialized's ATB line range from the *Stumpjumper Sport* at $535, to the *Stumpjumper SC* at $899. The bike I tested, the $799 *Stumpjumper* (Fig. 61), is an extremely comfortable machine in several ways. First, it smooths out the bumps, the slings and arrows of rough trails, almost to flat road quality. Not quite, but

*Fig. 61:* Specialized's *Stumpjumper* model ATB is equipped here with front and rear carriers and Madden panniers for off-road touring. However, your author has not removed the Streetstomper tires, which he would change to a more aggressive pattern for an off-road trip.

close. Second, steering is very quick. I could whip around corners at speeds and at steep angles I'd never get away with on a road bike. On the descents this bike was as steady as a rock, until I hit one. Even then the bike could be controlled, with an assist from friendly geometry. If the other bikes in the Specialized line match this one in quality of frame, components, and user-friendly design, then they are bikes to consider seriously.

There are three other ATBs in the Specialized line. They all have frames of chrome-moly double-butted tubing, a reinforcement sleeve in the steering head, and computer-designed gear ratios. Top of the line is the $899 *Stumpjumper SC*, a limited production model in 19.5-, 20.5-, 21.5-, and 22.5-inch frame sizes. It comes with brazed-on fittings for two bottle mounts, rear rack mounts, fender mounts, and chain hangar. The frame is hand finished and looks it. This bike is fitted with Shimano's revolutionary Biopace chainwheel set, which evens out the pedal stroke for the greater pedaling efficiency previously described.

The *Stumpjumper Sport XT* costs $599 and comes in the same sizes as the *Stumpjumper SC*. It has one bottle-cage braze-on. The *Stumpjumper Sport* should be especially interesting to short people and to youngsters who want a high-quality small-frame ATB with wide-ratio gearing. This model comes in 16.5-, 17.5-, 19.5-, 20.5-, 21.5-, and 22.5-inch sizes. The 16.5-inch size has 24-inch wheels that should fit people from 5' to 5'6" tall. It retails for $535. The *Stumpjumper Sport* has a high gear of 85 and a low gear of 22.5. The 24-inch-wheel model has a high gear of 79 and a low of 21. Because the Biopace only comes with a 28-tooth small ring, the *Stumpjumper SC* has a high gear of 89 and a low of 24. I can recommend all of these excellent bikes.

### TREK ATBs

Aside from the small companies in the hand-made frame area listed below, Trek, Ross, and Cannondale are the only U.S.-made models I have tested. I road tested both Trek models, the *830* (Fig. 62) and the *850* (Fig. 63), in the glacial Moraine hills of southeast Wisconsin. I pedaled along old logging roads, which, after a few miles into the pine woods, were virtually untouched by human foot, or, from the feel of the washboard surface, by anything else. I can report that both the *830* and the *850* performed admirably. Frame geometry is fairly radical, in my opinion, with chainstays of around 19 inches, wheelbase of 43 inches, a 1.78-inch fork rake, a head-tube angle of 71.5 degrees, and a seat tube angle of 71 degrees. Chainstays are an inch or so longer than other ATBs I tested. The longer chainstays did put my center of gravity a bit more forward than I was used to, and so in a fast downhill run I had to compensate for this new center of gravity

*Fig. 62:* Trek makes a handsome ATB, as this photo of their model *830* shows, with long chainstays and relatively short fork rake.

*Fig. 63:* Another Trek with the same frame geometry as in Fig. 62. This is Trek's model *850*.

by consciously thrusting my nether extremity as far rearward as possible. As a result, I found steering somewhat hard to control on the bumps, although I feel reasonably confident I could, in time, learn to adjust to this new geometry. On the plus side, both models were a lot of fun to ride on the flats and on the narrow tire paths of this logging trail. Steering was unusually quick and accurate, and I could whip both bikes around sharp corners easily and accurately. Both models, the *830* and the *850*, have absolutely top grade parts for their price. The *830* has a Reynolds 501 chrome-moly single-gage frame. The *850* has Reynolds 531P double-butted main tubes. Both are lugged and brazed, and very attractively styled and finished. Frame sizes are a bit unusual. They are, for both models, 18, 19.8, 21.8, and 24.3 inches. The *850* comes with bottle cage and bottle. Both have braze-ons for two water bottles, cable guides and stops, rear rack mounts, down tube cable stops, and chain hangar. The *830* lists for $469 and the *850* for $669.

### UNIVEGA ATBs

Of the five ATBs made by Univega, I was able to test the *Alpina Pro*, second to the top-of-the-line *Alpina Ultima*. The *Alpina Pro* has a TIG welded frame of chrome-moly tubing. Something must be right with the geometry because I took this bike on a century run in the California high desert country (where the two water-bottle braze-ons were appreciated) and did the 100 miles, not easily but I did it. The route took me over back ranch roads and trails, a lot of which were rutted and pitted. I didn't break any speed records but can report that this machine handled beautifully. In fact this author pulled a highly successful wheely over a rattlesnake sunning on the trail, out of sight just around a corner. Well, the wheely was successful as far as I was concerned because the front wheel cleared the critter. I don't think

*Fig. 64:* The Univega *Alpina Pro* ATB.

the back wheel did. I left in too much of a hurry to find out. Frame sizes are 19.5, 21, and 23 inches. High gear is 96, low is 26, which on this bike seemed adequate to get me up some fairly steep hills. I do like the looks of this bike, as well as the way it handles, and include it here as one I believe to be a good and honest buy at around $550.

## Fine Hand-Made All-Terrain Bicycles, Over $650

I have selected eight makes of the expedition-quality super ATBs to discuss. Prices go all the way from $650 to $1,500. These are very fine machines with top-quality components, great attention to frame design and construction, and in most cases unique features which contribute substantially to strength as well as to beauty. Because you can rest assured that only the finest parts will be used on these machines, I am not going to list them here. Also, parts selections will vary as improvements in them are made. I am including the address of each of the makers in case you can't order one through your bicycle dealer. I recommend that you write to the maker for more complete information.

Ride testing these machines seemed to be almost gilding the lily, like ride testing a Rolls Royce for comfort, or a Maserati for performance. These very fine ATBs have several construction elements in common, which are discussed below.

### REINFORCED SEAT CLUSTER OR SEAT TUBE

These fine machines have reinforced seat collars. Reinforcements are made in different ways, but the end result is a very strong seat post where the quick release binder bolt is mounted (Fig. 65). The reason why this reinforcement is so important is because on a ride you will be moving the seat to various heights; up for hill climbing and on the flats, down for descents at high speed (see chapter 3, on riding techniques). Tightening and loosening the quick release seat post bolt creates stresses at the seat post cluster. These stresses can cause the seat post cluster, or the seat tube to stretch or tear. Overtightening the quick release can also flatten the quick release bosses so you cannot get the seat post tight enough; the seat won't stay put. Reinforcements in this area prevent this type of damage. (You don't move the seat up and down on a road bike.) Fig. 66 shows a seat post cluster that is not in the super-fine bike category, although it does use a lug as a reinforcement, taking the place of a collar. However, Fig. 50 (on page 67) does show that there is not a lot of brass used in mounting the seat binder tube, a weak point.

*Fig. 65* (above, left): Highest quality hand-built ATBs have a reinforced seat collar, as this photo of a Fisher MountainBike shows. This is a good example of a very fine, lugless, fillet-brazed frame.

*Fig. 66* (above, right): Here's a mass produced ATB with seat collar reinforcement.

## CHAINSTAYS

One problem all makers of ATBs have to solve is how to widen the chainstays to make room for the fat tire. Producers of mass production stock bikes solve this problem in several ways. Some make a double bend in the chainstays (Fig. 67), which creates stress at the curve, a weak point. Another way to make room for fat tires is to have the chainstays come out straighter, with a gradual bend (Fig. 68), which eliminates some of the stress. But many of these chainstays are crimped or indented, to provide tire clearance or chainwheel clearance (Fig. 69). These crimps or indentations are stress risers, weak points where failure can occur. One of the ways the top custom frame builders work around this problem is by using specially made tubing with a gradual taper, without indentations or crimps. A typical builder, MountainBikes, uses a single-bend oval-to-round chainstay that is claimed to keep stiffness in the drive train, as in Fig. 70. The tubing is oval where it meets the bottom bracket shell, for full contact with the shell.

*Fig. 67:* Double bend in chainstays is made so fat tires will fit between stays. This method produces stress points where tubing is bent. Left chainstay also has a crimp or indent for tire clearance, another weak spot.

*Fig. 68:* A more gradually tapered chainstay design, but still with a bend near the outer edge of the tire. The right chainstay is crimped or indented for clearance for the large chainwheel, another weak point.

*Fig. 69:* Finger at top points at crimp or indent in chainstay that allows chainwheel clearance but which is also a potential area of stress-related failure.

*Fig. 70:* Here's the way to build an ATB with gradually curved chainstays, without bends or crimps. This makes for the strongest frame. This is a Fisher MountainBike *Everest 84* ATB.

## THE FORK

In an ATB, the fork takes a terrific beating from road shock. If the fork does not absorb some of this shock, all the impact will be transmitted to the rider's hands and arms. The custom builders have designed forks that provide flexibility parallel to the bike frame, without sacrificing lateral stiffness. Side-to-side stiffness in a fork is essential for accurate steering control on loose surfaces. Some of the stock ATBs also have forks with lateral stiffness but at the expense of stiffness in the direction of ride (i.e. they are not flexible in forward/rearward motion).

A popular fork design is called the Unicrown by one maker, a Uni-Fork by another (Fig. 71). As described by one of its designers, Joe Breeze of Mill Valley, California, it has "a one-piece fork crown and blade. Each side is made of one curved and tapered length of tubing. This design offers very good strength-to-weight ratios because of the fork's capabilities of evenly distributing riding stresses throughout the entire length of the fork." (Others contributing to the design are Gary Fisher of MountainBikes and Charlie Cunningham of Wilderness Bicycles, see page 89.)

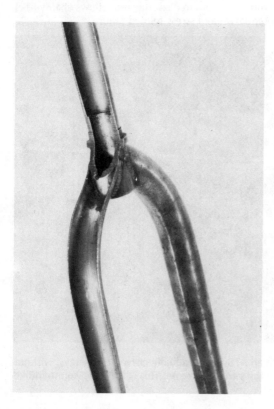

*Fig. 71:* A Unicrown fork used on top hand-built ATBs, showing the reinforced steering tube and fork blade area.

## STRONG LUGGED OR FILLETED FRAMES

Another characteristic of these fine custom ATBs is the care, good design, and quality of workmanship that goes into frame building. Lugless frames made by these high-quality builders are a work of both skill and art. Tubes are heated only enough to provide for maximum adhesion of the brass brazing material to the tubing (Fig. 72). The brazing material is skillfully flowed to build up a strong fillet at the joint, which is then hand finished and tapered (Fig. 73). The final joint, when finished and painted, is a joint of flowing beauty and strength (Fig. 74).

*Fig. 72:* This fork is being carefully brazed in Tom Ritchey's shop, so as to apply no more heat than necessary to effect a strong joint but not remove heat treatment from tubing.

*Fig. 73:* An excellent example of a well-brazed filleted lugless frame joint. Note the gradual buildup of brass brazing material that holds tubing together, without stress risers.

*Fig. 74:* This Ritchey frameset is a good example of the good looks a fine brazing job combined with a top paint-finish can impart to a frameset. Note sealed bearing bottom bracket.

## CUNNINGHAM WILDERNESS TRAIL BIKES

Here is a truly different all-terrain bicycle. It's the aluminum frame bike (Fig. 75), built by innovator and design expert Charlie Cunningham in his small shop in Fairfax, California. This is the bike that's ridden by the U.S. women's ATB racing champion, Jacquie Phelan. If you think aluminum frames are weaker than steel ones, think again. You should see, as I have, Jacquie fly down rough mountain roads, hair flying, seemingly glued to the trail, passing men as well as women. She does even better on hill climbs.

Cunningham ATB frames are built of heat-treated, oversized aluminum tubing, which provides the same strength as high-quality chrome-moly steel tubing. The fork is chrome-moly steel, especially designed to resist what Cunningham calls "autosteer," the tendency of a bicycle fork to flex or bend under the weight of the rider and the

*Fig. 75:* Jacquie Phelan, left, holds her Cunningham aluminum frame ATB on which she has won many ATB races and on which she has retained her U.S. women's championship in this bike category. At right is Casey Patterson, also a racing ATBer who runs ATB tours (see chapter 4).

impact from the front wheel as it goes over bumps. Autosteer flexing causes flex that in turn tends to steer the bike in directions you don't want to go. The Cunningham fork has internally butted blades that help prevent fork flex or bend. His forks also have a large outside diameter for further strength, with a thin wall diameter for lightness. This may explain why Phelan can hot dog down hills so fast.

The Cunningham frameset is 2.5 to 3 pounds lighter and at least as strong, according to the maker, as a same size lugless, chrome-moly, high-quality frameset. My ride test showed that this unique bicycle had excellent side-to-side stiffness, and thus little energy-wasting lateral flex, yet this stiffness did not make the frame any less shock absorbing than fine steel frames. Frames are TIG welded and heat treated to relieve stress and regain strength. Alignment is maintained throughout the process. Frames are lifetime guaranteed, and any repairs are generally made within seventy-two hours. Cunningham makes three different ATB framestyles. All include Spiedel alloy headset; replaceable, sealed bearing-bottom bracket, with Phil Wood heavy-duty spindle; seat post quick release; Shimano cantilever brakes (or Cunningham's own design of very powerful cam action brakes, Fig. 76); SunTour Cyclone II front derailleur; water bottle

*Fig. 76:* **The Cunningham cam action brake on an ATB. This brake is very powerful, takes less muscle to apply, yet gives excellent braking control.**

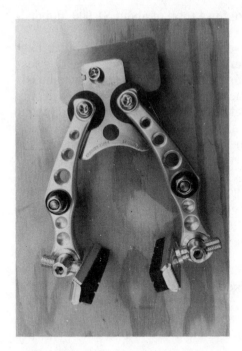

*Fig. 77:* **The SunTour version of the Cunningham cam action brake.**

cage mounts; cable stops; and threaded bosses for carrier on rear dropouts. By the way, SunTour now makes a version of the Cunningham cam action brakes (Fig. 77). These are not designed as an aftermarket item because you have to align and braze special bosses on the frame. Conventional cantilever brake bosses won't accept them. If you braze them on yourself, you will be faced with a frame refinishing job. There is a way, however, you can mount these brakes without brazing on a boss, and that's with special clamp-on bosses that should be on the market at about the time this book is available. As of this writing, prices aren't out yet on the SunTour cam action brake, or the clamp-on boss, but I would guess the brakes will be at least $85 a pair and the clamp-on bosses around $14 a pair. These bosses are made by Moots Cycles (see report on their ATB, below, for address). Charlie Cunningham is himself an avid all-terrain bicyclist, and a tough competitor in races. He is one of the sponsors of Jacquie Phelan. As with all custom-made ATBs, you may have any gear set-up you want, within the limits of practicality.

The *Indian* is for the off-trail rider who wants a stable, all-round machine for wilderness touring and a comfortable ride. The wheelbase is a long 43.5 inches and the chainstays only 17.5 inches, for traction on the hills and control on descents. Sizes are 19 inch to 23 inch, in one-inch increments. The frameset alone is $1,495. Cunningham will make this up into a complete bike for a total of about $1,900, depending on components.

The *Racer* has a short frameset with steep angles for quick handling. It's designed for the all-terrain expert rider who wants a fast bike for competition or high performance. The wheelbase is 42 inches and the chainstays a short 17.1 inches. Sizes are 19 to 22 inches in one-inch increments. Price: Frameset only, $1,565; complete bike, about $2,200, depending on components.

The "Little People's Bike": One way to get a bike small enough for short people is to use 24-inch wheels. That solution offers less traction and steering control than the bigger 26-inch wheels and that is why Cunningham sticks to 26-inch wheels and still comes up with a frame that has a top-tube-to-ground clearance of only 26.5 inches. This is the bike to buy if you want a fine machine and are under 5½ feet tall. Price: $1,295 for frameset, about $1,800 for a complete bike, depending on components.

**Address:** Wilderness Trail Bikes, Charlie Cunningham, 121 Wood Lane, Fairfax, CA 94930
**Phone:** (415) 457-1779

### FAT CITY CYCLES

If you live on the East Coast, Fat City Cycles is a builder of high-quality ATBs in your area. The "Fat City" name of course refers to the fat balloon tires used on ATBs. Despite its name, this company is

*Fig. 78:* Here's a good example of a hand-made ATB. It's from Fat City Cycles, one of the few builders in the East Coast area.

serious about building high-quality hand-made frames of the best Reynolds 531 double-butted chrome-moly steel tubing. The touring model, the *Real Fat Chance* (Fig. 78), also has a Unicrown fork made by Ishiwata of Japan, out of Tange tubing. The seat-tube collar and steering head is reinforced. Chainstays are short, around 17 inches, with a 2.25-inch fork rake, making for lively steering on the flats, good control on the descents, and good traction all the time. This bike comes with water bottle, cable guides and stops, rack and fender mounts, and a chain hangar. Gearing is 96 and 21 inches. The *Real Fat Chance,* complete, costs $895, not a bad price for this quality bike. The *Team Compe* is a lighter version, for racing, with the same basic specifications as the *Real Fat Chance,* that costs $1,395.

**Address:** Fat City Cycles, Inc., 3310 Somerville Ave., Somerville, MA 02143
**Phone:** (617) 625-4922

### FISHER MOUNTAIN BIKES

Fisher makes very elegant ATBs indeed. The frames are a fine example of the builder's art (Fig. 79). All four of these models incorporate the Unicrown fork previously mentioned (Fig. 80). On the *Ever-*

*Fig. 79:* Here's a prime example of a well-made, hand-fillet-brazed, lugless ATB frame. It's the *Everest 84* made by Fisher Mountain Bikes.

*Fig. 80:* A view of a Unicrown fork on a Fisher Mountain Bike *Everest 84*. This fork offers good lateral rigidity, coupled with good shock absorption.

*est 84*, *Mt. Tam*, and *Competition* models, the seat collar or cluster (see Fig. 65 on page 83) and heat tube are reinforced. These three models are lugless, fillet brass-brazed frames. They all have oversize cable guide and cable stop braze-ons, so heavier motorcycle cables can be used (Fig. 81). Bottom-bracket chainstays are single bend, oval to round, and gradually tapered to eliminate stress risers and provide strength at this critical point, as noted earlier (see Fig. 70 on page 85).

The model I tested seemed almost to have a life of its own, even going up steep hills. That's the *Everest 84*, which, while not inexpensive at $1,656 for the complete bike or $1,053 for the frameset, is well worth the money if you are truly serious about all-terrain bicycling. I must tell you that I have seen a number of dedicated cyclists who earn quite modest salaries, riding bikes as costly as the *Everest 84*, when caught by the ATB bug or when the hobbyist's "want" has turned into need. The *Everest 84* has a hand-built frame of oversized, double-butted chrome-moly steel tubing. Frame sizes are 16, 18, 19, 19.75, 20.5, 22, 23, and 24.5 inches. This bike weighs only 28.5 pounds. Braze-ons include two water-bottle cage bosses and two rack bosses.

The *Mt. Tam* is a TIG welded version of the *Everest 84*, with the

*Fig. 81:* Closeup showing oversized cable guides on this high-quality ATB. Guides permit use of stronger motorcycle brake cable.

same high quality tubing, Unicrown fork, and other features already noted. It costs $999 complete or $599 for the frame only.

The lowest priced bike in the Fisher line is the *Montare*, which is quite a bargain at $650, in my opinion. This is a TIG welded frame of double-butted chrome-moly steel tubing, single-bend tapered chain-stays, and reinforced seat collar. Braze-ons include cable guides and stops, double water-bottle cage bosses, and rear rack mounts. Fisher will hang almost any reasonable gear combination you want on his bikes. The *Montare* has a high gear of 96, a low of 21. The *Mt. Tam* has a high of 92, a low of 21. The *Everest 84* has a high gear of 92 and a low of 20. The *Competition* also includes the Unicrown, and is designed for the racing all-terrain cyclist. It has all the great features of the *Everest 84*, plus tubing and components selected for both strength, performance, and lightness. This model costs around $1,500.

Fisher All-Terrain Tandems: You'd think an all-terrain tandem would have to be articulated, like those double-jointed busses that bend around corners, to make it around the narrow sharp corners of mountain trails. Not the tandems I have selected for this book. One of these is the Fisher and like the others, it handles almost as quickly as a single. In the hands of experts, it tears around corners and up and down hills, at a pace no single bike can match. Even as an all-terrain tandem it weighs only 49 pounds, or less than 25 pounds per rider, compared with the 28 to 30 or more pounds per single-rider bike. Frames have all the usual braze-ons. Front and rear brakes are Shimano DeOre XT cantilevers. In addition to the standard rear brake is an Arai drum brake. Gears on this machine cover a very wide range, from a high of 108 (on which two strong riders can get up real speed), to a low of 30. Price: $2,524.

**Address:** Fisher Mountain Bikes, 1421 Franciscan Road, San Rafael, CA 94905.
**Phone:** (415) 459-2247

## IBIS CYCLES

Earlier in this chapter, I mentioned that TIG welding can, by eliminating the time and labor of hand brazing, cut about 30 percent off the price of a fine ATB (Fig. 82). Here's a prime example of that statement. It's the TIG welded Ibis ATB made by Scot Nicol (Fig. 83). He also makes beautiful fillet-brazed frames, for about 31 percent more than his TIG-welded frameset. I rode an Ibis up a steep, curving, loose soil trail in the Sierra Mountains, and I can report that it went up the hill like a startled gazelle. The traction this bike had on a loose dirt road was just amazing. The bike was so responsive, it seemed to be an extension of my body. A Nicol TIG-welded frameset costs $625, a complete bike around $850. The hand-brazed fillet frameset costs $850, the complete bike, around $1,000. At these prices, they're a good buy indeed.

**Address:** Scot Nicol, Ibis Cycles, P.O. Box 275, Sebastopol, CA 95472
**Phone:** (707) 829-5615

## KLEIN MOUNTAIN BIKES

Gary Klein, resident genius at Klein Bicycles, has just introduced his design of an ATB. Like his road bikes, Klein ATBs are different, with a vengeance. First, his ATBs are made of heat-treated, large-diameter tubing. Well, almost. What strikes the eye immediately are the chainstays, those pieces of tubing that go from the bottom bracket to the rear of the bike, parallel to the chain. Klein ATB chainstays are square-shaped for strength in this highly stressed area. The model I tested, a 19-inch frame, was easy to control up and down the narrow, twisty, bumpy trails that wind through hilly Lewis and Clark State Park, not far from the Klein factory in Chehalis, Washington.

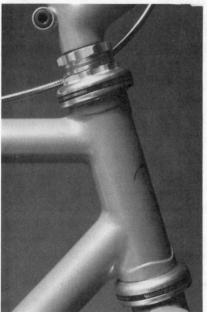

*Fig. 82:* Here's a close-up example of a fine TIG welded frame by master frame builder Scott Nicol. Frame is as strong as the best hand brazed lugged or filleted frame, but costs less because TIG welding requires fewer man-hours.

*Fig. 83:* Scott Nicol makes this hand-built TIG welded Ibis ATB. A hand-brazed model is also available. (Photo: Maury Cohen.)

Klein claims, and I believe him, that there's nothing very unusual about his ATBs except for the square chainstays, high-quality aluminum tubing, painstaking attention to detail in frame building, and high-quality components. The 19-inch model I rode weighed a tad over 26 pounds.

A minor difference is the use of a quick release on the front wheel for convenience in wheel removal. The theory here is that you won't want to ride the ATB on the road if it's equipped with high-rolling-resistance knobby tires for the trail. I agree with this theory. Certainly, it makes no sense to mount less aggressive fat tires for road use, then sling a couple of knobbies around your neck for when you get to the off-road trail. Where do you put the road tires? You sure can't risk strangling yourself by carrying them around your neck where they can catch on protruding branches on a narrow trail. Fat tires resist being folded up so you can carry them on your bike, but you could try. Klein is not worried about the quick-release lever opening as it snags on a branch, thus permitting the front wheel to fall out. His theory is that if you close the lever so it faces toward the rear of the bike, it won't snag on anything. Time will tell.

Klein ATBs use standard cantilever brakes on the front and Sun-Tour cam-action brakes on the rear, mounted on the chainstays. All cables run inside the tubing, which makes for a neat appearance. The front fork is a standard Unicrown design, similar to that used on Fisher and other high-quality ATBs. Frames come in 19-inch, 21-inch

*Fig. 83A:* Gary Klein's version of an all-terrain bicycle is unusual. For example, it has square chainstays, all cables run inside frame tubing, and main frame tubing is aluminum.

and 23-inch sizes. Frame size is measured as if the tube is horizontal, although it actually slopes slightly downward from front to rear. Wheels are standard 26 inches. Klein says the sloping top tube gives more seat adjustment by letting you put the saddle further down than you could on a conventional frame, which gets your center of gravity as low as possible for safer, more controllable descents.

Klein framesets alone are $495. The complete ATB costs from $900 to $1,100, depending on which components you specify.

**Address:** Klein Bicycle Corporation, 207 South Prairie Road, Chehalis, Washington 98532
  **Phone:** (206) 262-9823

## MOOTS CYCLES

The people at Moots make two very fine ATBs. The *Mountaineer 90M* is made of Columbus and Reynolds tubing, mitered, lugged, and low-temperature hand-brazed. Forks have Reynolds tandem blades, and the fork crown is Moots-made of chrome-moly steel. The down-tube is Columbus double-butted tandem tubing. The top and seat tubes are Reynolds 531 19–2 gage. Rear triangle is Tange chrome-

*Fig. 84:* Moots Cycles makes this ATB. Note the carrier strap on the top tube and the unique clamp-on cantilever brake bosses. Bosses can be positioned for 24, 26, and 27 inch, as well as 650- or 700-cm tire sizes.

moly steel with large diameter chainstays. Braze-ons include cable guides and stops, bottle mount, portage pad mount (Fig. 84), and fender mounts. Frame sizes come in an incredible nine sizes from 16.5 to 24.5 in one-half-inch increments. Cantilever brakes are mounted on Moots-made clamp-on bosses. You may never want to do this, but you could move the bosses should you wish to relocate the brakes to accommodate wheel sizes other than the 26-inch wheels that come with the bike. For example, by ordering a bicycle with 24-inch wheels you can get this bike in a 15.5-inch frame size and lower gears. The complete bike is $1,345. The frameset alone is $800. The *Mountaineer 70M* is similar to the *90M* except for the frame tube set which is Tange chrome-moly steel. The complete ATB is $1,150, the frameset alone is $650.

### MOUNTAINGOAT ATBs

These bikes are in a class by themselves. They're hand made by one of the top craftsmen in the field, and have outstanding lugwork and finish. The investment fork crown has a sculptured mountain goat head right in it (Fig. 85). Components are all top grade.

These bikes have very stiff lateral displacement, so muscle power is effectively transferred to the rear wheel. Yet the bike is responsive, with excellent traction and handling (Fig. 86). MountainGoat frames are individually built to suit the rider's body dimensions and his type and style of riding. Thus the size and frame design are tailored to the

*Fig. 85:* Insignia of a mountain goat is cast into the fork crown of a Lindsey MountainGoat ATB. This is a limited production, high-quality ATB.

*Fig. 86:* Jeff Lindsey, right, and friend, have pedaled up (scaled is more like it) California's Mt. Lassen on ATBs. Here he is, at the peak, with his well-named "MountainGoat" behind him. Photo was taken at the 10,453-foot peak. Which proves that a good ATB is a "go anywhere" bike.

individual. The top-of-the-line model, the *MountainGoat*, has frame tubes that are accurately mitered and hand finished for a close fit. Custom lugs are specially cut and hand finished. The tubes are silver brazed joined. Oversize frame tubes are 4130 chrome-moly. Handlebars are one-piece chrome-moly, with handsome nickel plating. Braze-ons for water-bottle cages, carriers, and cables guides and stops are standard. Price of the *MountainGoat* is $1,505. A less expensive version with scaled down components, is $1,205. The *EscapeGoat* is $950. The major difference being a frame that's heli-arc welded instead of silver brazed, saving a lot of costly handwork. Frame strength remains unchanged.

MountainGoat Tandems: Use oval chrome-moly tubing throughout. Have steeper geometry than single bikes, to fit two riders (Fig. 87). Price: $2,450.

**Address:** MountainGoat Cycles, P.O. Box 3923, Chico, CA 95927
**Phone:** (916) 342-4628

### RITCHEY USA

Tom Ritchey (Fig. 88) has been making ATBs, and fine ones, longer than any other builder. He is one of the pioneers of what has de-

*Fig. 87:* A MountainGoat tandem in the chill of a desert morning in central California. This is not an ordinary, everyday tandem, by any means. It's designed to be super-strong, to withstand the pounding of high-speed descents on bumpy roads, yet nimble enough to whip around narrow trail corners.

*Fig. 88:* Tom Ritchey is one of the pioneers in the design and building of high-quality ATBs, and today his machines are trendsetters.

veloped into today's high performance all-terrain bicycle. He is probably the largest producer of hand-made ATBs in the US at this time. All of his ATBs represent the state-of-the-art in ATB frames. His frames are made of Ritchey-designed double-butted chrome-moly tubing, and are lugless fillet-brazed.

The *Timber Wolf* model is Ritchey's lower priced ATB. It has the Ritchey Unifork. This bike is designed for use on city streets and paved highways, as well as for off-road cycling. Frame sizes are 19 to 24 inches, in one-inch increments. Price is $575 for the frameset alone, $995 for the complete bike. This would be the high-technology bike to buy if you plan to ride on paved roads as well as on the trail.

The Ritchey *Annapurna* is a truly luxurious cruiser for long day rides, week-long or longer jaunts into the wilderness, or for city riding or paved road cycling. This is the bike that will get you out there and also get you home. The frame is made of oversize double-butted chrome-moly tubing. For added strength, there's a Ritchey scalloped sleeve at each important tube joint.

This is the one bike that comes in a size for the very tall. Frame sizes: 19 inch through 25 inch. Price: $1,045 for frameset, $1,495 for a complete bike, depending on components.

The Ritchey *Team Comp* is a strictly high-performance off-road bike, built to take you up the hills efficiently, down the mountainside at full blast. It's built for the racer but suitable for the day rider who wants a fast-response machine. Features include custom double-butted Columbus tubing, custom racing Twin Strut handlebars. This is the bike that wins races. Frame sizes are from 19 inches to 23 inches in one-inch increments. Price: Frameset only, $975, complete bike, $1,345.

**Address:** Ritchey USA, Route 2, Box 405, La Honda, CA 94020
**Phone:** (415) 851-3254

### STEVE POTTS

Steve Potts, with Mark Slate, makes hand brazed, filletted, lugless framesets in seven sizes in his small machine shop (Fig. 89). Frame sizes are 17.5, 19, 20, 21, 22, 23, and 24 inches. All joints are finished to a smooth radius (Fig. 90), which not only makes for a beautiful transition but also provides a smooth stress flow throughout the frameset. Potts uses the Unicrown fork, previously mentioned. He makes his own stems in many different angles to suit the needs of the rider. He also makes his own shifter mounting system, which puts shifters next to brake levers, a more natural position. A neat touch is Potts' remachined tire pump, which fits into the seat post where you can't lose it on the trail or run over it. The frameset alone is $850, the

*Fig. 89:* Steve Potts, right, at work in his ATB shop in California. This is a typical small producer's factory from which emerge top grade, hand-built ATBs. His partner, Mark Slate, is at left.

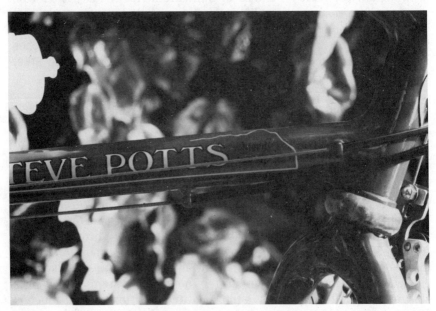

*Fig. 90:* Another example of a high-quality Potts lugless frame. Note the smooth, stressless transitions where tubes meet.

*Fig. 91:* Steve Potts makes some of the finest lugless hand-made ATBs on the market. This is one of them.

*Fig. 92:* Steve Potts also makes tandems, and here he is, left, demonstrating maneuverability of this bike so necessary on narrow, twisty, mountain trails.

complete bike around $1,600, or around $1,975 with Cunningham roller-cam brakes (Fig. 91). Potts also makes a production TIG and brass-welded model in 18-, 20-, 21-, 22-, and 23-inch frame sizes. Price will be $900 to $1,250, depending on components. Potts also makes great tandems (Fig. 92), one of which I rode and that I can report handled like a single. I could whip it around corners, make tight S-turns with no problem. The tandem sells for $3,300, including Cunningham roller-cam brakes.

**Address:** Steve Potts, 105 Montford Avenue, Mill Valley, CA 94041
**Phone:** (415) 388-4593

### EXPERIMENTAL PLASTIC ATB

Here's a plastic and metal ATB that, while in the developmental stage at this writing, seems to offer promise. It's the *ACR-3* (Figs. 93

*Fig. 93:* A prototype plastic ATB that Ron Anderson, its maker, claims is exceptionally strong and stable. Photo taken by author at an ATB rally in Carissa Plains, California.

*Fig. 94:* A rear view of the Anderson plastic ATB, at left. In background is the San Andreas earthquake fault, where the hills begin.

and 94), being developed by plastics expert Ron Anderson of Irvine, California. I saw this bike in action at an all-terrain bicycle rally in Carissa Plains, California, and I must say it was a crowd stopper. Ron claims its advantages include a "well damped ride" which means it absorbs road shock well, and he claims that the frame has "greater yield strength and elongation" than chrome-moly steel frames. The frame and fork are made of "carbon and S-glass fibers in a polyester resin surrounding rigid urethane foam." Metal components are mounted in aluminum inserts bonded in the frame structure. Ron is the Anderson in Anderson Cycle Research, Inc., P.O. Box 18765, Irvine, CA 92713.

# 3

## How to Ride Over (Almost) any Terrain, Safely and Efficiently (And Some Tips about Equipment and Preride Safety Checks)

Riding an all-terrain bicycle is a lot different than pedaling a conventional road bike. Even on a flat, paved road, riding technique is much different. On the paved flats, for example, the high bottom bracket road clearance and more stable frame geometry of an ATB let you take sharp corners at speeds and at angles of lean that would have a road bike's pedals scraping the ground and even, possibly, dumping you.

Cornering technique is important in trail riding. You never know what's around the next turn. Even how sharp a turn it is can't always be gauged in advance. You may have to make a tight left turn immediately after making a sharp right one, for example. In this context, I like the motto of the U.S. Coast Guard, *Semper Paratus*—always prepared. I'd amend that to "Always be prepared for anything on the trail, in terms of your mental attitude, physical alertness, and quickness of response."

In this chapter we will cover safe and sane off-road riding techniques to help you pedal uphill more efficiently. You will learn how to safely enjoy the thrill of fast descents down mountain fire lanes (a lot like skiing). Cornering, jumping over obstacles that would stump a road bike, forcing your way through mud and sand, and fording will be covered here. Since clothing, especially shoes, are so important, we'll review the basics of sensible garb for this new sport. We'll also cover winter riding tips through snow and over ice. The riding techniques in this chapter apply to general off-road cycling, as well as to ATB racing. Chapter 6 has more information on racing, types of events, National Off-Road Bicycle Association rules governing racing, and where you can find out about races in your area. Here's how to have fun, safely, on the trail.

## Bike Check Comes First

Before you can ride safely, you must have a bike that's safe to ride. Never assume that because your ATB was O.K. on your last ride, or because it's brand new, just out of the shop, that it's going to be reliable on your next ride.

Chapter 5 gives you a lot of information on bike repair and maintenance, and I suggest you review that data before embarking on your first ride, or any ride. To make sure we cover all the bike safety basics, though, here's what you should look for in a preride check. First, your mind-set should be that life and limb can depend on your bike's performance (pilots and small boat sailors have this mind-set). You need brakes that work effectively, handlebar and stem bolts tight, tires properly inflated. Here's a preride checklist. If you find anything wrong with your bike chapter 5 tells you how to fix it:

1. *Brakes:* Squeeze levers tightly. Cables should not slip out of cable bridges (sometimes called "cable carriers"), and brake shoes should return without binding to about ⅛-inch from rim flats (Fig. 95). Check cables for any sign of wear, such as frayed strands. Check near other end for broken strands.

2. *Wheels* should run true. Feel spokes for looseness. Adjust as necessary. Check tightness of axle bolts.

3. *Hubs* should show no evidence of sideplay or binding. Make sure axles aren't bent (a common occurrence on rough trails).

4. *Headset* should show no evidence of looseness. Note: Headsets do need adjustment more frequently than on road bikes.

5. *Cranks and pedals* should show no evidence of sideplay or binding.

6. *Chainwheel binder bolts* (Fig. 96) should be checked for tightness. Loose bolts can cause spread between chainwheels and then the

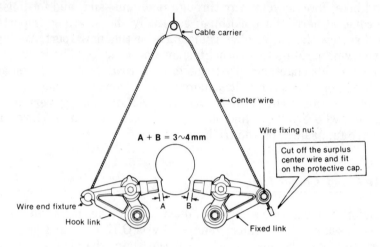

Cable carrier

Center wire

A + B = 3∿4mm

Wire fixing nut

Cut off the surplus center wire and fit on the protective cap.

Wire end fixture

Hook link

A    B

Fixed link

*Fig. 95:* **Preride safety check includes making sure cable is tight in the cable carrier, and that brake shoes are close to rim flats.**

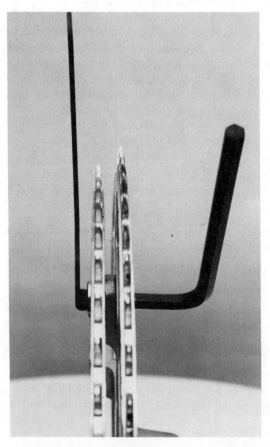

*Fig. 96:* **Check tightness of chainwheel binder bolts every couple of months. They can work loose and then the chainwheels can spread, let chain drop between wheels, lock cranks, and cause you to fall. This is a dual chainwheel set. On triple sets, small chainwheel will have to be removed to tighten two larger chainwheels.**

chain can fall between instead of on chainwheels and cause an accident.

7. *Check tires* for cuts, bruises, correct pressure (see recommendations on page 247). Make sure you have the right tire for the surface you ride on (see chapter 2).

8. *Check derailleur* operation. Shifting should be smooth throughout all gears. Check cables for signs of wear, such as frayed strands. Check at other end for broken strands. Make sure chain can't be thrown past outer cogs or chainwheels.

9. *Levers* should be tight on the handlebar. Check by trying to twist brake and shift levers.

10. *Bikepacks and racks* should be checked for tightness. Check all bolts. If you are carrying bikepacks, make sure all clips and straps holding the packs on the racks are securely fastened.

11. *Bolts and nuts* should be checked for tightness. I have mentioned most of them, but also check brake mounting bolts, derailleur mounts, and water-bottle cage bolts. If a brake-shoe mounting bolt, that holds the brake shoe in place, is not tight, the shoe could tilt up or down. You could lose braking or suddenly get too much braking if the brake shoe wedges under the rim—not really a healthy situation. I found that brake shoes with a knurled (serrated) shaft (see "A" in Fig. 95) can be twisted by hand, and are difficult to tighten enough to prevent twisting. Check brake pad alignment. The pad should strike the upper portion of the rim flat (never the tire, of course), so when squeezed real hard, the pad won't dive under the rim. A *worn* pad may also dive under the rim when squeezed hard, so check for pad wear and replace if necessary.

12. *The chain* should be checked for wear, cleaned and lubricated, and replaced if necessary. Plan on a new chain before any major, lengthy trip, it's good insurance. You'll need a new chain much more frequently than you're used to on your road bike. Chains are the fastest wearing item on an ATB, next to the rider. *Keep it oiled!* The No. 1 cause of chain death and friction is due to a dry chain.

13. *Take nothing for granted.* In the wilderness especially, you are strictly on your own. A bike mechanic is *not* going to be in the next town because in the wilderness, the next town is the one you just left. If you're racing, NORBA rules require that if it breaks, you fix it on the race course. Helper mechanics are not allowed. The reason for this rule is to help you develop a trouble-free bike. Please see chapters 4 and 5 if you find anything that needs fixing, and for the tools to bring on the trip. Don't forget a wrench so you can loosen the wheel

nut if you have to remove the wheel to repair a puncture, and a pump, patch kit, and spare tube!

## The Right Tire Pressure

The fat tires on ATBs have recommended tire pressure on the sidewall. It's usually 30 to 40 pounds per square inch (psi). That pressure is O.K. for average trail riding. If you weigh 150 pounds or less, around 30 psi is fine for average trail riding. If you're heavier, edge it up to 40 psi, depending on your weight. For street riding, on paved roads, though, you want lower rolling resistance. For that you can pump these fatso tires up to 70 to 90 psi, depending on your weight. Be advised, though, that inflation above what's printed on the tire will void that tire's warranty. Personally, I ride these tires on the street at 90 psi. I weighed 155 last time I had enough courage to step on the scale. In mud or loose sand, I cut tire pressure down to around 20 psi. The lower pressure spreads the tire out more for better traction. If the tire "bottoms out" when it hits a sharp rock, you could have a blow-out. Be aware of how much of an indent the tire makes as it strikes rocks and bumps and adjust tire pressure so the tube does not get crushed between the obstruction and the rim.

## Toe Clips and Straps

If you're used to toe clips and straps (Fig. 97) on a road bike, you know how to keep the straps loose in city riding so you can get your feet out in a hurry if you need legs to stay upright in, say, a panic stop. If you're not used to toe clips and straps, you may wonder why I advocate them, especially since most all-terrain bikes usually don't come with them.

Toe clips and straps are important on ATBs for many reasons. They keep your feet from sliding off the pedals when you're pedaling hard uphill. If feet do slip, you could lose control of the bike, possibly even dump it and yourself. With clips and straps you can pull up with one foot, push down with the other and get much more pedaling efficiency.

On fast downhill runs you may feel safer with feet dangling outboard. *Nothing* could be further from the truth. As we will mention later, keeping feet on pedals is vital to safety when going downhill. Toe clips and straps can be a big help in keeping feet on the pedals, particularly when the going is rough and fast. With clips and straps to help hold feet on the pedals, you can ride with leg muscles much more relaxed. More about clips and straps later when we discuss downhill techniques.

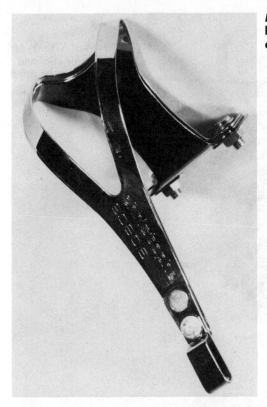

*Fig. 97:* **Two toe clips riveted and bolted together, furnish sturdy clips for ATBs.**

The toe clips I like are made of super-tough plastic, almost impossible to break. They don't rust, and they last a lot longer than metal ones. You'll pay more for them, around $15 a pair. They come in three sizes. I use the large size in winter when I wear felt lined boots, the medium size at other times. If your bike store doesn't have them, write A C International Sales, 16811 S. Maurice St., Cerritos, CA 90701. You can also use double clips (see Fig. 97, above). Remember, you may have to come down on them hard at times when you can't get your feet in them on a rough trail and you want them to stand up under this treatment. If, for example, your feet are off the pedals to avoid a fall, you won't be able to look down to get your feet back to the clips, so you may have to stomp on top of the clips for balance as you bounce on down the hill.

## A Word About Pedals

Most ATBs come with either Shimano platform (Fig. 98) or Sun-Tour XC-II "bear trap" pedals (Fig. 99). The Shimano pedals have slightly raised spikes and built-in reflectors, so you can wear thinner

*Fig. 98:* Most ATBs do not come with toe clips and straps. They can be fitted to pedals, as shown.

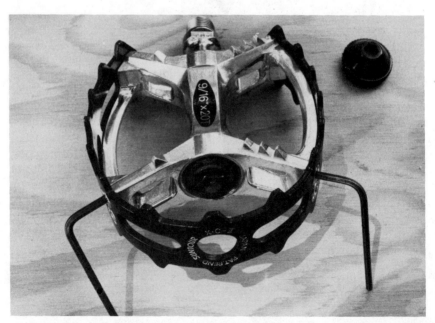

*Fig. 99:* **This "bear trap" pedal has removeable serrated section. Note Allen wrenches in bear trap mounting bolts.**

soled shoes, such as tennis or running shoes. Shimano pedals are well suited to city riding. As you can see in Fig. 98, on page 114, you can install toe clips and, of course, straps, on the Shimano pedal. SunTour pedals have much more aggressive spikes, so you need thick-soled shoes to avoid pain. The "bear trap" part of SunTour pedals is removeable and so replaceable.

## Safety, Trail Courtesy, Helmets, and Animals

Let's start with *helmets*. The National Off-Road Bicycle Association (NORBA), requires that helmets be worn on all official events such as races and rallies. And with good reason. You may think you don't need a helmet because you are far from auto traffic, on a nice, quiet, country dirt road or mountain lane. **WRONG!**

You *do* need a helmet, always and under all conditions. You just never know when you're going to fall. It could be just rounding a sharp curve on a narrow trail and snagging a wheel on a projecting branch, hitting a hidden rock or bump on a fast descent, not quite making a small jump over an obstacle. Your noggin is the most vulnerable part of your body. Your brain floats inside your skull, protected from the bony protrusions on the inside of your skull to some extent. But one hard fall and you could instantly be transformed from a biped into a noped, a paraplegic or a quadraplegic. I'm not going to get into the medical aspects of the brain and how vulnerable it is to impact damage. You will find lots of good reading material on this subject in the Appendix. Nor am I going to delve into the mysteries of Snell Laboratory impact, retention, penetration, and other helmet tests, for which, again, please see Appendix references. I do want to briefly mention helmets that have passed all the Snell tests with flying colors. One more word before I go further, though. I serve as an expert witness in bicycle accident litigation. I work with attorneys all over the country. I can tell you I am horror struck at the number of brain-damaged cyclists I run across in these accidents, whose injuries need not have been as severe (those that are still alive), had they been wearing helmets. You may think that a quiet country lane, with soft humus soil, does not require a helmet. But what about those hard trees lining the road, the steep fall off the side of the road down a ravine, the rocks on the side of the trail? Your brainbox, dear reader, is a jillion times more important than the $35 to $50 price of a good bike helmet. Well, enough of this hard sell on why you should wear a helmet. I just hope you do, that's all. Now here are the helmets I can recommend.

The Snell Foundation has been testing motorcycle helmets for many years. Recently they have done definitive work on testing bicycle helmets as well. They have completed tests on current models of helmets (as of this writing). From these tests, six helmets emerge as offering excellent, very good, or good protection on impacts from 3'3" to 6'; good retention on impact; good fit; coolness; and overall comfort. These helmets range in price from $42.50 to $57. They are the Bell Biker II, Bell TourLite, Bell VIPro, Bailen, and the MSR (Mine Safety Research) (Figs. 100–106).

Remember, do not wear a visor on your helmet. If you fall on it, or it is pushed into you as you slide on the ground after a fall, you can be hurt. One final point. Any helmet that meets ANSI Z90-4 standards as to area of protection, shock absorbance, penetration resistance, strength, and retention (on your head in case of impact) is a good helmet.

*Fig. 100:* Bell Biker II helmet has padded interior, hard shell lining, D-ring chin strap.

*Fig. 101:* Bell Tourlite is popular with touring cyclists. I would remove the visor, because if you fall on it, or it is pushed into you as you slide on the ground, you could be hurt. It also has padded interior, with snap chin-strap fastening.

*Fig. 102:* Bell VIPro helmet is popular with racing cyclists. It gives good ventilation, is light and offers infinitely more protection than the leather covered foam strip "hair nets" which are virtually useless, yet favored by many racers.

*Fig. 103:* This Bailen helmet was designed by a physician after seeing head injuries suffered by helmetless cyclists. Head is suspended by lining, for ventilation, yet shell and inner liner give excellent penetration and impact resistance.

*Fig. 104:* Interior view of Bailen helmet.

*Fig. 105:* Helmet by Mountain Safety Research. Patterned after MSR's climbing helmet, with holes for ventilation. Has excellent retention and penetration resistance.

*Fig. 106:* Inside view of MSR helmet. Molded inner liner offers good shock and impact resistance.

## COURTESY ON THE TRAIL

This advice comes from the National Off-Road Bicycle Association Code. The Code is designed to win over backpackers, equestrians, park officials, and the general public to the sport of off-road cycling. We want to demonstrate that we are good people, that we respect the rights of others in the wilderness, and the wilderness itself. To paraphase the Sierra Club, from a wilderness trip we want to leave nothing behind but our fat tire prints. NORBA says:

1. **Yield** even if it seems inconvenient. Sensitivity to others will assure a positive image for your sport. Restrictions caused by negative encounters can be minimized or turned aside. Remember, bikers in the back country are new to hikers and horses. Let's do all we can to reduce resistance to our new sport.

2. **Pass with care.** Let others know you are there. A cheery greeting, the tinkle of a bar bell, will do it. Never pass a hiker without some warning. Remember, you may not be heard, and startling a hiker out of the quiet contemplation induced by the backwoods, may anger the most gentle of souls. We want to avoid any startled rush of adrenalin as we glide silently past the hiker. Be especially careful as you pass a horse. As you approach, ask the rider if the horse is easily spooked. If so, you should get off and walk the bike past. That way the equestrian knows you understand and will be more tolerant and regard you as a friend, rather than as an enemy. There may also be times when you will have to stop and lift your bike off the trail to let others pass.

3. **Stay on trails.** Riding on meadows and other fragile ecosystems can damage them. Never cut switchbacks. It's a temptation, but stay on the trail. Be aware of the soil type you plan to ride on. If it's clay, wait three or four days after a rain before using it, or choose an alternate route, preferably of shale or of decomposed granite surface.

4. **Control your speed.** Safe speeds should be relative to the terrain. Make turns in anticipation of someone around the bend. I would add, always ride up to a sharp turn on a narrow trail as though something actually *is* there, such as a fallen log. I would also add this caveat for road cyclists who are new to off-road cycling: Don't draft, don't get any closer to the cyclist ahead than three or four bike lengths. If you stay too close to the rider ahead, you won't see danger that the rider in front of you sees, in time for *you* to avoid it. Trail riding requires some attention to the terrain, to the trail, so you don't run into the myriad obstructions you can so easily avoid if you see them in time.

*Fig. 107:* Skidding the trail as in this photo is definitely bad practice. Such a skid leaves marks that can contribute to trail damage and, if deep enough, will probably remain long enough to be spotted by rangers or others concerned with trail preservation. Don't do it!

5. **Try to avoid braking so that you skid,** as shown in Fig. 107. If you skid, slide, or slip, you will probably leave a mark on the trail that can contribute to trail erosion. Others not as friendly to ATBers may also see the skid marks.

6. **Don't run livestock.** You will occasionally come upon a herd of cows, for example. They can be panicked if you charge at them. (I have never had a bull charge at me, but it could happen.) You might also be aware that in cattle grazing country, cow plates, cow flops, call them what you will, are kinda slippery, and when dried on your bike frame, are hard to clean off.

7. **Don't litter.** Pack out what you pack in. If you have room in your panniers, pack out more than your share.

8. **Use permits.** Always check with local authorities regarding fire and entry permits. Check with landowners before trespassing on private roads or trails. Sometimes a "no trespassing" sign really means "O.K., if you ask first."

9. **Plan ahead.** Expect weather changes. Bring emergency rations, tools, cold weather gear even it's only a plastic sack you can punch a hole through for an emergency poncho and hypothermia preventor. You can buy an emergency, aluminum-lined plastic sheet that could save your life, and that when folded is no bigger than a Sony Walkman. (I was going to say, "than a pack of you-know-whats," but I gave them up a long time ago.)

To the above I would add a few thoughts gleaned from forest rangers. It's a good idea to leave a trip route with the local ranger. *He should know when you leave, where you can be reached at various check points, and when you will be back.* That makes it easier for you to be reached in an emergency. I've tried five watt CB radios and find them of very limited value, especially in the mountains.

Glenn Odell, NORBA executive secretary, also offers other advice, such as:

1. Yield trail use to faster travelers.

2. Avoid overuse areas. You'll have more fun in less crowded areas. (I would add: If you see a "Yuckabagoe," bike away like mad!)

3. Ride defensively, assume the worst and be prepared.

4. Know and ride within your limits.

5. Establish eye contact with those you meet on the trail. (It makes them feel you have seen them, so you won't run into them.)

6. Stick to the middle of the trail. Trail shoulders protect against washouts.

7. Keep a low profile. Try not to be seen, or be heard.

8. Dress for trail conditions, be prepared to cross water and mud. (The motley crew in Fig. 108 may not be a model of sartorial cycling elegance, but they are prepared for the worst. They found it at the 4,800 foot level in the Sierra, near Placerville, California. The massed start racers in Fig. 109 are more elegant, but their clothing reflects where they are, in the central California desert, halfway between Bakersfield and San Luis Obispo, practically astride the San Andreas Fault. There's more about clothing later in this chapter.

One more point. If you're cycling on country farm roads, be aware that drivers often drift over to the center of the road. Listen for approaching cars, especially at blind intersections. As you go over the top of a hill, know that drivers can't see over the top, so stay on the far right-hand side of the road and have an escape route picked out. Be prepared for gravel or stones to be kicked up by passing cars. Eyeglasses can help keep out insects as well as small particles of dust and dirt. If you keep your mouth closed, you won't swallow as many bugs. I know dirt county roads in farm country are not exactly wilderness areas, but you may have to ride one to get there. So be careful out there.

*Fig. 108:* A massed-start mountain race, near Placerville, California, in the Sierra, shows that riders are highly individualistic as to clothing styles. They do have one thing in common, a helmet on the noggin.

*Fig. 109:* **Another massed-start race, in Carissa Plains, California, in the high desert country, not far from the San Andreas earthquake fault. Note the youngster on the BMX bike in the center. To the right of the BMX bike is Jacquie Phelan, U.S. women's off-road racing champion.**

## ABOUT SUNGLASSES

They are fine in bright, shiny weather. But sometimes, on the sunniest of days, the trail will lead you into a dense, overgrown, tree-lined area, where the shadows grow dense (Fig. 110). It takes a few minutes for your eyes to adjust to the darker area, so be doubly careful, slow down until you can see where you're going. Then, when you hit the bright sunny area, slow down again until you can see that cow right up ahead on the trail.

## HOW TO FALL (REASONABLY) SAFELY

There's no really safe way to fall off a moving bicycle, especially when the road is hard and you are moving fast. There are ways to fall, though, that can minimize damage to your body. The problem is that potentially damaging falls are so instantaneous, so split-second, that about the only thing you can do is practice falling on a pile of hay, or an old mattress, or into a sand box. I have never practiced any of these falls, but somehow, over the years I have learned the art of protective flying over the handlebars. Here are a few tips.

*Fig. 110:* **The rider on this narrow mountain trail is approaching two possible hazards. He's in the super bright California sun and is wearing sunglasses. In a moment he'll be in dense shadow. His eyes will take a few seconds to readjust to the reduced light level, so he won't be able to see trail hazards clearly. He's also approaching a blind turn, around which could be anything from a tree fallen across the trail to a rider on horseback taking up the entire trail width.**

*Fig. 111:* **This rider is just beginning to go into the classic tuck position to minimize bodily damage on impact. He's correctly holding onto the handlebars, so as not to take impact on wrists and arms. He'll land and roll on back of shoulders (I know, I took this picture).**

I collect pictures of bicycle falls. I've been doing so for years. (Don't ask me why I have been doing this, I don't know. Possibly it's some morbid preoccupation.) Looking over this collection, I can see that in a frontal impact, as when you hit a bump or a stone or a log, the tendency is for the bike to stop and for you to keep going forward. My advice is to hold onto the handlebars and let the bike take the shock (Fig. 111). It's instinctive, I know, to put your hands out to absorb the fall. That's a good way to get a sprained or even a broken wrist.

If you go into a skid, or manage to fall off sideways, as happens, try the "tuck and roll" maneuver used by skilled cyclists, motorcyclists, skiers, and speed skaters. What you do is turn away from the direction of impact. Let the back of your shoulder take most of the impact. Just before you hit the turf, tuck your head down and slide out on your back and shoulder. Don't try to use your arms to break the fall; you'll likely break one of them or a wrist instead. Then, when you are on the ground, wrap your arms around your head, so you protect the extremely vulnerable back of your neck. If you should sever the spinal cord there, you have nothing left from the neck down. A safe way to learn how to fall correctly is to practice on a trampoline, or an old mattress or some other, more forgiving surface.

I'm not going to get into first aid on the trail in this book because there are so very many excellent works on this subject. You will find several first aid references in any sporting goods store. Learn how to deal with dehydration, sunstroke, poison oak, snakebites, hypothermia, hypoglycemia (we cyclists call it the "bonks" and it's when you run out of steam, i.e., low blood sugar), contusions, concussions and signs thereof, shock, fractures, cuts, and other manner of catastastrokes than can beset the human body in unforeseen ways. If it's a long ride you're planning, better learn, too, about diet for maximum energy. There are good references on trail food in the Appendix. Nutritionists have all this figured out for you.

### Shoes and Other Clothing

Shoes are important, so let's start with them. Your feet take a lot of punishment and pressure. You need shoes that will protect the soles of your feet from pain caused by the pins on the pedals. You need shoes that will also give you a firm grip on the ground if you need it. Which type of shoe is best depends a lot on where you will be cycling. If you're commuting to work, or riding mostly on flat, firm ground, cycling shoes will work fine. I have used and can recommend Rivat cyclo cross, Avocet, and Sidi shoes (Fig. 112). Cleats aren't advisable

*Fig. 112:* **Underside of recommended shoes. Note differences in tread pattern. Left to right—Nike, Avocet, Asolo, and Sidi. The more aggressive soles of the Nike and Asolo are favored for rough terrain because of their superior ground gripping. The other two shoes are fine for smooth terrain riding, such as paved roads.**

(metal or plastic frames, fastened to shoe sole, with a tunnel that fits over pedal cross section) because there will be times when you need to get your feet off the pedals fast, and cleats could slow that down. Fig. 113 shows male and female versions of the kinds of shoes I found others wearing, in this case just after an ATB race in the California desert country.

For serious trail riding in the wilds, though, conventional cycle shoes simply do not have enough sole grip. As I said earlier, there are times when you need to get your feet out quickly. You can't tell what kind of surface you will be placing your foot on. It could be rock or sand. In either case you need a waffle type gripper sole, such as the Nike Approach or the Asollo Supertrek S. Both of these shoes also give you good ankle protection. The Supertrek S (Fig. 114) costs around $97 and is one of the toughest, sturdiest hiking boots on the market. Its upper is of 2 mm full-grain smooth leather and Cordura, it has D-ring and hook lacing, a gusseted tongue, a cushioned insole, and outer waterproofing. The size 8 weighs 2 pounds, 3 ounces. The Nike Approach has a laminated upper of Cordura, Gore-Tex, and Cambrelle, with a Perma-Foam sock liner. The size 8 weighs about 1

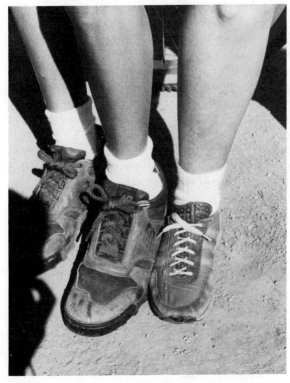

*Fig. 113:* Footwear for off-road riding doesn't have to be Gucci-elegant. It just has to give support, protection against sharp pedal points, and give good ground traction, which these shoes do.

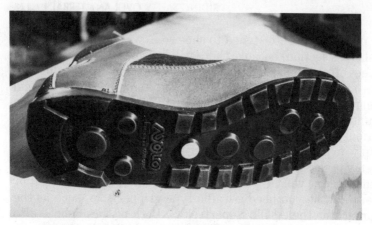

*Fig. 114:* **Close-up of excellent ground gripping Asolo sole.**

pound. It costs around $70. I have worn both and like them both. The Supertrek is tougher and gives more protection. It's the shoe I take on long overnight or week-long trips. I like the Nike for day trips, it's lighter and breathes a bit better than the Supertrek.

I have seen off-road riders also wearing $12 Astroturf Brand X baseball shoes. Their little pencil size fingers seem to grip the trail well and pedal well, I am told. The Nike Lavadome is also a popular shoe. The Rivat bike shoe has a fairly decent gripping tread for uphill walking (which you will do, believe me) and for running uphill. It has removeable cleats in the heel which are helpful when you have to get a purchase in mud. The Rivat is easy to get into the toe clip, and has a good stiff sole which flexes when you want to run, but is still enough for foot protection on bear trap pedals.

The ideal shoe for cold weather riding is a rubber/leather felt lined boot, the kind you find in Army-Navy stores, or in the L. L. Bean catalog. (See Appendix for that and lots of other catalogs for everything you might ever need for off-road cycling, and more.)

Since you can't foretell what kind of weather you'll face on the trail, unless you live where the weather is predictable (i.e, always hot, as in the desert, or often wet, as in coastal areas) you need to be ready for anything except snow in July. In general, you need floppy, loose clothing that won't bind in the crotch. Knickers and knee socks are great, you don't need to worry about cuffs catching in the chain. On warm days, shorts with chamois reinforced crotch, worn with nothing underneath, are great. As a general rule, stay away from anything made from an oil well or coal mine. Plastic clothing won't breathe, you will sweat and smell. Pure wool and cotton fabrics are the most comfortable and breathe best. You can use half wool or cotton and half polypropylene or some other synthetic, if the wrinkled look bothers you. Personally, I like the wrinkled look.

Lycra cycling shorts may be "in" for road touring and racing. I don't like them for off-road cycling, but not only because they are plastic. They also catch on the nose of the saddle as you sit back down after having got up off the pedals, which you will do a lot, as you will learn later in this chapter. When the crotch of these shorts catches on the nose of the saddle, you have to struggle to get free. At best it's a minor annoyance, at worst, it could cause an accident.

Layering is important. You can add or peel off layers of clothing as the heat or cold dictate. If you're heading for the heights, remember it gets a lot colder as you go up. And as you come back down you may have wind chill due to greater speed. Light windbreakers can be a big help, they can be rolled up and stuffed into a bar or saddle bag.

If you're going in for the really rough stuff, such as observed trials events which we discuss in chapter 6, you should consider clothing with padded everything; elbows, knees, and shoulders at least. This type of clothing is available from bike shops that cater to the BMX racing scene, and from motorcycle shops that serve the moto-cross motorcycle folk.

Gloves are very important. They give you protection against pressure on the ulnar nerve that runs up the middle of the hand. Such pressure can be painful if continuous. The best glove has a heavily padded palm. Look for bike gloves with a "visco elastic polymer, such as Spenco." It does a good job of absorbing road shock laterally across the glove. Spenco bar grips are also great for shock absorbance.

Raingear is important. The cheapest is a simple plastic garbage bag, which I have mentioned before. Just cut a hole in the top, use it as a poncho. The best raingear is a combination jacket and separate pants of Gore-Tex that keeps out water and lets out sweat. Less expensive and practical raingear is the bike poncho and chaps combination made by North by Northeast. Ask your bike shop for them. North by Northeast is located in Pawtucket, Rhode Island. For foot protection, you can use a small plastic bag over wool socks. Works well in cold weather, too.

## Animals and Other Critters

The Bambi syndrome is probably responsible for more human injury and death caused by animals than any other factor. This syndrome portrays wild animals as warm, loving, almost human creatures. Wild animals are *not* the sweet, cuddly, loveable beasts they may appear to be. Stay away from them, don't feed them. Be aware that male animals are particularly feisty during the rutting season from August into late winter. If you have ever seen deer, elk or moose clashing antlers during that period, you know what I mean.

Elk and moose are unpredictable at any season. Give them as wide a berth as possible. In general, try to avoid surprising any wild animal with your presence. (Humans too, as mentioned earlier.) In chapter 1, I mentioned a quick wheelie I pulled over a rattler. The rattlesnake and I were both surprised. You need to be aware of and have respect for wildlife, as well as be cautious near them for your own sake. Even on a bike you could be bitten by a snake if you come too close to one and surprise it. Remember, poisonous snakes can strike lightning fast.

For the material on animal confrontation that follows, I am indebted to Ken Kawata, General Curator, Milwaukee (Wisconsin) County Zoo, one of the major zoos in the U.S., and to the rangers of Yosemite and Sequoia National Parks in California.

In general, don't go near or feed any wild animal. Remember, they are not domesticated and are not predictable. The most dangerous animal you could confront is a grizzly or brown bear. If you should be so unfortunate as to come upon one, some authorities recommend that you pretend you're dead. This has worked in the past, but not always. You could turn and bike away as fast as possible, which adrenalin flow should make very fast in this instance. But be warned that grizzlies can run for a long time at 20 mph and have been known to go faster in short spurts. You will only find grizzlies in the wilds of the western United States and Canada, however.

Black bears are more ubiquitous and can be found in wilderness areas in many places in the U.S. They are more likely to run from than at you. But *never* get between a bear cub and its mother. Bears with cubs are, in general, more defensive and are more likely to attack if they feel the cub is threatened. Some authorities recommend going rapidly in a direction away from the bear, and, above all, doing nothing threatening. Others recommend you stomp, wave the bike around, whistle, scream, shout, blow a whistle, so the bear knows you are a human and not to be eaten. What makes the bear think you are human after those shenanigans I'll never know, or will I? Remember, too, that black bears can climb trees like crazy, so if you have to run, don't try it up a tree. The bear can chase you up and out on a limb (so *that's* where that phrase comes from) and he may think nothing of shaking you off it.

Members of the cat family, such as mountain lions, panthers, and bobcats, are unlikely to be a problem. These animals generally stay well clear of humans. Of course, if they feel threatened by anything you do, beware!

If a small animal, such as a squirrel, chipmunk, raccoon, or skunk appears to be friendly and comes up to you, it's probably rabid. To be on the safe side, it's best to consider it so. Snuggling up to humans is abnormal behavior for a wild animal. The incidence of rabies in wild animals can be high, so if one bites you, bike back to civilization and get to the first aid room of the nearest hospital or to the closest physician. If you are days from medical aid, try to get help from rangers. See chapter 4 for official ground-to-air rescue signals.

Apropos of summoning help, I always carry a signalling mirror. It's useful to attract the attention of people on far ridges or in cabins across the valley, or passing aircraft. As I said earlier, CB radios are practically useless in the mountains.

## How to Ride Down Steep Hills Safely, and Have Fun Doing It

An experienced off-road rider will leave an experienced road rider way behind on any kind of trail riding, uphill or down. That's because riding techniques for off-road cycling are so different from anything you've learned from paved road riding. On really steep, fast downhill runs, the technique you use is more akin to skiing than to road riding.

The inexperienced rider, starting a descent, even on a mild downhill grade, often makes the mistake of sticking a foot out to one side, sometimes both feet (Fig. 115). That's a mistake, for three reasons. First, one foot out unbalances the bike, and if you hit a bump you

*Fig. 115:* **With both feet out, this rider is definitely in an unbalanced position and could spill. He's just landed after a jump, and you can see his rear wheel is still airborne after landing on the front wheel first.**

could fall. Second, one foot out means the other foot is on the pedal and the pedal is at the 6 o'clock position. In that position, there's minimum clearance between the ground and the pedal. If you turn in the direction of the pedal that's down, you could drag that pedal on the ground and fall. Three, with one or both feet down, you're sitting on the saddle, and that puts your center of gravity up high, and, again, you could topple.

Ideally, you should get your saddle down low, your tuckus back as far as possible, and your weight on the pedals, as shown in Figs. 116 or 117. Pedals should be parallel to the ground for maximum road clearance. All this gets your center of gravity as low as possible for maximum stability. By the way, there's a new spring device on the market, designed by Joe Breeze and Josh Angell, of Mill Valley, California. It's called the Hite Rite (Fig. 118). Properly installed, it lets you reach back, flip open the seat post quick release, get the saddle down for descents, and retighten the quick release lever, without dismounting. Then, once at the bottom of the hill, and still on the saddle, you can reach down again, loosen the quick release lever, get your weight up off the saddle, and the Hite Rite shoves the saddle back up to your normal riding height. It's great for races where seconds count. This device also keeps the seat post in line with the frame, no matter at what height you adjust it, or how often you make an adjustment. It's also a confidence builder because it helps makes descents safer. If you can't find one in your bike shop, write to Breeze

*Fig. 116:* **The right stuff for fast downhill riding on a bumpy trail. Here the rider has his weight back over the rear wheel, feet on pedals more or less parallel to ground. This way he gets his center of gravity down as low as possible.**

*Fig. 117:* **Here's good form for high speed rough trail descents. This is a race, so the rider wants to keep upright, yet go as fast as possible. Note front wheel has jumped off the ground. The rider has front wheel pointing straight ahead, which means he'll have better control when it lands. If it were cocked, he would probably spill on landing.**

and Angell Development Co., 28 Country Club Drive, Mill Valley, CA 94942.

It's appropriate to give you an explanation regarding the use of the seat post binder bolt (Fig. 50 on page 67). This is exactly the same mechanism that's used on conventional road bikes to lock wheels in place. The binder bolt quick-release mechanism is a cam action device. It is *not* a bolt to be turned or tightened. All you do is turn the quick-release lever inward, toward the bike frame, to tighten it. If the saddle is still loose, this mechanism should be readjusted by turning the nut on the opposite side of the lever a few turns or by turning the lever itself clockwise a half turn or so, while the lever is in the open position (and then the lever should be closed).

Lowering the saddle also gives you better control on slides and other radical turns. And here's a technique you'd never learn on pavement. If you know how to snowplow, to traverse a really steep slope, you know what I mean by traversing on your ATB. Some slopes you hit are so steep you can't even walk down them. But you can ride

*Fig. 118:* **For off-road cycling, you need to raise your saddle up for hill climbs, down for descents. This device lets you do it without stopping. At left, saddle is low for descent, at right, the Hite Rite saddle adjustor has moved saddle to preselected maximum height. It maintains seat-to-frame alignment, too.**

down if you know how. What you do is use both brakes on the turns (i.e., only brake as you traverse, let go to make your turn into the next traverse, brake again, etc.), to keep speed under control. Then you just shift your body around to "snowplow" around rocks, trees, anything else that's in your way. But be careful if you "ski" downhill. If you try that on a soft, sandy slope you could cut grooves in them, and that's bound to be bad for our image and make things a lot tougher for others, when the ranger catches up to the damage. And on really, really steep hills you may have to get your body so far back it's right over the rear wheel.

Sometimes you can get on such a really steep hill that panic can set in. The situation is similar to that faced by a skier who suddenly finds himself pointing straight down the slope, accelerating at a frightening rate. The good skier and the good cyclist keep speed under control by traversing. That is, by swinging from one side of the trail to the other, using both brakes only after a turn, letting go the front brake to make another turn, and so forth, until they get to the bottom of the hill.

Remember, as a general technique, you need to ride and brake downhill so that you never lock up the front wheel. If you do, you'll go in the direction the wheel was pointing (Fig. 119). What generally happens here is that the wheel twists to one side or the other if you're not careful in braking or steering. But the bike wasn't going in that direction. It wants to go in whatever direction you were headed before the wheel twisted. This conflict usually winds up dumping the rider over the handlebars, in what sailors call a classic "pitchpole," where the boat's bow goes down, the stern goes up, and the whole thing goes ass over teakettle.

I should reemphasize here that a good rider never breaks traction and skids so the trail is torn up, as in Fig. 107. Trail erosion, especially in the West, is a major problem we don't, as cyclists, want to exacerbate. This is particularly true of the narrower trails. So never, if you can, and certainly not consciously, leave skid marks on a trail.

I have asked many skilled downhill ATB racers, usually people in their late teens or early twenties, how they could go so fast for so long without dumping. The stock answer almost always was: "Hey, you just relax, float with it, go with it. Be fluid, move with it." In only a

*Fig. 119:* **This is not good form for jumping. Front wheel is pointed away from direction bike is heading. When rider lands, front wheel wants to turn left, but bike is going another direction. Conflict is resolved as rider loses control and dumps the bike. This type of spill can be avoided by a skilled rider, but it takes lots of practice.**

few cases could I get some real specifics. It reminds me of the early space flights, with the astronauts trying to tell people what the world looked like from up there, and all we got was, "Wow, great, terrific." The mind boggles. You need to learn, so it's instinctive, the jillion tiny little body movements one has to make to keep upright, lean one way or the other, coax the bike around the trail to avoid bumps and rocks and stumps. It takes a lot of practice. Being cool, relaxed, is where it's at, keeping the techniques in this chapter in mind all along, of course. All I can give you are general rules. The rest is learned behavior, virtually instinctive because you have to react faster than you can think. Sometimes the body has a wisdom greater than the mind that is supposed to control it. So get that saddle down, butt back, keep control on fast descents by, among other things, reading the trail well in front of you. Make your turns by keeping body weight (i.e., center of gravity) as neutral as possible so it doesn't influence which way the bike turns (a learned technique words can't convey, really). Make your turns by putting all your weight downward on the pedal that's on the *outside* of the turn. The pedal on the *inside* of the turn will then be at the 12 o'clock position to give you maximum clearance between pedal and ground. That way you won't scrape the ground with the pedal as you lean into the turn. What you want are careful, slight, quick movements that are extremely controlled. A little "body english" is all you need in extremely fast downhill turns. Subtlety of movement is the key to control. Remember, too, that the shallower, less steep head angles of an ATB require the rider to lean more for a given speed and radius turn than necessary for the same turn on a road bike. The higher bottom bracket of an ATB lets you do this with less chance of the pedals scraping the ground, should you happen not to have the pedals at the correct position on the turn.

## How to Be a Climber

Look at the stem on your ATB. You'll notice that it's forward of the headset. That's so you can lean forward on hill climbs, so you can power and steer at the same time. There's a fine point, in hill climbing, between keeping traction on the rear wheel and maintaining steering control on the front wheel. Moving your weight backward, more over the rear wheel, gives you traction. Moving it forward puts weight on the front wheel and that helps you steer accurately.

Uphill climbing is an exercise in balance and weight control. In my experience, riding bicycle training rollers, the kind where you balance the bike on rollers and not the kind where the bike is bolted down, gives you balance training you need to ride up hills successfully. The motions one makes reminds me of a slow-motion ballet or a slow mime. On really steep grades you may have to get up off the saddle and stand on the pedals. In such a case you'll need to keep part of your body back for traction, and part of you forward for steering control, as shown in Fig. 120. Be warned, though, that standing on the pedals (Fig. 121) for uphill climbs is extremely demanding and requires top physical condition. If you're not in good shape, I suggest you walk up.

Walking uphill is nothing to be ashamed of. Champion off-road mountain racers do it sometimes (Fig. 122). Beginners do it more often (Fig. 123).

Don't wait to shift down to a lower, hill-climbing Granny gear until you are straining up the grade. Torque on the chain makes for erratic shifting, and you may not be able to shift at all. In that case you will have to traverse the trail from side to side so you can ease off on pedal pressure while you coax gears to shift down. You may even have to stop, lift the rear wheel, rotate the pedals and shift down. It takes three hands, or two hands and a leg, to do this. Best way is to shift

*Fig. 120:* Good form for uphill riding. This rider, Gavin Chilcott, a U.S. professional racer, has weight about equally over the rear wheel, for traction, and over the front wheel for wheel grip on this loose terrain. Front wheel grip is important for steering.

*Fig. 121:* Here is good form in hill climbing while standing on the pedals.

*Fig. 123:* Sometimes you have to walk up steep hills. Beginner ATBers walk up more often than more experienced riders, as these novices demonstrate.

*Fig. 122:* Even experienced riders have to walk up some very steep hills, as shown here during a race in Carissa Plains, California (about halfway between San Luis Obispo and Bakersfield).

down *before* you need the gear, while you can ease off on pedal pressure without stalling the bike.

If you stall out, best way to get going again is to straddle the top tube, then put your strongest leg on the pedal at the 1:30 o'clock position. Push down hard while at the same time pushing off and hoisting yourself up into the saddle. If the grade is too steep, or if you apply too much pedal pressure at once, if you can't get traction enough to traverse, why not give up gracefully and walk. As I said, it's no disgrace. As you do walk, stay on the left side of the bike, away from the chain and chainwheel. Put the left crank either directly in front or directly behind you, parallel to the ground, so you don't hit it with your shin or the back of your calf as you strain while pushing the bike uphill.

I know I've said this before, but I'll say it again: *wear a helmet; wear a helmet; wear a helmet; wear a helmet!* The head you save will be your own. Just because you're in the country doesn't mean you won't fall. If anything, there are more rocks, crevasses, stumps, bumps, and humps on the trail than on the road any day. The skillful rider will avoid 99 percent of them. It's the 1 percent you can't avoid that makes a helmet such a lifesaver.

## Jumps and Wheelies

A jump and a wheelie may seem alike. They are not. A jump is when you come upon a small cliff, say a drop of two, three, or four feet on the trail, where perhaps it has eroded. A garden variety of wheelie is where you pull up on the bars to get the front wheel up in the air to go over an obstacle in the trail.

In a jump situation, you may not be able to stop, and you suddenly find yourself airborne (Fig. 124). If you have been watching the trail ahead and have some experience behind you, you can see where the vegetation drops. Bushes seem to show just the tops, whereas bushes where you are can be seen in their entirety. You will, most of the time, be able to sense when the trail is about to drop off under you. At that point you have the choice of stopping and possibly working your way around or walking down the jump or flying airborne over it. If you elect to jump, keep your balance on the saddle, don't make any exaggerated movements, "be fluid, keep your cool." Try to get the machine to land on both wheels at once for maximum stability. After you hit the ground move backward a bit to get weight off the front wheel. If you start to wobble while airborne, try gripping the saddle between your thighs so you don't wobble more. Be aware that as you land, the impact could dump you. All jumps can be hazardous. It's a good idea to practice small jumps, starting at 6 inches or so, and work up to 18

*Fig. 124:* Making a jump. Note pedals are parallel to ground, rider has weight toward rear of bike, but is also using body english to keep bike going straight.

*Fig. 125:* Jumping a ditch with an ATB.

or 24 inches. Wear protective clothing with padding at knees, elbows, and shoulders, gloves and a helmet, while you do so.

If you want to, or have to, jump a ditch (Fig. 125), be sure you have enough speed to do it. You may have to release brakes to build up the speed you need to clear the ditch. If the ditch is too big to jump, it's big enough to ride through. In that case, as you go into the depression, push your weight forward on the bars, then, as you emerge on the other side, push your weight back on the saddle, so you'll have the traction you need to climb out. In other words, you move your body mass forward as you enter the ditch, backward as you leave it.

## Wheelies and Bunny Hops

The kind of wheelies I am serious about are *not* the kind you see youngsters doing on their BMX bikes wherever they can find a little hill, or during BMX races over a staged course. Those break dancing bunny hops, with all their attendant dangers to life and limb, are deliberate and, for the most part, made safely after lots of practice. What I mean to discuss are hops you sometimes have to take, or decide to take, during the course of an ordinary trail ride, to clear an obstacle (Fig. 126).

Sometimes I wheelie over a small stump or a curb when I don't have to, just for the fun of it and for practice. Pulling a wheelie is not the bunny hop you may have imagined. You can, of course, approach an obstacle, such as a curb, and as you come up to it, jerk up on the handlebars. The upward jerk will pull the front wheel off the ground. If you pulled upward on the bars hard enough you may have pulled the front wheel up far enough to top whatever you're jumping over.

The trouble with the handlebar pull-up, bunny-hop wheelie is that it does nothing for the rear wheel. The front wheel may clear the obstruction, but the rear wheel will hit it hard. Results of this type of hop are bent or broken axles, out-of-true wheels or actual flattened rims and blown tires. If tire pressure is too low, bottomed out tubes are squeezed between what you jump over and the rim, and blow out.

The bunny hop is useful for going over logs or a ditch you didn't see until you were on it, or a curb you need to hop over to avoid an oncoming car. To bunny hop, yank up the front wheel by the handlebars, shove your weight backward and fly over the obstruction. As the front wheel clears whatever you are hopping over, push down on the bars, move your weight forward as far as possible and get the rear wheel moving over the obstacle with as little impact as possible on that wheel. If you practice, you should be able to hop over an obstacle of 16 inches or higher. Practice this maneuver so that the hop is one smooth motion, raising both wheels off the ground at the same time

*Fig. 126:* Here rider is hopping over an obstacle in the trail by pulling back on bars to get front wheel up. As he clears, he will push down on bars to get rear wheel over the obstacle with minimum impact.

by pulling up on the bars as you come to the curb, with your weight to the rear, then pushing down on the bars with your weight forward as the front wheel clears the curb. In other words, a wheelie is a technique to be learned by doing. Here are some tips. Do all moves virtually at once, or within split seconds. Accelerate up to the obstacle fast, in low gear. Bow your back and push your body as far backward as possible. Do all this while pushing forward and up on the handlebars. If you do it right, the front wheel will come up. As the front wheel clears the obstacle, quickly lean your weight forward, to get the rear wheel up or at least minimize rear wheel impact on the obstacle. Use the rear brake only to keep speed under control.

John Olsen, one of the country's most expert observed trials events riders, and his friends in Issaquah, Washington, near Seattle, practice the ultimate wheelie. It involves going over a fallen log about 36 inches high (Figs. 127 to 130). They also go over a rock-strewn stream bed and other assorted impediments to forward motion. Rumor has it that this gang can ride right over a Ford Pinto, the long way, and I believe it.

*Fig. 127:* Not everyone can climb 36-inch-high logs. Here rider John Olsen, in the rain forest near Issaquah, Washington, demonstrates technique for log hopping in an observed trials event. Object is to negotiate obstacles without feet touching ground or obstacles. If foot does touch, a penalty is assessed. This is a specially built bike for this type of event. Note small chainring. Note also protective clothing worn by rider.

*Fig. 128:* It's up and over the log shown in Fig. 127.

*Fig. 129:* Coming down the other side of the log, rider has successfully negotiated this obstacle. Not to worry, *you* won't have to do this on a trail ride, unless you're into observed trials riding.

*Fig. 130:* You can learn how to hop over smaller obstacles, such as this 12-inch-high log, as this rider is doing.

## Fording Rivers (or at Least Streams)

I have seen ATB riders going downriver, water up to the neck, bike completely submerged. For fun, of course. But what a way to cool off on a hot summer day, surprise canoeists, anger anglers, and surprise fish!

More seriously, fording shallow rivers and streams can be an everyday occurrence in the wilderness. Here's how to do it. First, you make sure the water is fordable. Going downstream, with the current, up to your neck in water, may be feasible. But crossing a swiftly flowing river at neck height is definitely not advisable, the stream could knock you over, which is not the healthiest situation for person or bike. Walk through first, make sure the water is not above bottom bracket height. While you're at it, check for holes and rocks in the stream bed. I once saw a rider assume that the stream was as shallow at the end of a small piece of land jutting out into the stream as it was where the trail entered the stream, next to that little peninsula. He was in a race and thought he'd cut some 10 feet off the course by riding out that far into the stream. He hadn't checked out the depth of water at the point of the land, hit about three feet of water (Fig. 131), and dumped the bike (Fig. 132).

*Fig. 131:* **This rider went out on a small peninsula before checking stream depth.**

*Fig. 132:* The rider in Fig. 131 landed in deep water, could not proceed, and dumped the bike. The moral: know the stream is not so deep that you can't pedal across, before you try. At least in a race, ride down the trail and ford any streams first, so you know what you're getting into.

*Fig. 133:* Best way to ride through a shallow stream is at full speed. Hit the water as fast as possible, with the chain in an intermediate gear. Power your way through. If you hesitate or slow down, you'll probably fall over. Remember, water is highly resistant to your forward motion, so give pedaling all you've got to make it across.

Once you have checked out the stream, get on the bike far enough away from the stream to get up a good speed, in a medium gear, say 26 front, 24 rear. Hit the water as fast as you can (Fig. 133) and keep on pedaling hard. If you slacken, you will fall over, no ifs, ands, or buts about it.

Mud is a slightly different matter. Here, too, you must keep pedaling, but in low gear. Balance carefully, you will not be going very fast. Shift your body weight around to keep upright. Watch for grooves that could catch a wheel and throw you. Use the rear brake first, to keep steering under control. If you're on a muddy uphill slope, apply only enough pedal pressure to keep going, so you don't skid and lose traction. Keep in a low gear for the power you need if you hit a pocket of mud.

### Keep It on Ice

As I noted in chapter 2, you can ride on ice with studded tires. Don't do it on an ice-slick highway, though. You might not skid, but a car could, right into you. Lake riding is fun, however. It takes a lot of balancing skill. You could stud your own knobby tires with sheet metal screws, backed by a liner such as Mr. Tuffy, to protect the tube. Someday, I hope, a manufacturer will produce tungsten studded ice tires for all-terrain bicycles.

### Riding in the Snow

You can ride in snow, certainly up to 3 inches deep. Again, though, don't do it on city streets for obvious reasons. But riding through softly falling snow on a rural road or country trail is my idea of Heaven. For snow riding, use the most aggressive knobby tire you can find (see chapter 2). Shift down in snow so you will have power enough to plow through deep spots.

Now, let's go to chapter 4, and get into off-road tripping and the equipment you need to do it.

# 4

## ATBing Around the World (Where to Go, What to Take, Bike Packing Tips and Notes)

In this chapter you will learn how to select a bike pack, racks for packs, sleeping bags, and tents. We will also cover tools and spare parts to take on wilderness trips. The best stoves and cookware, a bit about foods for wilderness bike trips, and tips on health, safety, orienteering, map reading, rescue signaling, and first aid will be given. Finally, off-road touring opportunities in the U.S. and abroad will be reviewed. Now, let's start with packs and racks.

### Packs and Racks

Bikepacks (Fig. 134) are also called panniers. I prefer the term "bikepacks." After all, hikers use the term "backpacks," so bicyclists can call them "bikepacks." In this book, I'll just call them packs. One more item of nomenclature. The item that supports packs are called "carriers" by some makers, "racks" by others. I prefer the shorter term, so when I refer to a "rack" (Fig. 135), you'll know what I mean. Here is what to look for in selecting a pack for your ATB:

*Fig. 134:* Here's a fully loaded ATB, ready tor the trail. Packs are by Kirtland.

1. **First, a word about stability.** If you have ever had an un-balanced front wheel, or worn front end on your car, you probably have experienced front-wheel shimmy. You know how such shimmy can shake the front of your four wheeler around. This shimmy can be handled by braking till the shimmy stops. But on a two wheeler it can easily lead to an accident. Front wheel shimmy on a bike can cause loss of control in seconds, because each side to side movement of the front wheel increases intensity (amplitude) and frequency of swing in milliseconds. I know. It happened to me on a bike going down a steep hill in the Austrian Alps a few years ago. Coming up the hill, toward me, was a loaded Mercedes logging truck. On my right there was a 1,000-foot drop. I was going about 40 mph when the bike suddenly got the DT's and began to shake and shimmy like a belly dancer. Braking only seemed to make the shaking worse, so I just dropped the bike on its side and sat on it till it stopped. No harm done, other than shot nerves, some scrapes on the bike and me. A check of the bike revealed no visible reason for the shimmy, until I checked the packs. They were loose, could be pushed from side to side and front to rear. The pack mounting system consisted of two U-shaped hooks that clipped to the top of the rack, and one strap that was to be looped behind the rack to hold the pack in place. Obviously this mounting system was less than adequate. In addition, the load inside the packs could bounce around. Further, I found the rack itself to be unstable. I could grasp it and

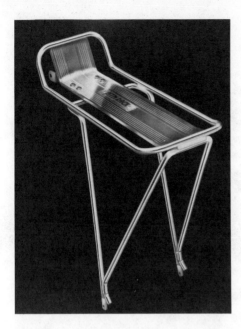

*Fig. 135:* Designed for ATBs, this Blackburn aluminum alloy rack should fit most frames.

easily move it from side to side. Fortunately, packs and racks have been vastly improved since that time (1974). There is one other contributor to instability and possible loss of control on an ATB, and that is fat tires, particularly if underinflated. I suggest that if you are carrying a loaded pack, you add four or five additional pounds of pressure to the tires.

2. **Secure mounting on the rack.** Back in 1972, I was bouncing along a cobblestone street in Brussels, in the midst of traffic, when my left bikepack jumped off the rack and fell into the street. That was the pack that was carrying, among other items, my prized $1,200 Hasselblad camera. I think I broke all records for instant dismount and pack retrieval before a car could run over it. Ideally, the pack should be secured to the rack so well as to be virtually a part of it. There should also be no pack sidesway that could cause instability of the bike.

3. **No load shifting inside the pack.** What you're carrying inside the pack should stay put. If it moves around as you pedal, the weight shift could reduce the stability of the bike. Well-placed interior and/or exterior compression straps (Fig. 136), can keep the load from shifting around.

4. **Proper load distribution inside the pack.** Heavy items should be placed in the forward part of both front and rear packs. Weight as far forward as possible helps keep the front wheel on the ground, particularly on loose terrain, for better steering control. For example,

*Fig. 136:* **One of the best designed, high-quality bikepacks. Needle Works has compression straps that keep the pack securely in place for cycling stability.**

you may suddenly have to steer to avoid an obstacle on the trail. You want the bike to go where you point it, and proper load distribution will help you do it. Forward placement of the load in the rear rack puts the weight closer to the bottom bracket and aids front wheel adhesion.

5. **Packs should be mounted as far forward as possible.** The rack should permit the packs to be as far toward the front of the bike as possible, yet give ample heel clearance on the rear pack, again, for optimum weight distribution on both wheels. In addition, the closer the load is to the center of the bike, the less frame flexing and twisting stress there will be on the bike frame. Placement of the front pack should not interfere with steering. Packs should not obstruct movement of the cantilever brake arms or cables.

6. **Packs should also be as low as possible.** The bottom of the rear pack should be about even with the rear derailleur (Fig. 137), but should not interfere with its operation. A low mounted pack is more stable than a higher mounted pack. Ideally, about one-third of the front pack should be below the front wheel axle (Fig. 138).

*Fig. 137:* These front racks keep front packs low for a stable ride and better front wheel adhesion, for accurate steering, especially on loose terrain.

*Fig. 138:* Eclipse front packs mount low, clear cantilever brakes.

**7. Rectangular shape packs give better side clearance.** A pack that's more rectangular in shape (see Fig. 134 on page 150) is better than a pack that's more square in shape, with the same cubic capacity, because it will not bulge out as much as a square bag. The rectangular pack gives you a thinner profile for clearance on narrow off-road trails. You don't want the pack to catch on anything projecting from the side of the trail, such as tree branches.

**8. Load isolation is important.** The pack should be compartmented (Fig. 139), so you can stow items for convenient retrieval. When you want something you should be able to find it, without an exasperating and time wasting search through the load.

**9. Other pack design features to look for.** Check for loose, unstitched fabric inside the pack, behind zippers. If there is such fabric, I guarantee it will fray and the loose ends and threads will catch in zippers, a major cause of zipper failure and lost tempers. Fabric ends inside as well as outside the pack should be neatly stitched, as in Fig. 139. Back stiffeners should be removeable and replaceable because they can become bent and warped. Tie-downs and other straps should not dangle where they can be caught in the spokes. A rain cover, one

*Fig. 139:* Best bags have many internal compartments, some of which are adjustable so heavier items can be placed toward the front, as in this Needle Works pack.

that's durable and easy to install, is a real plus for two reasons other than rain protection. The cover protects the pack from wear and tear on the trail, as from sharp trail projections or from tears that might occur if you dump the bike. It's a lot easier and less expensive to repair or replace a cover than the pack itself. Second, a cover makes the pack less attractive to thieves because it's more difficult and slower to get into. Every extra second a thief has to spend getting to the target increases the likelihood of his (or her) being caught. (A cable and lock will be yet another deterrent, especially when you camp, but be sure to tie the bike to a tree.) Now let's take a look at the bike racks that carry your bikepacks.

## How to Select a Bike Rack

Not all bike racks are alike. You will have more difficulty fitting some onto your ATB. Some are stronger and more expensive than others. Here's what to look for when shopping for a rack.

1. **The rack should fit your bike.** Not every rack fits every bike. Manufacturers, for example, have yet to standardize the location of

*Fig. 140:* **Racks should fasten securely to bike frame, and be rigid, without sidesway. This Bruce Gordon hand-brazed, mitered, tubular steel rack is an exceptionally well made unit that's very stable.**

*Fig. 141:* Front Gordon rack, showing attachment to fork blade braze-ons. Clamps are also available if there are no braze-ons.

braze-on rack mounting fittings on seat stays and fork blades. Bigger bike frames have longer stays and forks than smaller bikes, which either require location of braze-ons to compensate for frame size, or adaptability of the rack to fit a variety of makes and frame sizes. If your ATB has braze-ons for mounting the racks, you should be able to use these fittings to bolt the rack to the frame, as shown in Figs. 140 and 141. Clamps will work if you don't have braze-on fittings, but they tend to loosen. If clamps loosen, the frame can move, slide around, interfere with brakes and affect overall bike stability. (As a safety measure, it's best to get into the habit of checking the tightness of all rack mount points before every trip.) The rack should either be made to fit your particular make and size of bike, or have enough adjustments so it can be fitted easily and accurately, without a lot of bending and twisting that can weaken metal components. One further point about stability. If the load shifts around, it sets up movement that works against you. You should not have to fight against a load shift one way, while you're trying to pedal or balance in another direction.

2. **The rack should be sturdy.** If the rack breaks on the trail, and you're carrying a lot of camping gear, you will be faced with a major decision. You can abandon all but absolutely necessary gear, and hide the rest in the woods. If you're lucky, it will still be there when you get back, if you can find it. What's necessary depends on how far you are from civilization and the weather. In a pinch you could do without your tent and sleeping bag if you have warm clothes. You will need your food, though you may be able to ditch the stove and cookware if you have enough food that does not require cooking to get you back. If you can get back within the day, then of course you can hide your gear and hope it's still there when you return. A discrete blaze mark on a tree can help you locate it on the return trip.

Ideally, though, you should have a rack strong enough that it won't break. It should have cross bracing for strength and rigidity (Figs. 142 and 143). The rack should be able to withstand the stresses and rigors of trail riding, and have the strength to stay together should the bike fall on its side or collide with a solid object, such as a boulder or tree trunk.

3. **Other features to look for.** The rack should be adjustable so the top can be flat, parallel to the ground. If the frame tilts toward the rear, the pack tends to slide in that direction, which puts load weight toward the rear instead of toward the front of the bike. When fastened to the frame it should not move when pushed from side to side.

*Fig. 142:* **Like the Gordon rack in Fig. 141, this Blackburn welded aluminum front rack permits carrying the packs low for greater cycling stability.**

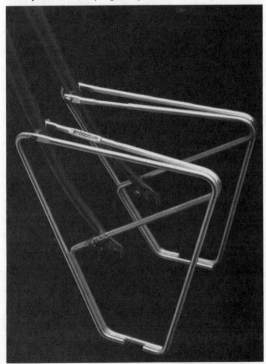

*Fig. 143:* This Blackburn rear bike rack has cross struts to provide stability and minimize sidesway.

The rack should virtually be part of the frame. You should be able to remove the front wheel without removing the rack.

**4. Racks, fat tires, and fenders.** Be careful about buying a rack that's not made specifically for an ATB. Racks made for skinny tire street bikes often do not have enough clearance for the fat rear tire. Check this point out *before* you pay for the rack and go to all the trouble of installing it. Or trying to install it.

If you plan to ride in the rain, there are fenders made to fit over fat tires. That way you'll avoid a streak of dirty water and/or mud up your back and all over the bike and bikepacks, and you won't foul the chain and other moving parts. One rack maker offers a splash guard attachment (see page 169) for his rack. But the problem here is that if you use the biggest fat tire (2.125 inches), it may scrape on the inside of the rack, especially on bike frames smaller than 19.5 inches.

## Pack Selections

Here are recommended bikepacks. If you find a make or model not mentioned, its absence in this book implies nothing whatsoever about it, except that a sample could not be obtained in time for my deadline for this book. The packs are discussed in alphabetical order.

### ECLIPSE, USA

Eclipse makes a very large rear pack, big enough to contain your tent and sleeping bag as well as all the other gear you will need for an extended trip far from supermarkets and the deli. This is their *Professional* pack that has 12 pockets. Total capacity is 2,790 cubic inches. Eclipse makes a street bike rack for this pack, but it won't clear the 2.125 fat tires of an ATB, so use one of the racks described on pages 149 to 158. The loaded pack is about 8-inches wide, maximum. Two packs add about 16 inches to the bike's width, which really is less than the 24- to 27-inch width of the handlebars. If bars clear the trail, the packs should too, unless you're going down a narrow trail overgrown with projecting bushes at hub level. There is some excess fabric, about ⅜-inch inside behind the zippers, but if it frays, you can snip off the excess fabric. The Professional costs $139 a pair. A front pack, the Superlite, has two pockets, a total of 1,107 cu. in., costs $65 a pair. Both packs have removeable stiffeners, high quality zippers, and are made of 8-ounce Cordura fabric, but do not come with compression straps. Total capacity of both packs is 3,897 cu. in. If that seems too cramped, I suggest you're carrying too much stuff. (Whatever you decide to leave out, *Don't leave out the stove* [Fig. 144]). Few things are more frustrating than trying to cook breakfast in the damp of the morning when the fire won't start and you're dying for a cup of coffee. Further, you'll choke on smoke from damp wood. If you've never tasted smoke coffee (water impregnated with smoke odors) you're

*Fig. 144:* Be sure to take one of the excellent small camp stoves along. Depending on damp wood to make a quick breakfast can be one of the more frustrating experiences of outdoor life.

*Fig. 145:* Eclipse Professional model bar pack has a detachable map case. Note the special adapter onto which the pack frame fits, on the center of the handlebars. This adapter is available from bike shops. Be sure to check tightness of its Allen bolts from time to time. If they work loose, the pack can fall off and drop down on front wheel.

lucky. Besides, a wood fire leaves a mess, is hazardous in dry timber areas, and is generally a nuisance. Eclipse also makes rain covers for small packs (won't fit the Professional model), for $16 a pair. Eclipse also makes a dandy bar pack, with a detachable map case. To mount on handlebars you use the adapter shown in Fig. 145, available in bike stores. The only problem I have found with this adapter is that the inside is smooth, the bars are slick and smooth, so if you don't tighten down the two Allen bolts that hold the adapter on the bar, the adapter can tilt upward and the pack will fall off and perhaps cause an accident. So if you use this adapter, check its tightness before you start out. The adapter won't fit on "slingshot" stems (see Fig. 24 on page 40) because the front brake cable guide is in the way. The Eclipse Professional bar pack costs $65.

### KANGAROO PACKS

Kangaroo packs are very sturdy. They're made of 11-ounce "ballistic" nylon, which they claim is 66 percent stronger than ordinary nylon. Inside the packs, seams are neatly stitched, with no excess fabric to snarl zippers. "Mountain" packs have a mounting system consisting of ¾-inch nylon cross straps which hold the pack on the rack securely. These packs are fitted with compression straps. The model I tested is the Trail Ridge (Fig. 146), which has just two compartments with a total of 2,400 cubic inches of interior space. It costs $89.95 a pair and can be used on the rear rack or as a low rider pack on a front rack. This model would be fine for a trip of a few days. For longer trips I prefer Kangaroo's "Butte Mountain" model, which has nine pockets and 3,000 cu. in. of space. It costs $110 a pair. For day rides, the "Klunker Frame Bagg" attaches with Velcro tabs to the top and head tubes, will hold a 35mm camera, film, a wallet, a sandwich, and an apple, at least. Its price is $16.95 and well worth it. I carried my camera on many trips in this bag and the mounting system kept the camera intact even on some pretty rough trails. The sandwich held up O.K., too. The larger packs have nonremoveable aluminum stiffeners to which the mounting straps are riveted.

### KIRTLAND PACKS

Kirtland makes a full range of packs for ATBs, from one suitable for day trips (see Fig. 134 on page 150), to expedition size and quality packs. Judging from the samples they sent to me, these are well constructed and designed packs. The packs for rack mounting use a unique "Lever Lock" system (Fig. 147), which clamps two U-hooks

*Fig. 146:* **This Kangaroo rear pack has compression straps and is an excellent bikepack.**

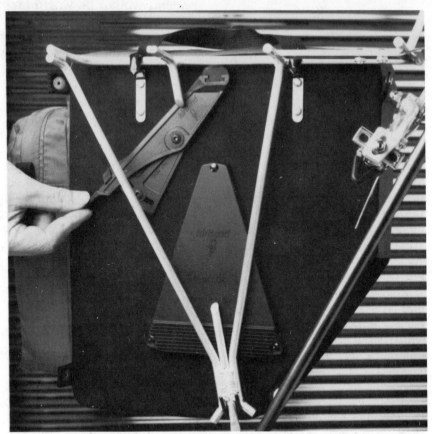

*Fig. 147:* Kirtland bikepacks are held on rack's top tube by the locking unit shown, clamping the pack securely in place.

per pack onto the rack top rod. A spring loaded hook, which clips to the bottom of the rack, also holds the pack in place. The pack I tested, the XT II, has a 1,900 cu. in. capacity and four pockets. (Other Kirtland packs have greater capacity, more pockets.) The XT II is very nicely finished, with double stitching and no loose fabric inside. A reflective stripe runs around the outside of all packs. The XT II sells for around $130 a pair. A bar bag (Fig. 148), with a map case that can be Velcro fastened to any ATB handlebar, is excellent for a day trip. It can hold a spare tube, patch kit, and an adjustable wrench for wheel removal.

### LONE PEAK

Packs from Lone Peak are good quality, and an excellent value. Their biggest pack, the 2,200 cu. in. King's Peak MB-300 (Fig. 149), costs only $98 a pair. It has a hook and elastic shock cord attachment that isn't as reliable as a more positive rack attachment, but you could wrap a couple of elastic shock cords (bungee straps) around it to keep

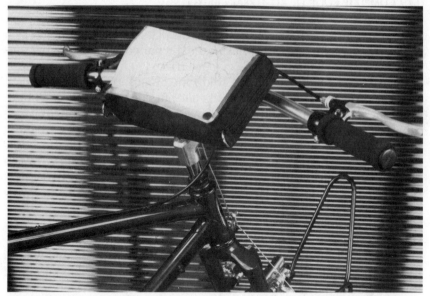

*Fig. 148:* Small Kirtland bar bag has map holder. Velcro fastens it to handlebars.

*Fig. 149:* King's Peak MB-300 by Lone Peak has 2,200 cu. in. of storage space, and costs only $98 a pair.

it from bouncing off the rack. It comes with a compression strap, a removeable plastic stiffener, has two external pockets plus a big single pocket, and is made of 8.5-oz. Cordura nylon fabric.

Lone Peak's front pack is the Red Pine Mountain MBH-298, which has a 1,200 cu. in. capacity, including one outside pocket. So with both sets, the MB-300 and the MBH-298, you would have 3,400 cu. in. capacity and 5 pockets. The MBH-298 costs $60 a pair.

This company also makes a bar pack, the MBH-50 Pfeifferhorn, with 230 cu. in. of space. Two Fastex buckle straps fasten it to the bars and two shock cords clip to the bottom of a rack. The MBH-50 is small as bar bags go, but it's secure and sturdy. It doesn't have a map case. It costs $22.50.

### MADDEN

These bikepacks (Fig. 150) use U-hooks, shock cords and Velcro Fastex adjustable straps to keep packs on the racks. One advantage of this method is quick removal from the rack, but for off-road cycling I don't see this as a major feature. Packs are of 11.5-oz. Cordura. The rear pack has 1,925 cu. in. and only one big pocket and the cost is $77.50 a pair. The front pack has 1,225 cu. in., costs $69 a pair, and has one big pocket. A rack-top carrier for tent and sleeping bag has 1,450 cu. in. and costs $39.50. None have compression straps.

*Fig. 150:* These Madden bikepacks are sturdy, well made, and hold lots of gear.

## NEEDLE WORKS

Here are the Rolls-Royce of bikepacks, with prices to match. But if you are going on a trek into the wilds, these are the packs that have the greatest capacity, the most pockets, the sturdiest construction and most meticulous attention to detail of those I have tested. The model I like for off-road touring is the World Tour (Fig. 151). Each of the two packs that make a set have five internal compartments, one of which is removeable so you can stow a larger item. That's ten compartments for the rear pack set and ten for the front pack set. I prefer internal compartments over external pockets with zippers. First, the zippers are a nuisance on the heavy fabric used in packs, especially on the smaller pockets. With internal compartments you just open up the one big cover and you have instant access to all the contents. The compartments provide good load isolation that keeps contents from shifting around as you pedal. Capacity of the front and rear packset is immense; 2,175 cu. in. in the rear and 1,850 cu. in. in the front packset, a total of 4,025 cu. in., yet the packs have a narrow trail profile

*Fig. 151:* Needle Works packs are really superb in both design and workmanship, have the greatest capacity of those checked.

despite all this stowage space. Each bag in the packset also has an external nylon mesh pocket which I use for drying damp clothes as I pedal and for stowing munchies during the day. Rack retention is excellent (Fig. 152). Packs are mounted with stainless steel U-hooks, plus two adjustable Fastex quick release fasteners. When tightened down, the fasteners hold the packs securely in place. In addition, the packs come with three compression straps that keep pack contents from shifting. This is the most stable of the bikepack systems I have seen. Packs are of 8-ounce ParPac nylon duck. Bottoms of the pack are of 11-ounce nylon Cordura, as are the top covers and the back section. Stiffeners are fastened by stainless steel Allen bolts and are removeable. All straps, including a shoulder strap, are fastened to three layers of pack fabric. The World Tour packset costs $135 a pair for each of the front and rear sets, $270 for both. A pack cover, which is much sturdier than a rain cover, is available for $35. You would need four covers. The covers are made of 11-ounce Cordura, and are designed to protect the pack against rips and tears as well as from rain. On all packs, zippers and seams are double stitched so there are no loose fabric ends inside to fray and snag zippers. These packs are not sold in stores, but can be ordered directly from the manufacturer. Other, smaller packs are also available at less cost. For information, write: Needle Works, 769 Monroe St., Eugene, Ore. 97402.

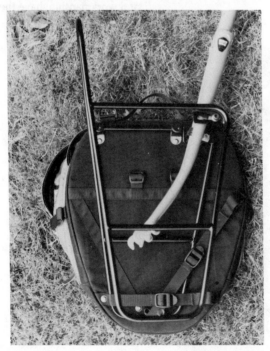

*Fig. 152:* Needle Works front and rear packs fasten securely to racks with two straps and two U-hooks. Note how low the pack can be located, again, for added stability and steering accuracy.

## TAILWIND

These packs are aerodynamically designed, according to the maker, for decreased wind resistance. That feature really isn't important for off-road riding, though it will help cut drag if you ride on the pavement. The packs are stiffened to retain shape, with a smooth outer surface that presents nothing to snag or tangle on the trail. There are no pockets or compartments. Instead there are four color coded stuff sacks you can buy for each bag. When the sacks are full there is still room for either two more sacks, or other items such as clothing. Each pack will hold up to six sacks. The mounting system consists of three hooks with a positive retention system that is claimed to keep the pack from jumping off the rack. The Blackburn LowRider front rack (see below) has a hole drilled in a side strut on each to hold the pack down. Rear packs are $80 a pair, front are $70 a pair. Stuff sacks are four for $14. Tailwind also makes a small utility "Moose Bag" which fastens to any ATB stem with three adjustable straps. It costs around $14.

## About Racks

For off-road riding you need a very strong rack that will support your loaded bikepacks. Of the many racks on the market, I have selected three that in my opinion have excellent strength, durability, and ease of mounting on the bike.

### BLACKBURN RACKS

Blackburn racks have become pretty much the standard of the industry since their introduction about ten years ago. The MTN Rack (see Fig. 135, on page 151) has two four-way adjustable stainless steel extenders that permit it to fit seat tube braze-ons or to be clamped to the seat tube. The Blackburn LowRider front rack comes in two versions. The FL-1 model (see Fig. 142, on page 157) is designed to fit Blackburn braze-on fittings on the fork blades, which is the best way to fasten a front rack. The standard model LowRider can clamp onto fork blades. Both racks are made of Reynolds T-6 6061 heat-treated aluminum alloy rod. The rear rack has a protective platform, so if you don't use fenders, it will at least keep water and dirt from streaking your back in foul weather. The platform also adds to rigidity and strength of the rack. The rear rack comes in two sizes. The MTN-1 is for bikes up to 22 inches in size. All models allow plenty of room for fat tires. The MTN-2 fits bigger bikes. Both racks cost about $18 each.

## BRUCE GORDON RACKS

Here's a set of racks that match the Needle Works packs in quality and price. Bruce Gordon makes fine hand brazed bike frames, and now, fine racks for ATBs. His racks (see Fig. 141, on page 156) are made of 4130 aircraft chrome-moly steel tubing, which is rated at 93,000 pounds per square inch tensile strength (about twice the strength of T-6 aluminum). The rack tubing is machine mitered for an accurate fit and hand brazed, just like a fine bike frame. There's no question but that this rack is the strongest you can buy, and it's not much heavier than solid aluminum-rod racks. What is much greater is the price. The rear rack is $75, the front rack (Fig. 153) is $60. Oh well, if you want the very best rack that, for its size, is as strong as your ATB frame, that won't break on the trail, whose mounting system is adjustable and very rigid, that's the rack to buy. These racks are sold direct, not through bike stores. Gordon will want to know measurements of your bike so his rack will fit accurately. He can be reached at: Bruce Gordon Cycles, 1070 W. 2nd St., Eugene, Ore. 97402.

*Fig. 153:* Another view of the Gordon front rack. Note that the rack is canted outward, so front wheel can be easily removed.

## CANNONDALE RACKS

Everything Cannondale makes seems to be nontraditional. Now it's a new type of nonwelded aluminum rack with triangular struts. Struts and mounting fixtures are adjustable so they will fit any bike. The modular rack is put together with Allen bolts, so parts are replaceable, unlike a welded aluminum rack. The rack comes assembled and includes an Allen wrench. Rear rack costs $29.50, front rack $26.50.

## RACK MATE

If you don't want fenders on your ATB and your rear rack doesn't have a splash guard, you can buy a Rack Mate that snaps on top of your rack, for about $6. Rack Mate also makes a splash guard that snaps on the downtube to keep water off your legs, face, and chest, for about $8.50.

## Car-Top Carriers

If you live in the city but like to bike in the country on off-road trails, chances are you'll want to car-lift your bike to the trails. If so, there are a number of excellent carriers on the market. There are carriers that fit on the roof, on the rear trunk or bolt on the bumper. Trunk and bumper mounted carriers are most convenient. If you get one that fits your car, you can open the trunk without having to remove the carrier. Lifting the bike to a trunk carrier is a lot easier than mounting it on the roof. On the minus side, trunk carriers involve putting the bike frame in direct contact with carrier arms, a great way to scratch bike paint. Some trunk carriers mount on some cars so that parts of the bike, such as cantilever brake arms or pedals, hit and scratch car paint. I have both roof and trunk carriers, and I find myself using the trunk carrier for short trips, and the roof carrier for longer trips where I want more protection for both bike and car.

There are three roof carriers I have used and can recommend. They all cost around $140 and are fitted to carry two ATBs, but can carry four with optional extra mounting fixtures (Fig. 154). They are all well-designed to keep your expensive bike tied down. It's darn disconcerting to see your expensive ATB in your rear view mirror, taking off to total destruction, airborne down the highway. It has happened.

The Thule Swedish-made carrier is the most versatile—it fits cars with a short roof—because the bike mounts by the handlebars and the saddle, the two shortest tie-down points on a bike. The Thule System 1050-19 has a key-lock on the carrier roof mounts and on the handlebar mount. The carrier is lockable to the roof of your car so it will be there when you come back off the trail to the car. The bike can be

*Fig. 154:* The Burkhard carrier will hold up to four bicycles. In this photo, the carrier holds one ATB and two pairs of skis. Bike is firmly held by quick release clamps on the fork, by straps around the rear wheel. Front wheel is removed, carried separately as shown.

locked to the carrier so you can stop for lunch and not have to worry about its security.

The Yakima roof carrier also fits cars with short roofs, such as slantbacks, and has a version for cars with no rain gutters. The Burkhard Bicycle Rack (Fig. 154) is another sturdy, very secure carrier that locks the bike in place by a front wheel clamp. The rear wheel is strapped securely into a "V" mount.

If you often carry your bike on a plane, you may want to invest in a sturdy box with external wheels made for this purpose. This is one way to guarantee that your fine ATB will arrive at the baggage claim center intact. It's not cheap, but good insurance if you need it. The Bike Travellier costs $279 and can be obtained at your bike shop. It's made by Product Protectors, Prado Mall, 5600 Roswell Rd., N.E., Atlanta, GA 30342. Some bike stores rent them.

### Tools and Spare Parts for a Trip

Even if you're going on a day trip, there are certain tools and spare parts you really should bring along. You'll see most of them in Fig. 155. Here they are, along with the reasons why you should bring each one along. The entire set is really not all that heavy, and can easily fit in a small pocket of a bikepack or in a bar bag:

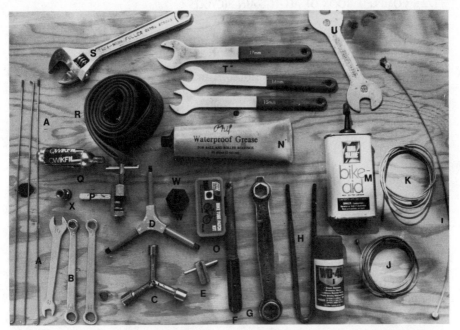

*Fig. 155:* Here's what you should take on an off-road trip, even a day trip. See text for description of each item in the photo. These are the basic tools, tire repair items and spare parts you need to take along.

A. **Extra spokes.** If you break one, your wheel will instantly tilt to one side. Wheel clearance is minimal on some ATBs and you could have wheel rub on chainstays, which acts as a dragging brake.

B. **Set of 8, 9, 10, and 11 mm wrenches** you need to tighten brake cables, replace cables, or tighten front freewheel binder bolts.

C. **Three-in-One 8, 9, and 10 mm socket wrench.** You'll find a use for it.

D. **Three-in-One 4, 5, and 6 mm Allen wrench.** Fits brake shoes, most headset binder bolts, chainwheel binder bolts, derailleur mounting bolts, some derailleur cable binder bolts, and brake and shift lever binder bolts.

E. **Spoke wrench. Don't leave home without it.** A "must" for replacing broken spokes and truing wheels.

F. **Tire removal tool.** Makes it easy to remove fat tires when you have to fix a flat.

G. **Three-in-one 14, 15, and 16 mm wrench.** Screwdriver end fits bottom bracket dust caps. Fits crank bolts and wheel axle nuts. You should tighten crank bolts every 50 miles for the first 200 miles. If the softer aluminum crank gets loose, you can quickly ruin the square hole inside as it moves on the harder steel spindle (see chapter 5).

H. **Pin wrench. Fits most bottom-bracket adjustable cups.** However, you will also need a bottom-bracket wrench if you have to do field repairs on nonsealed bottom-bracket hubs (Fig. 156). You could use a screwdriver and a rock to bang the lock nut loose in an emergency, but why gouge your good locknut when you can use the proper tool?

I. **Small spray can of chain lube, such as WD-40.** Useful for chains, brake, derailleur, and derailleur pivot points (see chapter 5).

J, K, and L. **One brake, one derailleur, and one brake-yoke cable.** Cables have been known to break.

M. **Can of general purpose light oil (about 20 grade SAE).**

N. **Tube of grease** for nonsealed hub, headset, or bottom-bracket bearings. You'll need it if you go over sand or through water. You can relube sealed bearings (see chapter 5).

O. **Patch kit** for when, not if, you have to patch a puncture.

P. **Chain rivet remover.** A "must" tool (Fig. 157) for repairing broken chains (see chapter 5). This is a tool you should never leave behind.

Q. **Tube of $CO_2$.** This item could come in handy if you lose your frame pump or break it. Actually, you should bring along six of these

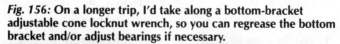

*Fig. 156:* On a longer trip, I'd take along a bottom-bracket adjustable cone locknut wrench, so you can regrease the bottom bracket and/or adjust bearings if necessary.

*Fig. 157:* A chain rivet remover is an absolute necessity on any trip, however short. If the chain breaks and you don't have this tool, you'll have a real problem removing the broken link and fitting the chain back together. I've had to do this on a road trip in Wisconsin with a rock and a nail I found on the road. But you are unlikely to find a nail on the trail, so make sure this little tool is in your kit. If you travel with others, there's no need to bring more than one set of tools.

cartridges because it takes one to pump the tube up enough to find the leak, and two more to inflate a fat tire. Make sure the cartridges fit your tubes; they're made for either Presta (skinny European) or Schraeder (fat U.S.) valve stems. Make sure you read manufacturer's instructions for their safe use.

R. **At least one spare tube.** You can patch a leak, but what if you cut a big gouge or blow a hole in a tube? Besides, when you're in a hurry, changing a tube instead of patching one can be a lot quicker. Save patching tubes till you pitch camp or get home. But do be sure to bring a small roll of duct tape to patch gouges in the tire: That's the gray, 1-inch-wide tape used to seal heating duct joints. It's ideal for patching rips and tears in the thin sides of fat tires well enough to get you home.

S. **An adjustable crescent wrench** for odd size bolts and nuts, such as on some racks, or for straightening a bent chainwheel or rear derailleur cage.

T and U. **Thin hub cone wrenches** let you disassemble and re-grease nonsealed hub bearings. You may need to do this in the field on a long trip, if you pedal through sand or water very often.

W. **Freewheel remover tool.** Be sure to buy one that fits your freewheel, there's about a dozen different configurations. Fig. 158 shows a few. You will also need a box or open-end wrench that fits this tool (not shown above). (See chapter 5 for instructions.)

X. **If you use Presta valves, an adapter to convert valve stem** to Schraeder size can be handy if your pump breaks or is lost and another ATBer on the ride only has a Schraeder pump.

**Not shown, but a pair of needle nose pliers** can be very helpful in cable slack removal or cable replacement.

I urge you to review chapter 5, with emphasis on: chains, hubs, bottom brackets, brakes, and derailleurs, so you know what to do if any of these components brings you to a halt on the trail.

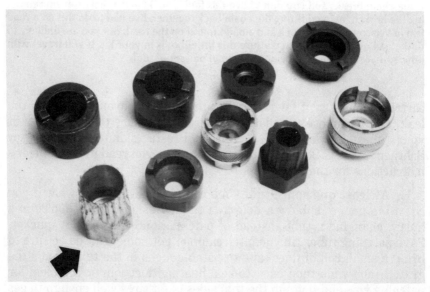

*Fig. 158:* A few of the many configurations of freewheel removers. I despair of ever getting the European and Japanese freewheel makers to standardize on one tool. Even the same makers don't do it from year to year. Arrow points to the easiest tool to use. The little projections on the other tools are easy to break off or round off, so the tool is useless. Take the tool that fits your freewheel on the trip, because if you break a spoke on the freewheel side, you probably won't be able to replace the spoke without removing the freewheel.

## Camplights

I've used an ordinary flashlight for years, until the new Tekna Lite flashlights came along. They cost more than a regular flashlight. But in terms of lightness, rugged construction, and durability, they are far, far superior to a conventional flashlight. I especially like the little Tekna Lite 2 which weighs only 3 ounces, including two AA batteries, and throws a piercing beam from its sturdy 5.5-inch body. This light costs around $12. It, and its big brother the Tekna Lite 4, is available at most sporting goods stores. The Tekna Lite 4 uses a Krypton-gas-filled bulb and four AA batteries, a combination that throws a truly high intensity beam a long distance. It weighs nine ounces with batteries, is 4.5 inches long, and costs around $25. Be sure to take extra batteries and bulbs along.

## A Word About Camping Gear

There have been so many excellent articles and books written during the past few years about stoves, cooking gear, food to bring on hikes, and everything else about wilderness camping, that I see no point in reinventing the wheel, so to speak.

For example, I have used every minicamp stove on the market, and I like them all. The stoves that use Butane or LP gas light instantly at the touch of a match. You don't have to mess with gasoline. On the minus side, you have to pack and pack out about three Butane containers for each week of the trip. Butane stoves take longer to heat than gasoline. It takes Butane about 8.5 minutes to boil a quart of water. A gas stove can do it in from 3 to 4 minutes. If you cook for two, for example, one 6.5-ounce Butane cylinder lasts for at least two days. You get about 2.5 to 3 hours of use out of a cylinder. I use from two to three cylinders a week on a trail ride.

Butane stoves are inexpensive, about $20. The cartridges for them weigh about 10 ounces and cost about $2 each. One stove with cartridge weighs around 22 ounces.

Gas stoves cost a lot more, but they also give you a lot more heat. Going all the way up the price scale, the MSR X-GK stove boils a quart of water in just three minutes (at sea level), burns for 99.8 minutes on a 2-pint container of fuel, burns almost anything including all auto fuels including gas, kerosene, No. 1 and 2 diesel fuel, and several kinds of solvents. This is a rather expensive stove, at $79.95, but it's the best one on the market, in my opinion. On the basis of some rather extensive bikepack trips in this country and abroad, my experience has been that it takes about 15 minutes of stove time to prepare the average meal, but that depends on how much heat the stove puts out. I was able to get by with about 60 ounces of unleaded gas for a week with the MSR, which is not a lot to carry. How much fuel to carry is a matter of what and how much you will cook. If you bring mostly dehydrated foods, you will need only to heat water and can get by with very little fuel. I suggest you practice cooking at home on the stove you will take. Cook the kind of food you will pack and check cooking times and fuel consumption. Don't take anybody's word for this. Don't guess, know for sure.

The Coleman Peak I stove (Fig. 159) has been recently improved, and the new version, which boils a quart of water in about 4.5 minutes at sea level, uses unleaded gas. The tank holds 11.8 oz. of fuel, which will last one hour and fifteen minutes at full blast or will simmer for 2.5 hours. It costs $45.

The camper's standby, a stove I had been using for at least the past 10 years and finally gave to one of my sons, is the brass Swedish SVEA (Fig. 160). It throws a very hot blast but is a bit tricky to light in a brisk wind. I have no figures on how long it takes to boil a quart of water at sea level, but my recollection is that it does so quickly, in around 3 minutes. It costs about $45.

*Fig. 159:* This Coleman Peak I camp stove uses unleaded gas. It boils a quart of water at sea level in about 4.5 minutes.

*Fig. 160:* **The old stand-by, this Swedish-made SVEA gas stove is a bit tricky to light in a breeze, but is light and reliable.**

A new very compact stove that can double as a camplight is the Hank Roberts. It uses LP gas cartridges that cost $3 each and burns at full blast for around three hours. The stove itself, with camplight adapter, costs $39. It's slow though, taking 7 minutes to boil a quart of water at sea level.

## About Tents and Sleeping Bags

Again, there have been reams of words written about how to select a tent and a sleeping bag. You don't need me to repeat them. I will sum up all this material, though, and leave you to select these items from your local sporting goods store or from one of the very excellent catalog houses. You will find reputable and reliable mail order suppliers of tents, sleeping bags, stoves, cookware, dehydrated foods, and everything else you will need. Their catalogs are listed in the Appendix. However, as a general guide, I will briefly review what you should look for in a sleeping bag and a tent.

### SLEEPING BAGS

1. **How cold will it get?:** That's the first question to ask about the climate in the area where you will be cycling. Remember, even in summer, high altitudes can still produce below freezing temperatures at night. I have always been comfortably warm at night with a sleeping bag rated from +5°F to +10°F.

2. **Down vs. synthetic fillers:** Without getting into the millions of words written about this comparison (see Appendix for references), I will just say that in my experience a high-quality, down-filled sleeping bag is warmer for the weight and is more compressible so it can be stuffed into a smaller sack than a synthetic-fill bag. However, some of the newer synthetics are very close to down in compressibility. If a down bag gets wet, it's hell to dry and impossible to sleep in. A synthetic-filled bag dries fast, and you *can* sleep in it even when it's wet. A down bag should either be hand washed or dry cleaned only by a special process (ask the cleaner for a guarantee) that will not remove the natural oils from the down. A synthetic-filled bag can be washed by any process. But *never* dry *any* bag in a hot clothes dryer. The heat can destroy both the filler and the bag's fabric. I speak from experience, brothers and sisters.

3. **A down bag costs a lot more than a synthetic filled bag:** A good down bag costs from about $150 to $200. A synthetic-fill bag of equal quality costs from $100 to $150. Personally, having used both down- and synthetic-filled bags, I prefer the synthetic-filled bags. When made right, they are comfortable, warm, compressible into an 8″ × 18″ stuff sack, and a lot less expensive.

4. **Shape is important:** I found a mummy shape (looks like an Egyptian mummy) difficult to get used to. There's little room in it to move around. I had a mild case of claustrophobia. On the other hand, the body-clinging shape retains heat better and is more compact and lighter than a roomier rectangular-shape bag.

5. **Zippers:** Should be nonmetallic and be buried in fabric when closed. Metal zippers are really cold to the touch on a chilly night. Good bags never use them. If you're going with a compatible partner, zippers that open left and right let you zip two bags together.

6. **Head covering:** A sleeping bag that has some sort of head covering, such as a hood, makes for warm comfort. A lot of heat loss is from

your head, so if you keep your noggin covered, you'll be toasty warm at night. Sure you can use a hat of some kind, but be assured it will slip off your head as soon as you slip off to sleep.

7. **Bags I have used:** On a purely empirical basis, I have used two sleeping bags that I like very much, in recent years. One is the Cannondale Chesapeake bag. It has a temperature rating of +5°F, a draft proof wrap-around head cover, weighs about 5 pounds, and costs $130. Its modified mummy design was roomy enough for comfort. This really is a great sleeping bag. The Cannondale comes in one length for people up to 6'6" tall.

I have also camped with Early Winters' Silver Lining bag rated to +10°F. This too is a light, comfortable bag. It weighs about 4 pounds and costs $150 for the regular size (for people up to 5'10" tall), and $155 for the long size. (See Appendix for address.) Other than the above, I recommend that you review the literature on sleeping bag construction, costs, pros and cons of fillers, and overall ratings. See the Appendix for a bibliography of articles on this subject. One more point: a foam pad of some kind under your sleeping bag protects you against cold and moisture seeping through the tent bottom and also protects against the tiny pebbles and twigs you never seem to sweep away before pitching the tent.

### ABOUT TENTS

Here's a capsule review of tent features, based on my own camping experience.

1. **Fabric should be "breathable":** If your tent does not let body vapor out at night, it will condense on the inside of the tent and drip on your face all night. Further, if you don't turn that tent inside out every morning and wash it in warm soapy water, it will smell like a dozen skunks sprayed it all night. That odor will be there to stay, for life. I have had to throw a couple of tents away on this basis. A tent of GoreTex fabric will breathe, but will require sealing the seams with a liquid sealer before first use and repeated sealing each season.

2. **Capacity:** If you're traveling alone, a one-person tent will do just fine. It will be light, compact and keep off the bugs and rain. (I know a lot of people who don't even take a tent along. They simply spread a light tarp, held up by branches, over the bag if it rains. Personally I much prefer the security, imagined or real, of a tent, against things that go "bump" in the night. I also keep my wallet and other nonlosables inside the tent at night.) I do prefer, though, a bit bigger tent, say a one-and-a-half person tent, even if I'm alone. I like to spread out, have room to sit up, move around if I want to. There

are as many tent configurations as there are people who design them. In general, I prefer one that uses light, simple flyrod-like poles, to a tent with complicated rigging. I like a tent you can set up quickly, that won't blow away in a stiff wind while you're doing it, and that has a waterproof tub base that rises up about 4 inches all around the tent to keep you dry even in a torrential rain. ("Ditching," shoveling a trench around the tent to channel water away, is a definite no-no for ecological reasons.)

3. **Tents I like:** A lot has been written about what you should look for in a tent, which I am not going to repeat here. The Appendix has a bibliography that will lead you to this reference material. I can, however, report on the four tents I have used that have served me well, in recent years. The Cannondale "Wabash" is a spacious two-person tent. It has a vestibule over the front entrance that's big enough to stow gear such as bikepacks, out of the weather and away from the light fingered. This tent's fabric is urethane coated 1.9-oz. ripstop nylon in the sides and 1.9-oz. nylon tub in the floor. This tent is easy and quick to set up. It's not inexpensive at $325, but for a totally reliable, breathable and roomy tent for two, it's well worth the money. It does weigh a hefty 8 pounds, 12 ounces, but if there are two of you, one can carry the tent, the other the sleeping bags and cookware, so that would be 4 pounds, 6 ounces of tent per person.

At different times, I have used two makes of one-person tent on solo trips, both of which were breathable and kept the black forest and bugs at bay. Early Winters' Pocket Hotel (Fig. 161) is a GoreTex fabric design with plastic rods that make set up easy and fast. It costs $150, weighs just 2 pounds including stuff sack, and is 7¼ feet by 2 feet in size when set up.

The Hoop Tent (Fig. 162) uses either two wheels to hold it up (I have used fat tire wheels with this tent) or a set of Fiberglas rods. It, too, is light, weighs 2 pounds, 1 ounce, and has over 30 cu. ft. of interior space. A minor security point—if you use the wheels for end support and someone tries to make off with them, with you in the tent, you'll know about it. This tent costs $110. Poles for the tent (which I recommend, really) cost an extra $15.

If you want a one- or a companionable two-person tent that's beautifully made, it's the Moss Starlet (Fig. 163). The top is open to the skies, through a fine mesh fabric that screens out even no-see-ums, but lets you see the stars and the moon at night. A fly over the tent can be quickly erected if it rains. It has a small vestibule which gives you 8.5 sq. ft. of space outside the tent, to stow your bikepacks at night. You can even sit up in this tent, yet it packs into a tiny 16″ × 5″ bag. It weighs 4 pounds, 14 ounces and costs around $185. It's so

*Fig. 161:* Early Winters' one person "Pocket Hotel" only weighs 2 pounds, can be carried in bikepack, and is great if you travel or sleep alone.

*Fig. 162:* Unique "Hoop Tent" uses bike wheels at each end. Or you can use optional plastic rods. If you use wheels, you'll know if someone tries to make off with them while you're in the tent.

*Fig. 163:* This Moss Starlet tent is open to the sky at night, has a fine mesh top that keeps out no-see-ums as well as bigger bugs. Weighs 4 pounds, 14 ounces and sets up quickly, it has a fly cover for rainy nights. This tent is big enough for two, is very well made, and has a small vestibule in front, so you stow bikepacks inside, at night, without cluttering sleeping portion of tent.

beautifully designed and made that I consider it the Bentley of small bikepacker tents.

By the way, Fig. 164 was furnished by Eclipse, to show all the stuff the well-equipped bikepacker can take along. I'd kill the Frisbee, the dress shirts, and the cleated bike shoes, and add a sweater and another pair of shorts. The bikepacks look full, but I would guess they're paper stuffed so they sit up straight for the picture.

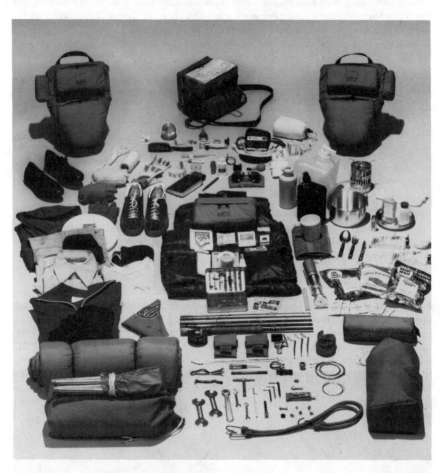

*Fig. 164:* From Eclipse comes this collection of what to take on an ATB trip. Well, actually, the collection was made for road cyclists, so you won't need the cleated shoes at top left, or the dress shirts on the left side. The fly rod and tackle are optional items but great if you cycle in trout country. Don't forget your fishing license!

## About Food for the Trail

As with tents, sleeping bags, stoves, and other impedimenta of camping gear, much has been written about foods for backpackers. I have selected a few pertinent books on this subject (see Appendix) that you can find in most sporting goods stores that cater to backpackers. The foods you should take along on any trip lasting more than a day are amply covered in these books, as are cooking tips, menus, and discussion of energy creating and energy maintaining diets. Because bikepacking on an ATB is no different than backpacking on your own two feet, the food requirement is the same for both.

## Safety on the Trail

In chapter 3 I covered what to do if confronted by a wild animal, and how to avoid such confrontation in the first place. In addition, I would urge you to become familiar with the basics of first aid, such as caring for fractures and concussions, avoiding and treating heat stroke, hypothermia (exposure to cold) and hypoglycemia (low blood-sugar level, which causes a real energy droop), CPR (dealing with a heart attack), poison ivy and poison oak exposure, and snakebites, to name a few possibilities. There are many books on administering first aid in the wilds. You'll find a few of the better ones listed in the Appendix. Some of these are compact enough to take on the trip.

Beside the basics of first aid, you really must know how to find out where you are, which involves the art of orienteering, use of a compass, and other skills. You should know how to read maps, including contour and topographic maps, so you can not only plot the route but the severity of hills you will have to climb. If you find yourself facing a lot of 15-percent hills, for example, you will probably have to walk up them, even with a "granny low gear" on your ATB, which isn't much fun if the bike is loaded with 30 pounds of gear. A 15-percent grade is a hill that goes up in elevation 15 feet for every 100 feet of trail. You'd climb 792 feet up for every mile on a hill, if the road grade was a uniform and revolting 15 percent all the way. Fortunately, few roads are that consistent. They usually level out for a bit, just to give you the illusion you have come to the top, but around another turn up they go again, straight to the sky. So you should learn how to read contour maps and plot your course to avoid hills you'd rather not face. Or at least most of them. There are lots of good books on map reading and orienteering, and the best ones are available in stores that cater to the backpacker, as well as those listed in the Appendix at the back of this book.

**Fig. 165:** Left to right, a signalling mirror that throws a sun-reflected beam for long distances, a mileage or distance reader for calculating distances from a map, and a good compass for orienteering, so you won't get lost.

A good compass (Fig. 165) is an absolute "must" on any trip, and you should learn how to use it so you don't get lost. A trip mileage gadget (Fig. 165), one of those things with a little wheel you push along a route to tell you how far it is between points on a map, can also help in planning your journey. On the trail, plan on no more than 20 miles a day, at least for a start. If the terrain is hilly, rough or hard to navigate, you may do no more than 15 miles a day. If the terrain is relatively flat and open, you can easily do 35 miles a day. But remember, you're not in a race. You're out there to enjoy the wilderness, to see the animal life, to get away from it all for a little while. You won't see castles, or museums or any of the man-made wonders of this world. You will see its natural wonders and beauty, though, and in this high-technology day and age, that's reward enough, for me at least, and I hope for you.

### If You Get Lost

As I said in chapter 3, if you're going to travel in the wilderness, you should always leave your itinerary with someone in authority who can come looking for you if you don't show up at a stop, or return, on time. Remember, many of our national and state parks require you to register and obtain a fire permit, even if you use a cook stove. If you do get lost, stay put. Don't move. You should bring along a signalling mirror (Fig. 165). It picks up and throws the sun's rays over a long distance. You can use it to signal passing aircraft, a house, cabin, or person on a distant hill. I have one, and to illustrate its power, I can stand a block away from my house and so vividly light up about a two foot square on the wall in a room that you'd think it was done by Klieg light. The mirror I advise *against* is the rear view kind you clip onto your glasses or helmet, so you can see what's behind you. These are fine for street use, but on the trail you won't find too many trucks coming up behind you and you will find the straight wire that holds the rear view mirror to be an eye-piercing hazard should you fall on it.

You might also bring along a pair of minibinoculars, available from any good sporting goods store for about $149. Get the kind that gives you eight-power magnification and that weigh about 9 ounces. With them you could see that person on horseback across the valley to whom you could signal with your signalling mirror, or see a variety of wildlife close up but from a safe distance.

As I said earlier in this book, I have tried five-watt CB radios in the mountains and find them wanting. Their signal does not travel far enough, apparently blocked by hills or mountains, though they might work to signal aircraft, if the pilot had a CB radio and it was turned on. Besides, the good ones are bulky and heavy.

## The Weather

Mark Twain once said: "Everybody complains abut the weather, but nobody does anything about it." Well, *you* can do something about it, learn to read all the signs of impending bad weather, for example, so you can avoid riding into storms just over the horizon, and weather them out in your tent. In the Appendix you will find listed at least one book on how to read clouds, the wind, and other signs of future bad or good weather.

## Emergency Ground-to-Air Signals

Say you have left word with a ranger or a friend as to when you will return, or where you can be found at a specific check point. Or, say, you arranged to pick up food and supplies from a village post-office or via an air-drop. But you are injured, or someone in your party is injured, and you aren't where you are supposed to be when you said you would be there. In your absence, an alarm is issued, people start to look for you. You need to be able to signal your needs in a way these searchers can quickly and accurately understand. Here are standard signals, understood by rangers and others in the business of rescuing people. First, select an open space, visible from the air. Gather tree limbs, or even rocks and arrange them in the patterns indicated below to signal your problem to aircraft or ground personnel:

1. **You need a doctor for a serious injury.** Lay out just one tree limb, pieces of colored fabric, stones or anything that will attract attention, in the shape of a capital I. Signals should at least be 10 feet in length to be big enough to be seen. As the aircraft swoops down, lie on the ground, with your arms stretched out straight behind your head.

2. **You need food and water.** Lay out two symbols in the shape of an F.

3. **You are lost, want to know which way to proceed.** Lay out a K.

4. **If there is room for the aircraft to land** put out a triangle. But only if you're sure that the aircraft above can make it. Forget it if it's a 747.

5. **If you don't need help,** put out two capital Ls (LL), and wave your right arm.

6. **If you have forgotten all these signals,** just get together enough objects to form an SOS.

7. **If the pilot understands your message,** he will signal a "yes" by dipping the plane's nose up and down. If not, he will fishtail, i.e., move the rudder section right and left.

### Should You Take the Kids?

Children can go along on short day trips, if they have decent ATBs. For a child from age eight to eleven or twelve, a good bike for an ATB is a converted BMX bike. You can buy a rear hub that will accept a five- or six-speed freewheel, put a rear derailleur on the bike, and you now have a dandy little 20-inch wheel bike that the child can ride on the trail. If the freewheel has 12 to 38 teeth, and the chainwheel has 44 teeth, this conversion gives you a low gear of 24 inches, which will get your child up any hill you can climb. The high gear isn't so great at 73 inches, but you're not out to win races anyway, so it should do fine on the flat part of the trail. Just remember that youngsters can put out tremendous spurts of energy, but they might not have the stamina you have, so plan on frequent rest stops and keep daily mileage within a child's limits. What those limits are depends on your child, and if you keep tuned into how he or she is doing you'll know soon enough when the energy level is ebbing. If you keep daily mileage expectations within a child's limits, I see no reason why you can't take kids on a longer trip, say lasting up to a week or so. The nice thing about off-road riding is that you and the kids don't get bored. Boredom is unlikely because they are *part* of the scenery, in it, involved in it, one with natural beauty. Besides, the National Off-Road Bicycle Association specifically forbids boredom on the trail (see Article NBA:1, entitled "No Boredom Allowed," subsection A, para. N). Also, NORBA regulations spell out the duties of children around the campsite, such as policing the grounds before leaving, cleaning up, helping pitch and strike the tent, and maintaining absolute silence after 10 PM.

After all this, I am sure you will welcome information on where you can ride your ATB, and where you can't. In searching for this data, the first thing I discovered was that it's very hard to find. There are, of course, lots and lots of books on where you can ride in all fifty states and abroad. But 99 percent of these planned and programmed rides are on paved roads. In describing rides, typical statements say "good paved roads, but narrow shoulders," or "you may have to ride on rough dirt roads." Gee, too bad about those dirt roads, folks, but that's what ATBs are for. What I am saying here is that so-called bike-trail or bike-route maps, free or otherwise, from private publishers or from a state, are very, very seldom of much use in planning a trip for off-road or trail riding. The routes are almost always designed for skinny-tired road bikes. But in perusing all of these routes and trails, a few good ones do surface, and I will mention them briefly below. But first, a word about the National Park System and riding in designated Wilderness Areas.

### Implications of the Wilderness Act

Public Law 88-577, passed by the 88th Congress on September 3, 1964, and otherwise known as "The Wilderness Act," contains a paragraph that the people who run our National Parks and Wildlife areas interpret as prohibiting bicycles from such parks and areas. The prohibition reads: *"there shall be in National Forest Wilderness . . . no use of motor vehicles, motorized equipment, motorboats, or other forms of mechanical transport. "Mechanical transport," as herein used, shall include any contrivance which travels over ground, snow or water on wheels, tracks, skids or by flotation and is propelled by a*

*nonliving power source contained or carried on or within the device."*
Since ATBs, or at least all of them I have seen, are powered by a
*living* power source, I really wonder, not being a lawyer, whether this
Act excludes ATBs?

This part of the Wilderness Act has, as ATBs become increasingly
popular, prompted park officials to restrict them to designated bike
trails or paved roads within these areas. Unfortunately, this attitude
has closed a large part of the open wilderness to everybody except
hikers and horseback riders.

This *is* unfortunate, because fat tire bikes, as I noted in chapter 1,
leave nothing but their fat tire prints behind, do not damage the
ecosystem of the trails. There are places where ATBs should not go,
such as off-trail riding over meadows and prairie land, nor ought
hikers or horsemen travel over these delicate ecosystems. We ATBers
need to join forces and back NORBA in its efforts to change this
attitude. We need to prove that fat-tire bikes, moving at the slow
speed they do, are harmless to wilderness trails. Glenn Odell notes in
a letter: *"Bicycling as a form of recreation is in harmony with the
parameters of Wilderness management. It was a means of travel in
primitive areas before the age of the automobile. Its physical impacts
on the environment are similar to those of the pedestrian and much
less than those of the equestrian . . . We are not asking for unlimited
access to all Wilderness Areas. We do expect access to certain trails
when the size and proximity of designated Wilderness Areas pose a
significant obstruction of point-to-points, on-trail travel."*

Since NORBA is *"initiating research to study the comparative environmental impact of off-road cycling to hikers and equestrians . . .
and encourages the maintenance of, and access to, trails appropriate
for the use of bicycles . . ."* I urge you to join this fine organization. As
a NORBA member you get:

1. Twenty-four-hour, anytime bicycle-accident coverage (second-
ary insurance) of $5,000 ($100 deductible) and accidental death and
dismemberment coverage of $5,000.

2. Monthly NORBA newsletter with nationwide event calendar,
dealer directory, and names of ATB experts and enthusiasts.

3. Active representation to government land managers and legis-
lators on behalf of all off-road bicycling enthusiasts.

4. Access to information on public lands open to bicyclists.

5. Copy of events rules and guidelines.

6. Organized competition from local to major, national championship, events. Membership card and logo decal.

An individual membership is $18. If you wish to join, and again I would urge you to do so, send your check to National Off-Road Bicycle Association, 2175 Holly Lane, Solvang, CA 93463. The phone number is 805/688-2325. NORBA would like to have, besides your name, address, and phone number, your age, gender, and, if you want to race, whether you consider yourself an expert or novice ATB racer.

## Professional Tours

There are a number of organizations that, for a fee, will take you on off-road tours in scenic areas. It costs more to go that way, but there are certain advantages to these tours that can make the added cost worth it. These advantages are:

1. **You won't get lost:** Routes are planned and in most cases ridden by the tour guides before you set wheel on the trail.

2. **No hassles:** Permits are taken care of. Food is supplied, in most cases. An expert mechanic is on hand. Cooking gear and tents may be provided by some tour outfits. Insurance coverage is usually provided (A.D.D., medical and dental). The route is planned well in advance and selected for scenic beauty. Most leaders are trained in first aid.

3. **You'll be with people:** It's a lot more fun to share the adventure with others.

On the minus side, you have to go when and where the trip is routed, can't deviate from the itinerary, or lay-over if you feel like it. You do lose a certain amount of freedom and independence. I like both kinds of trips, the professionally planned tour and the sturdily independent one. There's nothing that can go wrong with my bike that I can't fix, unless the frame breaks. But alone or with just one, two, or three others, I suppose I could get lost, or receive inadequate first aid (self-administered CPR leaves something to be desired). Each type of off-road touring has its benefits and drawbacks, each is worth doing. You pays your money and you takes your choice. There's a list of guided tour organizations at the end of this chapter.

Here are suggestions for places to go and trips to take on an ATB, state by state. I asked each state for their official attitude about the use of all-terrain bicycles in their parks, forests, and wilderness areas, and their responses are included here. I'm not sure this was a wise move on my part. I think in some cases I reminded park officials that ATBs are coming, although I took pains to remind them that ATBs are compatible with the use of these parks and are no more ecologically harmful than are hikers and less so than heavy-hoofed equestrians.

The Sierra Club has been, for so many years, as it is today, a protector of wilderness areas against the encroachment of motor driven vehicles, and a supporter of bicycling as an energy saver. However, the club has taken no stand I could discern on off-road bicycling in wilderness areas. I have checked with their national headquarters in San Francisco and with area clubs around the country, and so far the reaction is "We're studying the matter." It is to be hoped that the official attitude will be positive, as it is toward bicycling in general today.

## A Concise Guide to All-Terrain Bicycling in the U.S. and Abroad

To save space in listing where to go in each state and country, if a state has no policy, I am going to say simply "No policy," which means authorities are aware of ATBs and are studying the matter. Other rules will be equally succinctly stated. Remember, if you write for trail information, always spell out the word "bicycle" to eliminate any association with motorized trail bikes, which are the kiss of death so far as getting cooperation from park authorities is concerned, and rightly so, in my opinion. "No response" means just that some state officials did not answer my query as to their attitude toward ATBs in state parks. I take this as a "no policy" statement, but, to be sure, you probably should check with individual wilderness area management before you take off.

Remember that just because a state says "no" to ATBs on their State Parks and Forest trails, does not mean there aren't plenty of other places to ride. In the major cities of our land, people are taking to ATBs in droves. Ask any bike-shop owner. As I've said earlier in this book, the shock absorbancy, the comfort, the more upright stance, the sturdiness of these bikes, make them perfect for commuting. These same features also make them great for long-distance touring on any kind of terrain, including paved roads. States that have ruled out all bikes from their wilderness parks also have very scenic backroads that ATBs are ideally suited for. Rough, many of them, yes. Gravel, sand, washboard surfaces—an ATB eats them up where a skinny-tired road bike would jolt your arms off. Remember, fatigue can come from many sources. A major contributor to fatigue on a cross-country tour is road shock. That source is minimized by an ATB.

**Alabama:** Foot traffic only, but no stated policy as to ATBs as yet. (ATBs *are* foot traffic, no?) Of state parks, Gulf, Chewalco, Monte Sano, Oak Mountain, and Cheaha look promising. Department of Conservation and Natural Resources, 64 North Union Street, Montgomery, AL 36130.

**Alaska:** No policy. Lots of places to ride. Check out the Kenai Peninsula, the 11,000-acre Shuyak Island of the Kodiak Archipelago, Chugach State Park, Power Line Pass Trail, Bird Creek logging roads. There are more areas to wilderness bike than I have room to list. Send for a booklet entitled "Alaska State Parks" which lists over 100 of them and tells where to write for more specific data, including maps. Bill Garry, Sup't., Chugach State Park, 2601 Commercial Drive, Anchorage, AK 99501.

**Arkansas:** No response. Parks available include Pea Ridge, Lost Valley, Buffalo River, and Bear Creek Mountain. State Parks and Tourism Department, State Capital, Little Rock, AR 72201.

**California:** Ah, that Golden State! No response, but the authorities in Sacramento have closed off some of the most attractive scenic areas to ATBers. However, I spent a lot of time just before writing this book riding all-terrain bicycles in both state and national parks in California and can report that, with or without a state or federal policy, local rangers seemed kindly disposed and unwilling to thrust us onto paved roads. There are so many mountains, seashore areas, scenic wilderness trails in that state that it would fill up the rest of this book just to mention them. I recommend you pick your spot, call or write park management there for permission and maps. There are literally millions of acres of remote, beautiful, scenic wilderness areas available to you. In Northern California, good riding is available in these state parks: The Forest of Nisene Marks, Henry Cowell and Fall Creek Redwoods, Big Basin Redwoods, Butano, Annadel, Sugarloaf Ridge, Austin Creek, Armstrong Redwoods, Cow Mountain, Mt. Shasta, and Mt. Lassen. For information, write to the California Department of Transportation, P.O. Box 1499, Sacramento, CA 95807, and California Office of Tourism, 1030 13th St., Suite 200, Sacramento, CA 95841. Better yet, check the organized-tour guide, the professionally led tours, at the end of this chapter. There are many such off-road tours offered by these organizations in California.

**Colorado:** Like California, Colorado is an ATBers paradise. Lots and lots of trails and quiet mountain dirt roads are available in the Rockies, in the high country of Colorado. The famous Pearl Pass tour is a 17-mile jaunt, with a 3,835 foot vertical climb to the summit and an 18 mile, 4,915 ft. drop to Aspen, is well worth doing. The mountains around Crested Butte are famous for scenic trail riding. From Colorado authorities, however, no response. I am told that the rangers are well disposed toward all-terrain bicyclists, so pick any mountain that's within a state park or wildlife area and you should have no problems. Colorado Division of Commerce and Development, Office of Tourism, 1313 Sherman #523, Denver, CO 80203.

**Florida:** No bicycles allowed on hiking and nature trails, but O.K. on fire roads. The state says, however, that they hope to produce maps of off-road bicycle trails as part of their statewide bicycle-trails mapping effort. For off-road bicycling, try the St. Marks National Wildlife Refuge, and trails paralleling rivers such as the Suwannee. There's not much in the way of mountains, the state is mostly flat, but there are hundreds of miles of sandy beaches to ride on. Florida Department of Transportation, Haydon Burns Building, 650 Suwannee St., Tallahassee, FL 32301-8064.

**Hawaii:** I can't recommend this state for trail riding. The state is too crowded and I hear the crime rate is fairly high. If you do go, stay off Oahu, the most crowded island. For information, write Hawaii Visitors Bureau, 2270 Kalakaua Ave., Suite 801, Honolulu, HI 96815. (I may hear from them before you do, with this plug.)

**Idaho:** There is no official position on ATBs, but the state has a wait-and-see attitude. There are many great trails in the Idaho backcountry. Sun Valley is an ATB paradise. Try the Clearwater National Forest. For a list of the dozens of ATB opportunities, though, I suggest you write Todd Graef, State Trails Coordinator, Idaho Department of Parks and Recreation, Statehouse Mail, 2177 Warm Springs Ave., Boise, ID 83270.

**Illinois:** Treats an ATB as any other bicycle. I'm not sure what that statement means. I would doubt, however, based on my experience in state parks, that you'd be hassled by any authority figure so long as you stayed on the trail and didn't wander off through the prairie, a delicate ecosystem. The state has sent me a large packet of trails suitable for ATBs. In this packet are addresses of some 150 on- and off-road trails, and an equestrian-trail guide. I checked with the Forest Preserve District Managers who operate these. After I explained the nature of an ATB, they either encouraged their use on equestrian trails, or seemed to take a wait-and-see attitude. Some of these trails are paved, most are dirt or rough stone that would not faze an ATB. I suggest you write for this data to: Dan M. Troemper, Public Information Officer, Lands and Historic Sites, Illinois Department of Conservation, Lincoln Tower Plaza, 524 S. Second St., Springfield, IL 62701-1787.

**Indiana:** No reply. There are many small- to medium-sized state parks in Indiana. I found them unsuitable for off-road riding mostly because there were so few off-road trails. All of the listed rides in this state are highway affairs. Indiana does have twenty-one state parks, totaling about 66,000 acres, most of it flat to gently rolling. Like the rest of the Midwest, most of this state is farmland, not available to bicycling of any kind. Indiana Department of Commerce, Indiana

Commerce Center, One North Capitol Suite 700, Indianapolis, IN 46204, for state park information.

**Iowa:** The Tallcorn state takes a dim view of ATB trail riding. They say bikes can use all roads in state parks, but not hiking trails because "We do not feel it is appropriate to allow bicycles on hiking trails, not due to possible environmental damage; but rather, due to user conflicts. The hikers do not appreciate being 'buzzed' by the cyclists, and the cyclists do not appreciate having to dodge hikers." Open spaces in this state are mostly farmland, so off-road riding opportunities are minimal. For information, write Iowa Conservation Commission, Wallace State Office Building, Des Moines, IA 50319.

**Kansas:** I have driven across the width and breadth of this state, and I can only suggest that you rule out this pancake-flat area as an exciting place to off-road ride. However, you can write to the Kansas Department of Economic Development, Travel and Tourism Division, 503 Kansas Ave., Topeka, KS 66612, for any information on trail riding opportunities. There are state parks. I've been in some and they do not excite me. I am willing to be corrected, however. Also, no reply.

**Kentucky:** No reply. A fairly hilly state. However, between the coal mines, the farms, the distillers of bourbon, legal and otherwise, and the horse breeders, not much room is left for trail riding. You can guess who gets priority between horse and bicycle in the Kentucky Derby, Bluegrass state. If I'm wrong, the Kentucky Division of Tourism, Capital Plaza Tower, Frankfort, KY 42302, may change your mind.

**Louisiana:** No reply. Not much by way of a challenge to the ATBer in this state, so I'll take a pass on it. There are plenty of rutty back roads, mostly flat, which can get you across the state, but bring food and water. Louisiana Department of Transportation and Development, General Files Unit, P.O. Box 44245 Capitol Station, Baton Rouge, LA 70804.

**Maine:** No response. Not a terribly congested state, with many scenic parks. The natives tend to be taciturn, so bring all your own maps. For directions to parks and forest areas write Maine Publicity Bureau, 97 Winthrop St., Hallowell, ME 04347.

**Maryland:** No reply. This historic state has some ATB opportunities, such as Sugarloaf Regional Trails, maps for which can be obtained from the Maryland-National Park and Planning Commission, 8787 Georgia Avenue, Silver Spring, MD 20907.

**Massachusetts:** Now here's a state after my own heart. Gilbert A.

Bliss, Director of Forests and Parks, writes and says that "Until such time as a definite policy statement is made, Mountain Bicycles are allowed on hiking trails and fire roads within the Massachusetts Forests and Parks." So pick your park and go to it. Bliss notes that a Statewide Trails Committee of trail user groups has been formed and that mountain bikes will be discussed and that recommendations of this committee will influence the State's position as to their use. The state has many very scenic parks, some mountainous, others along the seashore. For information, write Gilbert A. Bliss, Director of Forests and Parks, 100 Cambridge St., Boston, MA 02202.

**Michigan:** No response. This state has many miles of scenic dunes along Lake Michigan, and many state parks that have miles of trails which, if not challenging in terms of hills, do offer the all-terrain cyclist many opportunities to pedal into the quiet of the rural countryside. For specifics, write to Bill Tansil, Supervisor, Highways and Non-Motorized Planning, Michigan Dep't. of Transportation, P. O. Box 30050, Lansing, MI 48909.

**Minnesota:** The land of sky-blue waters has a large acreage of quite wild and wooly forest land suitable for ATBers. Unfortunately, whoever's in charge of their parkland has not responded to my query, so let's assume all's well and we can bicycle on trails in this lovely state. For information write to Nancy Mahle, Chief, Bikeway Unit, Minnesota Dep't. of Transportation, 704 Transportation Building, St. Paul, MN 55101.

**Mississippi:** There are long forgotten trails that run alongside the Mississippi River that Mark Twain must have seen at one time or another, that would be just great for the ATBer. Or you might try the Natchez Trace, a path followed for generations by Natchez Indians and, later, British, Spanish, and French traders. I don't know what the state's park management has to say about ATBs; they did not respond to my query. However, you might write Bill Sheffield, Bicycle Coordinator, Mississippi Highway Department 85-01, P.O. Box 1850, Jackson, MS 39205.

**Missouri:** In this state I'd stick to the Ozarks, a fairly hilly and very scenic area. The hills can be quite challenging, with some 15-percent grades that aren't long, but mighty tough. Remember, the percent of grade is defined by how many feet the road rises in 100 feet of horizontal travel. On a 15-percent grade road, in 100 feet of forward travel you will go up 15 feet, so in a mile you'd rise 792 feet in elevation $(5,280 \times .15 = 792)$. There are many state parks, and the Ozark National Scenic Riverways, managed by the National Park Service, is available to you. Write Deborah Schnack, Planner, Division of Parks and Historic Preservation, P.O. Box 176, Jefferson City, MO 65102.

**Montana:** The state abounds with scenic areas that are state managed and which should be open to you. Montana is one of our largest states in geographic area, yet it has less than 800,000 people and lots of longhorn sheep. Check off-road riding with the Montana Travel Promotion Bureau, Dep't. of Commerce, 1424 9th Ave., Helena, MT 59620.

**Nebraska:** Another sparsely populated state with excellent off-road touring possibilities. For information, write Nebraska Division of Travel and Tourism, P.O. Box 94759, Lincoln, NE 68509. Although the state did not reply to my query as to whether or not ATBs are permitted on state park trails, my experience has been that sparsely populated states seldom make a fuss about judicious and careful bicycling on trails. In fact, I have a nice letter from Carl W. Wolfe, Outdoor Education Specialist, Nebraska Game and Parks Commission, in which he says the state has no prohibitions against the use of ATBs on hiking trails in their park system. He was also nice enough to report that "In checking with the U.S. Forest service, they do not have any prohibition on the use of these bicycles on their trails." For info, write Carl at the Nebraska Game and Parks Commission, 2200 N. 33rd St., P.O. Box 30370, Lincoln, NE 68503.

**Nevada:** Poor paved road riding but excellent off-road trails in state and national parks. No response to my query but you might do better. Write Nevada Department of Transportation, Map Section, Room 206, 1263 S. Stewart St., Carson City, NV 89712.

**New Hampshire:** New Hampshire says: "We would not permit the use of mountain bicycles where there would be a potential conflict . . . we have not had a request to use mountain bicycles on state park land. If the request to use this type of vehicle is presented, it would be handled on a case by case and park by park situation." My advice is to go ahead and use the trails, since ATBs are very popular in that state and they must be riding somewhere. If "conflicts" have not surfaced by now, with courtesy and consideration by all sides they should never exist. There are many opportunities for the off-road rider. Try the area around Dartmouth, the White Mountains, including Mt. Washington, and the Green Mountains. For information, write New Hampshire Department of Public Works, Hazen Dr., P.O. Box 483, Concord, NH 03301, and William H. Carpenter, Supervisor, New Hampshire Division of Parks and Recreation, 105 Loudon Road, P.O. Box 856, Concord, NH 03301.

**New Jersey:** No response. Opportunities for off-road cycling are not numerous in this densely populated, highly industrialized state. A few are the Watchung Mountains and the Pine Barrens section of the state, and the shoreline. There are other mountains in the Northwest.

Write William H. Feldman, Pedestrian/Bicycle Advocate, New Jersey Dep't. of Transportation, 1035 Parkway Ave., Trenton, NJ 08625.

**New Mexico:** No response. Off-road opportunities abound in this scenic state. You have a choice of desert, plains, or mountains, with plenty of trails for ATBs. State parks, so far, are quite lenient and permissive, so you should be able to ride on hiking trails and, of course, on the many fire roads and backcountry dirt roads. New Mexico Tourism and Travel Division, Bataan Memorial Building, Santa Fe, NM 87503.

**New York:** No response. Stay at least 50 miles from New York City, of course. Upstaters are friendly, and the parks and trails around Lake George, the Catskills (shades of Rip van Winkle), the Finger Lake district, and the Adirondacks offer superb bicycling and scenery. For information on Finger Lake area riding, write Finger Lake State Park & Recreation Commission, Rte. 3, Trumansburg, NY 14886, and the New York State Dep't. of Commerce, Tourism Div., 99 Washington Ave., Albany, NY 12245.

**North Carolina:** No response. Off-road riding opportunities abound in this state, notably in the Blue Ridge Mountains in the west section, the Outer Banks area in the East, and the Pisgah National Forest, to name a few. Write Mary Meletiou, North Carolina Dep't. of Transportation, P.O. Box 25201, Raleigh, NC 27611, and/or Curtis B. Yates, State Bicycle Coordinator, same address.

**North Dakota:** Well, there are a few state parks, the Badlands in the western section, and a lot of flat prairie. The Theodore Roosevelt National Park is also in the western section and offers off-road riding. You can get more information from Norlyn Schmidt, Transportation Planner, North Dakota State Highway Dep't., 600 E. Boulevard Ave., Bismarck, ND 58501.

**Ohio:** To judge from the response, Ohio is one of the least hospitable states for off-road cycling. Yet this is the state that's home to some of America's major bicycle companies, including Raleigh Cycle Company of America, which makes excellent ATBs. To quote from their response, Wayne R. Warren, Deputy Chief, Office of Outdoor Recreation Services, says: "Bicycles are prohibited at our state parks and state forests except on roads open to the public and on designated trails. We have two bikeways where mountain bicycles may be operated, the Little Miami Scenic Park and the Blackhand Gorge Section of the North Central Trail. We have no other facilities where bicycle use is permitted at this time." He sent me maps of these trails. The Little Miami Scenic Park is only partly available to ATBs, and the map says "13 miles of the trail are paved and suitable for use by bicyclists. Equestrians and hikers are also permitted on this stretch." The Blackhand Gorge section consists of a tremendously challenging *flat 4.5 miles* of an abandoned railway right-of-way. I assume the railway ties have been removed. Too bad. Obviously this state has little or no idea of what an all-terrain bicycle looks like and can do. Flat, paved trails suitable for bicyclists, indeed. How can we ATBers get the message across to desk-bound bureaucrats? I guess by joining forces and using political clout, the only message they seem to understand. For more information, write the Ohio Department of Natural Resources, Fountain Square, Columbus, OH 43224.

**Oklahoma:** The Sooner state is mostly flat, with lots of high wind on the plains. If you plan to ATB in Oklahoma, stick to state parks and forests in the east and southeast section. The state reports that it is "in the process of developing rules governing the use of ATBs on State Park lands." By the time this book is in your hands I would expect this policy to have been formulated. Write Dwayne Stutzman, Programs Coordinator, Planning and Development Division, State of Oklahoma, Tourism and Recreation Department (whew!), 500 Will Rogers Building, Oklahoma City, OK 73105.

**Oregon:** There's good news from this wonderful state. The authorities are by no means bureaucratic desk jockeys. What they did in formulating a policy regarding use of ATBs is an example of what other states should do. I quote from their response: "For about a year the Oregon Recreation Trails Advisory Council has been aware of a controversy developing around mountain bicycles, so they've been investigating the 'evidence' available. Following their October 1983 quarterly meeting at Kah-nee-tah they took the opportunity to ride mountain bikes which were loaned by a dealer in Bend, Oregon. The Council is aware that the Pacific Crest National Scenic Trail Advisory Council has recommended that the use of bicycles be prohibited on the Pacific Coast Trail. However, the Oregon Trails Council has not reached a consensus on the issue and has not yet recommended a specific policy for Oregon Recreation Trails. . . . There has been no indication of a problem with the use of them [ATBs] in State Parks." The letter is from Jack Remington, Coordinator, Recreation Trails System, Department of Transportation, Parks and Recreation Division, 525 Trade St. S.E., Salem, OR 97310.

The state abounds with so many state and national parks that I can only urge you to write, to pick a park, and to take off. I prefer the western section of the state; the eastern section is flatter except for outstanding mountain areas, such as the Sisters near Bend. The Umpquah National Forest in the west is an excellent example of a location for ATB riding. Get a fishing license, bring your trout rod (use of flies only, no live bait) and catch your dinner in the Umpquah River. Or try the Siskiyous, near Ashland, and in the summer you can bike down the mountain and attend the famous Shakespeare Festival in that city.

**Pennsylvania:** Well, there's good news and bad news from the commonwealth, for ATBers. First, the bad news. In his response, William C. Forrey, Director, Bureau of State Parks, says ". . .the mountain bicycles would not be allowed on our designated hiking trails." The good news is that he also states that: "The use of these bicycles on fire roads is permitted on state parks and state forest lands." Which leaves a lot of open off-highway terrain for ATBs. The state is loaded with parks and forests, and I suggest you send for the Pennsylvania Trail Guide listing them all. The Guide, kindly sent by Mr. Forrey, contains a description of each park and forest area, a map showing locations, and a roster of information sources where more data can be obtained. I found the *Source Data* very useful. Write for your copy to Pennsylvania Trails Coordinator, Pennsylvania Bureau of State Parks, P.O. Box 1467, Harrisburg, PA 17120. The guide also lists sources for National Parks and Trails information.

**Rhode Island:** This little pancake of a state has some excellent riding possibilities along the coast and in the forest and marshes of the southeastern section. For a good state map showing rural and back roads, write Rhode Island Department of Economic Development, Tourist Promotion Division, 7 Jackson Walkway, Providence, RI 02903.

**South Carolina:** There are rugged mountains in the northwest, notably the Piedmont section, which offer great off-road riding in areas of scenic beauty. The coastal and central areas are mostly flat. You can get a "Bicycle Guide to South Carolina" from the SC Department of Parks, Recreation and Tourism, Suite 110, E. Brown Building, 1205 Pendleton St., Columbia, SC 29201. The Guide is for the road biker, but it shows state parks and recreation areas.

**South Dakota:** No response, but data I have indicates that bikes are not permitted on trails. However, the Black Hills area does have many off-road trails and fire roads you may be able to use. I suggest you write SD Department of Tourism, 221 S. Central, Pierre, SD 57501, for maps and information.

**Tennessee:** East of Chattanooga are lots of state parks with trails and fire roads, and in the central area you can cruise along the Tennessee River. Forget the western section, it's quite flat. Tennessee Dep't. of Tourist Development, P.O. Box 23170, Nashville, TN 37202.

**Texas:** I have an interesting response from R. C. Hauser, Chief, Park Operations, Texas Parks and Wildlife Department (you can write them at 4200 Smith School Rd., Austin, TX 78744). Mr. Hauser says:

"The use of bicycles on trails and fire roads in Texas State Parks is prohibited with the exception of trails and fire roads that are specifically designated as hike and bike trails." The Lord giveth, and the Lord taketh away. Or, in this case, vice versa. Texas is so big it has just about every kind of ATB riding there is. I like the Padre Islands (be sure to oil the chain every day when you ride in sand or through salt water), the forest region in the east, the hill country in the west, and the back roads everywhere, once you are away from metro areas. I'd avoid the Panhandle, though, unless you like to eat wind-blown dust. For data on the hill country, write Kathryn Nichols, at the same address as for Mr. Hauser above.

**Utah:** This state is loaded with ATB rides ranging from easy to very, very difficult. It's advisable (always) to check map contours so you know you can handle the grade. A few of the many areas to check are Bryce and Zion National Parks, the Grand Canyon area, Yellowstone National Park (limited to paved trails, I'm afraid), and the Great Salt Lake area. For information, write John Morris, Utah D.O.T., Transportation Planning Division, 4501 South, 2700 West (yep, that's the address), Salt Lake City, UT 84114.

**Vermont:** ATBs are limited to "forest highways and other roads where motorized vehicles are permitted," according to George E. Plumb, Recreation Division Director. He points out that this stricture is ". . . in conformance with the Long Trail Management System Plan (the State's most extensive trail system) as adopted by the Green Mountain club." I've done a lot of biking in Vermont and I have noticed that roads in forest areas can be scenic and demanding in their own right, although I would prefer to use or at least have the option of using hiking trails as well. However, hiking trails in Eastern states are quite narrow, fairly heavily used by hikers in warm weather, so in a way I can understand the restriction. I hope that through education and exposure to ATBs this attitude will be softened enough to open up appropriate hiking trails to off-road bicycling. Mr. Plumb can be reached at the Vermont Agency of Environmental Conservation, Department of Forests, Parks and Recreation, Montpelier, VT 05602. Which for some reason reminds me, although I have said this before, that there's absolutely no reason why you should restrict yourself to wilderness trails and hiking trails. ATBs are great to ride on back roads, between towns, for savoring the scenery and camping out in state parks. I can heartily recommend Route 100, up the middle of the state. One campground in particular stands out vividly. It's the road from Route 100 to Calvin Coolidge State Park. If you want to experience for yourself a 15-percent grade, that's it. Because the road is paved and you have a low low gear, you should be able to make it, but it will be slowly. At least your rear wheel won't skid out from under you on the pavement. The back roads from Hanover down the Connecticut River and across to Vermont and down to Brattleboro are well worth taking.

**Virginia:** Virginia's Parks Commissioner, Ronald D. Sutton, wrote and told me that, "As the demand for more facilities for mountain bikes grows, the Division may have to develop a separate policy for them, but until such time, they will be treated as bicycles. Therefore, you may want to include Virginia State Parks in your listing of states with no position. Bicycles are permitted on all regular park roads and on all designated bicycle trails." Seems to me this position is fairly clear. Let's hope that the Division can see that ATBs are consistent with hiking by foot, with riding horses, that there really is no conflict between the three means of locomotion. Well, there are fortunately lots of good back roads in scenic mountain areas, even though we can't use hiking trails. The Blue Ridge section of the Appalachian chain, the Piedmont plains area, and the Shenandoah valley are areas of interest. For more information, write Ronald D. Sutton, Commissioner, Department of Conservation and Economic Development, Division of Parks and Recreation, 1201 Washington Building, Capital Square, Richmond, VA 23219.

**Washington:** In the summer, when it finally stops raining, this state has just about everything an off-road cyclist could want. You like the mountains? Washington gives you Mt. Rainier, Mt. Baker, Mt. Adam, the Cascades, the Olympics, and more. Do you like the seashore? She gives you Puget sound. Island hopping, starting from Seattle, taking the ferry, riding across an island, then another ferry, up to Vancouver, B.C., is a great trip. Do you like rivers? Try cycling along the Columbia river, from Vancouver to the great Bonneville dam and, enroute, cross the river into Oregon to view famous Multnomah Falls, a breathtaking view if ever there was one. Do you like the narrow, twisting trails of a rain forest? Within 20 miles of Seattle there's one you could get lost in if not careful. In some forests, where biking is taboo, there are former railroad paths, wagon trails, and other primitive roads that are like a trip back to the eighteenth century. Do you like volcanoes? Bike around Mt. St. Helens.

What is the state's attitude toward ATBs on trails in state parks and forests? In answer to this query, William A. Bush, Chief, Research and Long Range Planning, Parks and Recreation Commission, 7150 Clearwater Lane, MS KY-11, Olympia, WA 98504, sent me a copy of Chapter 352-20-WAC, regarding use of motor vehicles in state parks. Nowhere in this chapter is a bicycle of any kind mentioned. I can only conclude that there is no restriction as to the use of ATBs.

**West Virginia:** This is a very hilly state with lots of mountains. I did not hear from the Parks Division as to their policy about use of ATBs on trails, so I assume it's O.K. For a list of state parks and forests, write West Virginia Travel Development Div., 1900 Washington St. E., Charleston, WV 25305.

**Wisconsin:** This is one midwest state that's far from flat, even though it has few mountains, aside from Rib Mountain up north, worthy of the name. There's lots of scenic trail riding along the Mississippi river for hundreds of miles; trails in ancient Indian burial grounds, such as Kettle Moraine State Park in the east; miles of trails in picturesque Door County in the northeast, on Lake Michigan; and the cross state trail following, in one section, an abandoned railway right-of-way from Kenosha in the east, near Lake Michigan, some 350 miles to the west, at La Crosse on the Mississippi.

David L. Weizenicker, Director of the state's Department of Natural Resources, replied to my query that currently the state is posting self-guided nature trails to prohibit bicycles. I wouldn't worry about that. As Mr. Weizenicker points out, the state has over 1,900 miles of trails within its park system. There are hundreds of parks, so he suggests writing to individual park directors for maps and details. Send for the little booklet that lists every state park, forest, trail, and recreation area, entitled: "Wisconsin State Parks, Forests, Trails and Recreation Areas, Visitors Guide," Pub. 4-8400(84), from the Wisconsin Department of Natural Resources, Box 7921, Madison, WI 53707-7921.

**Wyoming:** In cycling through this state a few years ago, I had a frontiers sort of feeling about the state and the people in it, outside of the big cities, that is. (I wondered what signs saying "Open Range" meant, the first time I saw one. This Eastern boy thought it meant some sort of military firing range, and the cycling went gingerly. Then, over a rise, I saw the road clogged with cattle, and it came to me that the sign meant no fences. You learn something every day.)

I had no response to my query about ATBs in state parks. Yellowstone is in Wyoming and bicycles are O.K. there, but only on roads open to cars as well. This is also the state of the Grand Tetons, judged by some to be the most beautiful of all mountain areas in the U.S., the Wind River Range, and the Big Horn Mountains. For specifics, write the Wyoming Travel Commission, Frank Norris Jr. Travel Center, Cheyenne, WY 82002.

## Other Countries

Because off-road riding does require local knowledge as to trail conditions and availability, and weather conditions, I do believe it's best to go on a planned tour in other countries, at least at first. However, if you want to tour on paved roads, then the world is your oyster. I've bicycled pretty much throughout Europe, Great Britain, and Scandinavia. If you stick to "C" routes, which are the equivalent of U.S. county roads, you'll escape the traffic, see the countryside and enjoy quiet lanes and good food in rural inns. I can offer four tips on travel abroad. First, predeclare everything not made in the U.S.; your bike, watch, camera, etc. Just go to U.S. customs at the airport, bring what you're taking overseas with you, fill out a form for this purpose, and make sure the customs officer signs it. That way you won't have to pay duty twice. Second, make sure your bike is protected against damage. If you don't use the bike box mentioned earlier in this chapter, be sure to use a wood block or old axle in the dropouts so the fork and stays don't get bent. It's happened to me. Third, bring at least one spare tire, if you use 26-inch wheels. Tires that size may be hard to find overseas. If you're going to China or Africa, bring two spare tires. You can fold even the knobbiest fat tire in an "S"-shape, then fold it back over the "S" for a reasonably compact shape you can tie onto your rack. Four, write down whatever you buy abroad, no matter how inexpensive. The longer the list, the better. Then give this list, with date of purchase (inconsequential but impressive) along with item description and price paid, to the U.S. customs person on return. Customs people are always pleasantly surprised and pleased to see such a list, and it makes customs check quick and easy for you.

## Planned Tours at Home and Abroad

**Africa:** Bicycle Africa, 4247 135th Place S.E., Bellevue, WA 98006.

**Alaska:** Touring Exchange, Inc., Box 256, Port Townsend, WA 98368. This group also has tours in *California, Washington state, Baja, New Zealand, and Australia.*

**Australia:** Tropical Bicycle Odysseys, 26 Abbott Street, Cairns, Queensland, 4870, Australia.

**Austria:** Gerhard's Bicycle Odysseys, 4949 Southwest Macadam, Portland, OR 97201.

**California:** Wilderness Bicycle Tours, P.O. Box 692, Topanga CA 90290; Bicycle Touring Company, P.O. Box 115, Taylorsville, CA 95983. This outfit also has tours in *Oregon, Hawaii, Yucatan, and Baja.* Other CA tours by Backroads Bicycle Touring, P.O. Box 5534, Berkeley, CA 94705.

**China:** China Passage, 302 Fifth Ave., New York, N.Y. 10001.

**Colorado:** Mystic Wheels Bicycle Tours, 2820 W. Elizabeth, Fort Collins, CO 80521; Timberline Bicycle Tours, 3261 S. Oneida Way, Denver, CO 80244.

**Florida:** Suwannee Country Tours, P.O. Box 247, White Springs, FL 32095.

**Just about everywhere:** Bicycle Adventure Club, 3578½ Bayside Walk, San Diego, CA 92109.

**Maryland:** Cycling Tours, 140 W. 83rd St., New York, N.Y. 10024. They also have tours in the *Canadian Rockies*.

**New England:** DownHill Spokers Bicycle Tours, Inc., 121 Madison Ave., New York, N.Y. 10016. They also have tours in *California, England, Scotland, Ireland, France, New Zealand, North Carolina, New York, Pacific Northwest, Spain, Switzerland, and Italy.*

**New Mexico:** Santa Fe Trails, c/o Jim Manning Agency, La Fonda Hotel Lobby, Santa Fe, NM 87501; Bicycle Tours of the Great Southwest, 535 Cordova Rd., Suite 463, Santa Fe, NM 87501; New Mexico Bicycle Tours, 165 Cook St., Denver, CO 80206.

**North Carolina:** Eagle's Nest Camp, 43 Hart Road, Pisgah Forest, NC 28768.

**Scotland:** Hamish Tour Expeditions, Box 3, 4093 E. Spruceway, Vail, CO 81657.

**Vermont:** Vermont Bicycle Touring, Box 711, Briston, VT 05443; and Vermont Country Cyclers, Box 145, Waterbury Center, VT 05677.

**Washington (state):** Mountain Bike Tours, P.O. Box 31327, Seattle, WA 98103.

Now that you know what to take, and where to take it, you need to know how to maintain your bike so it will last as long as possible, be reliable and safe, no matter where you go. That's what the next chapter is all about.

# 5

## Tender Love and Care for Your All-Terrain Bicycle

Your new all-terrain bicycle can last you for years, and some models should hold up practically forever. Or, its moving parts can wear out in just one or two seasons. It can take you up hills, within your capability, or it can sit down and refuse to move, so to speak. Your ATB can be safe to ride downhill at speed, or unsafe at any speed on any hill. Your ATB can be reliable for months of riding on remote mountain trails, or break down within a few miles. It all depends on how well you adjust and care for its moving parts.

That's what this chapter is all about. You will learn how to adjust your brakes so you can control speed safely, how to care for your chain so it won't wear out in one or two rides, and the care, adjustment, and lubrication of all other moving parts on your ATB.

### Brakes

Because brakes are the one function of your ATB that must work reliably at all times, on which your very safety can depend, let's start this chapter with these speed controllers. Here is a step-by-step guide to cantilever brake care and adjustment:

**1. Brake lever adjustment.** There are two important adjustments to make to brake levers. The first is to place them on the handlebars in a position that you can reach easily. The second is to be able to control steering accurately while you apply the brakes. The first adjustment is to position the brake levers. To move the levers, loosen the clamp bolt (see arrow "E" in Fig. 166) and reposition levers. An angle of between 40 and 45 degrees downward is a normal angle for most people, an angle that lets your fingers rise naturally from the bars and reach out to the levers. The second adjustment I recommend is to have just enough cable slack so brakes only lock-up completely when the levers are almost touching the handlebars. This is heresy in road bicycling, but important in ATB riding. The reason: As you descend a bumpy trail at a fairly good clip, you're busy steering the bike, holding on to the bars to do it. At the same time, you must also keep speed under control. If the brakes begin to lock almost as soon as you pull on the brake levers, two things can happen. One, your fingers will be extended two or three inches from the bars, so you have to steer with most of your hand off the handlebars. That does not make for accurate steering control. Second, if you hit a bump hard and have to grip the bars for control, while you have fingers on the brake levers, you could lock the brakes as you hit the bump, which is not the safest way to control a bike. You could easily dump the bike in that situation.

*Fig. 166:* The lever at left is best for people with big hands. It also has a reach adjuster, "H," to set limit on lever travel. "E" shows where you should periodically check lever tightness with an Allen wrench.

Brake manufacturers recommend that brake shoes always be within 1/16 of an inch from the flat side of the wheel rim. That close a clearance can only be achieved with the brake cable adjusted so that brakes begin to lock up when the brake lever is squeezed about 1/4-inch. That's simply not a safe adjustment on an ATB, in my opinion. I keep my brake shoes about 1/4-inch from the rim flat. This gives me enough cable slack that when I grip the brake levers hard, the levers go to within 1/4-inch of the handlebars. This way I can have enough of my hands on the bars for good steering control, yet keep the brakes partially closed as I brake. SunTour has what they call a "reach adjuster" ("H" in Fig. 166) on the levers which controls, to some extent, brake-lever travel. You might want to play with this adjustment. It takes a 2-mm Allen wrench.

Brake lever clamp binder bolts take a 4- or a 6-mm Allen wrench, depending on make. You'll find an infuriating lack of standardization on all bikes, no matter who makes them or where they came from. Some parts even require special wrenches that fit nothing else in this world. This cavalier lack of any sort of standardization on the part of the bicycle industry has been going on for the past 100 years and I doubt it will ever change. Frederick Taylor, where are you when we need you?

While I'm on the subject of brake levers, take a look at Fig. 166. You'll see quite a difference in the shape and size of handhold areas. The lever that's best for big hands is the SunTour, at the left. The others are Shimano, center, and Dia-Compe, right, with the smallest area. If you have a big hand and a small grip area on the lever, you might exchange levers with a friend who has the opposite situation. You may have trouble buying levers separately, they're usually sold as a set with the brakes themselves.

2. **Removing cable slack:** Brake cables are made of strands of steel wire, twisted together. They do stretch a lot, particularly when new. As they stretch, brake shoes become farther away from the rim flat (Fig. 167) and if stretch is too great, you will find that the brake levers can be pulled all the way to the bars without stopping the bike. Cable slack removal is especially important if you follow my advice above about keeping brake shoes about 1/4-inch from the rim flat. On a new bike, pull brake levers as hard as you can, all the way to the bars if possible. Do it two or three times. You'll find that now brake cables have stretched and you may have to take up cable slack to keep brake shoes the correct distance from the rim. To remove cable slack, follow these steps:

a. *Squeeze brake shoes with a toe strap*, cord, or leather shoelace, so they touch the flat side of the wheel rim (or have a friend hold the brakes on the rim).

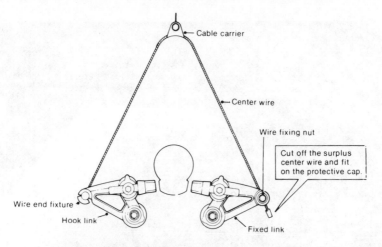

Cable carrier

Center wire

Wire fixing nut

Cut off the surplus
center wire and fit
on the protective cap.

Wire end fixture

Hook link

Fixed link

*Fig. 167:* Check tightness of carrier cable binder bolt before riding a new bike. Otherwise you could lose braking and/or the center wire could drop into spokes. See text for recommended brake shoe clearance to rim flats. (Shimano American Corp.)

*b. With two wrenches,* one to hold the cable carrier binder bolt "R," in Fig. 168, and one to loosen its nut "A," pull excess cable "H" through the carrier cable binder bolt.

*c. Retighten this bolt.* You can use a pair of needle-nose pliers to pull the cable through or, better yet, a Park Tool, "M," that pulls excess cable and holds it while you tighten the nut.

*Fig. 168:* Taking out cable slack, using a Park Tool "M" (or needle nose pliers), loosen nut "A," pull wire "H" through carrier "E." Hold nut "R" while moving "A." "L" is the crossover wire.

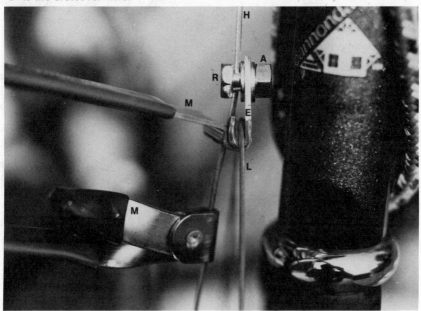

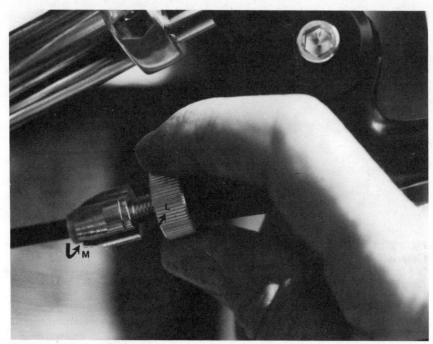

*Fig. 169:* You can also remove cable slack at brake levers. Squeeze brakes to rim, loosen locknut "L," turn "M" to remove slack, tighten locknut.

*Fig. 170:* Arrows point to cable stops where, on some bikes, you can also remove cable slack.

Once you have initial cable stretch removed, further cable stretch can be removed by an adjustment to the brake lever (Fig. 169). To make this adjustment, hold brake shoes against the rim, loosen the locknut, "L," and back off on the adjuster, "M," then retighten the locknut. Other micro-adjustment points on some bikes may also be found at brake cable stops, on seat stays, and on the handlebars, see arrows, in Fig. 170.

**3. Changing a brake cable:** Eventually brake cable strands fray, break, and unwind. If you see even one broken strand, it's time to install a new cable. To do it:

 *a. Strap brakes to rim.*
 *b. Loosen carrier binder bolt* and pull old cable through (see Fig. 168, on page 207).
 *c. Align slots in brake lever* so that adjuster and its locknut slots are aligned. See "N" and "O" in Fig. 171.
 *d. Pull cable housing out of adjuster,* lift it up and slide cable end "N" out of its slot in the lever (Fig. 172).

*Fig. 171:* **To remove brake cable, align slots in brake lever.**

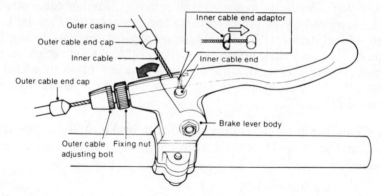

*Fig. 172:* **Remove cable, after disconnecting at carrier (Fig. 168), by pulling it out through lever slots. (Shimano American Corp.)**

*e. Install a new cable by following the above steps in reverse.*

**A word of caution.** When you go to buy a new cable, take the old one to the shop and make sure you get an exact duplicate. Road-bike cables have a bell or round lead end that won't fit in cantilever brake levers. A new cable should also have a new housing, and I recommend the kind with a Teflon liner so the cable slides easily in the housing (cable housing is also known as "spaghetti tubing"). These liners wear out in any case so it's a good idea to replace the housing when you replace the cable. There is also no standardization in the size of the cable end slot and you may need a little adapter spacer (see Fig. 172). Your brake cable may already have one on it, so save and use it, if you find much slack where the lead cable end fits into the brake lever. (If you drop this itty bitty spacer, Sloane's Law of Unconstant Recovery says you will *never* find it.) *See the Torque Table on p. 217 for specifications on tightening brake bolts and nuts.*

**Another caution!** You can put a lot of power into depressing brake levers. If the carrier binder bolt is not tight ("A" in Fig. 168) the brake cable ("H" in Fig. 168) can be pulled out of the binder bolt hole and you will have very little or no braking left. Retighten this bolt occasionally, using the torque values below. Another reason why this is important is that if you have, say, only an inch of cable ("H") left outside the carrier, so that it can be pulled entirely out of the carrier, then the carrier and/or the crossover cable can fall and tangle in the spokes or wedge between the rim and the brake shoe, lock the brake or the wheel, and cause an accident. If you leave about two inches of free cable ("H"), there will be less chance of these cables dropping off. If you have that sickening sensation of the brake lever suddenly going easily all the way to the bars, with no braking, you know instantly that this critical binder bolt was too loose. It's easy to prevent this accident causer. *This situation can exist on a brand new bike!*

*If you raise or lower the handlebar height* you will have to adjust the front brake cable. If you raise the bar, you will need to pull more cable through the carrier binder bolt and retighten. If you lower the bar, you will add cable slack and have to remove it as above. This is one drawback to cantilever brakes, but, given their extra power, one I'm willing to live with. Cantilever brakes are also the only ones, besides the Cunningham brake (see below) that opens wide enough so you can remove the fat tire.

*To remove the wheel:* ATB tires are too fat to fit between brake shoes. To remove a wheel, squeeze brake shoes tight against the rim and pull out the crossover wire free end from the brake arm (see Fig. 167, on page 207). On most bikes this is the right brake arm on the front and the left brake arm on the rear brake.

**4. Brake shoe adjustment:** There are basic adjustments you will need to make on your brake shoes. Both relate to your safety as well as to braking efficiency.

*a. Adjust the angle of the brake shoe* so it meets rim flats evenly (Fig. 173). The shoes should meet the angle of the rim flat squarely. There's no standardization as to rim-flat angle, but you should be able to eyeball it. Shoes should hit the rim flat so that all the shoe is on the rim, *none* on the tire. Shoes should also be toed-in slightly (Fig. 174), to eliminate brake squeal and give graduated braking control. Shimano has an adjuster for toe-in (Fig. 175).

**Note:** If wheel is out-of-line, brake shoes may rub on rim flats. This is another reason for the wider shoe clearance I recommend. Wheels get out-of-round more easily on ATBs, as they pound over the trail. Wheel-truing instructions are given later in this chapter.

*b. Adjust for brake shoe wear:* Readjust brake shoe clearance from rims as they wear. If you don't, the shoe may dive under the rim as you pull hard on the brake lever, get caught in the spokes and dump you. This is also another good reason to take out cable slack as the cables stretch.

*c. Replace brake shoes* when tread pattern wears smooth, or when the shoe is worn to within ⅛-inch of the metal shoe holder.

*Fig. 173:* Adjust brake shoes for correct clearance (see text) and alignment with angle of rim.

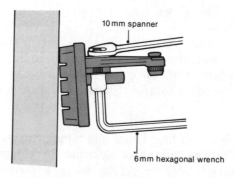

*Fig. 174:* Adjust brake shoes for toe-in toward front of bike, in direction of wheel rotation. (Shimano American Corp.)

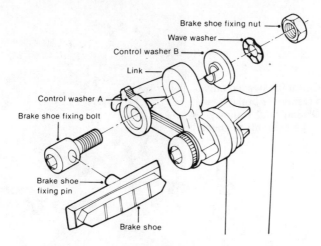

Brake shoe fixing nut

Wave washer

Control washer B

Link

Control washer A

Brake shoe fixing bolt

Brake shoe
fixing pin

Brake shoe

*Fig. 175:* **Exploded view of Shimano cantilever brake. (Shimano American Corp.)**

*Brake bosses should be brazed in boss mount:* In the early days of cantilever manufacture for ATBs, some makers only swaged the brake boss arm in the boss mount ("E" in Fig. 176). As a result, the arm eventually became loose and rotated as the brake was applied. Eventually the swaging wore, the arm became loose and braking erratic. If not repaired, the arm could even drop off and the brake assembly fall, with the danger of it becoming tangled in the spokes. Manufacturers soon recognized this, and printed instructions to the

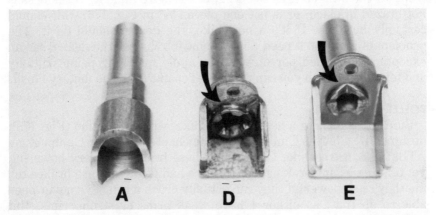

A      D      E

*Fig. 176:* **Cantilever brake boss shaft, "E," is only swaged in place, it could rotate if it becomes loose, and may break off. Boss "D" is brazed as well as swaged, and "A" is one solid piece of metal, both of which are safer.**

*Fig. 177:* Check for swaged only brazed-on cantilever brake boss shaft at "D" and "H." You may have to scrape paint off to check.

bicycle maker to braze the boss arm in place, as shown in "D" of Fig. 176. A better solution is "A," where the boss and arm are one machined piece. On most bikes you can look behind the brake boss braze-on and check to see if the arm is brazed over the swaging (Fig. 177). You'll probably need a flashlight and you may have to scrape some paint off the swaged area to check, but be sure to do it. If the boss is *not* brazed in place, or is not one piece ("A" in Fig. 176), this should certainly be done. If it's a new bike, the dealer should do it. The problem is that you'll need a new paint job, unless the dealer has an exceptionally skilled person who can apply matching paint skillfully and feather it out so you can't tell this repaint from the factory finish.

## ROLLER CAM BRAKES

SunTour is making a new type of brake, with cam action (Fig. 178), designed by Charles Cunningham (see chapter 2, under Cunningham ATBs) of San Anselmo, California. These brakes are very powerful, yet offer excellent braking control. I've had users of these brakes tell me they're so powerful they can actually crush a rim. I've never been able to do that, so either I have weak arms or strong rims. But powerful they are.

These brakes do have a major drawback, though. They, like cantilever brakes, require a brazed-on mounting fitting for installation. So if you're having a bike built by one of the custom makers, you can

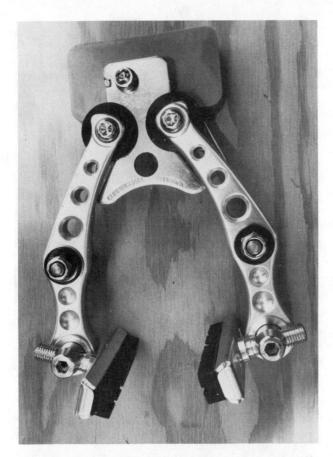

*Fig. 178:* Cunningham design roller cam brakes now made by SunTour. These very powerful brakes are ideal for ATBs.

order these brakes. If you want to retrofit them on an existing bike, you'd have to remove the old cantilever bosses (the Cunningham brake won't fit on them), and braze on the larger diameter bosses that come with the Cunningham brakes. If you do that, though, you're in for a repaint job. The heat from a brazing torch will sizzle the paint to about 5 or 6 inches from the braze-on location.

There is a possibility that by the time this book is out, you will be able to buy clamp-on fittings for the Cunningham brakes from Moots Cycles. Moots already makes clamp-on bosses for conventional cantilever brakes (Fig. 179). I sent a set of the Cunningham bosses to Moots and they tell me their clamp-on version should be on the market around January, 1986. The SunTour/Cunningham brakes will cost around $90 a pair (you supply your own levers). The Moots clamp-on fitting will cost about $18 per set of four. You can mount the Cunningham brakes on the fork, of course, but you can mount them either on the seatstays or on the chainstays, as well. Moots supplies installation

*Fig. 179:* Moots Cycles makes this clamp-on mount for cantilever brakes, and also one for roller cam brakes, so you can retro-fit these brakes to your bike.

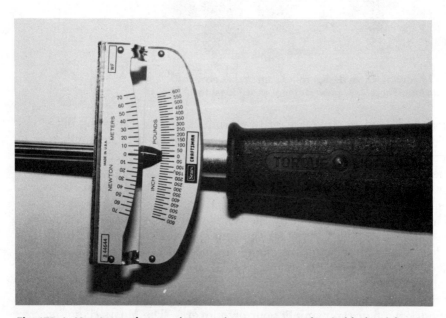

*Fig. 179-A:* Here's an adequate, inexpensive torque wrench suitable for tightening bolts and nuts on your bicycle. It costs around $20, and has a ⅜-inch drive for standard and Allen sockets. To use, determine correct torque from Torque Table (page 217), and turn wrench to tighten until pointer lines up with torque value.

instructions with their clamp-ons. To order, send your frame dimensions and contours of fork stays and either seatstays or chainstays (depending on where you want to mount the brakes) to Moots Cycles, P.O. Box 2480, Steamboat Springs, CO 80477.

**Torque Table**
(Values in this table are in inch/pounds)

| | |
|---|---|
| Front wheels with nut attachment | 264 |
| Rear wheels with nut attachment | 360 |
| Handlebar clamp bolt | 216 |
| Handlebar stem expander bolt | 180 |
| Cantilever brake shoe anchor nut | 72 |
| Brake cable anchor nut | 48 |
| Brake lever binder bolt | 60 |
| Brake shoe fixing bolt | 65 |
| Brake arm mounting bolt | 60 |
| Carrier binder bolt | 40 |
| Rear derailleur cable clamp nut | 36 |
| Front derailleur clamp bolt | 48 |
| Front derailleur cable clamp bolt | 36 |

Torque values are given in the Torque Table above. Torque is the safe, correct tightness for nuts and bolts on your all-terrain bicycle. Torque may be defined as the twisting movement which produces rotation about an axis, as when you tighten or loosen a bolt or a nut with a wrench. Such torque is measured in inch/pounds. To tighten bolts and nuts to these specifications, you will need a torque wrench. An inch/pound torque wrench is available (at press time) from Sears, Roebuck for around $22. It's Sears catalog No. 9 AP 44644. If you don't have a set of metric socket wrenches, you can buy them from most hardware or auto parts stores. Be sure they fit the ⅜-inch drive of the torque wrench described above. You will also need 4 mm, 5 mm and 6 mm Allen hex head bits to fit your torque wrench, also available from Sears, Roebuck (catalog No. 9 AP 42668) for around $22. To use a torque wrench, simply put the correct size socket tool on the wrench. Then put the socket on the nut or bolt you wish to tighten. Check the torque table above for the correct torque specification for that nut or bolt. Tighten the nut or bolt until the scale reaches the specified torque value.

## Chain Care

The chain on your all-terrain bicycle is exposed to a lot more wear and tear than the same chain on a road bike. Off-road riding is often over sand, mud, dirt, and other abrasive substances. You may also ride through streams that wash out protective lubricants. Therefore, once home you should remove the chain, clean it, lubricate it and put it back on the bike. On the trail, you should wipe off accumulated mud and dirt and spray it with a penetrating lubricant such as E.P. Liquid Grease. Here are steps in chain maintenance:

1. **I recommend you remove the chain** to clean it, but you can get by without doing that if you're in a hurry to get out and ride. Just use an oversize bottle brush, a can of "gunk" (the stuff used for cleaning auto parts), and a cup to hold the gunk. Brush the gunk on the chain. Use the brush to wash the chain with hot water. The gunk will fall, the chain will be cleaned. Gunk will clean off exterior abrasives, but will not remove all the lubricant from the chain's innards. While you're at it, use the brush and the gunk to clean sand and dirt off freewheel cogs, the chainwheels, and the rest of the bike, wash gunk off with warm water, and presto, chango, you're ready for the road. See Step 4 for lubricant recommendations.

2. **To remove the chain,** use a rivet remover (Fig. 180). Screw in the handle about six times to push the rivet out (Fig. 181). Try to leave about ¹⁄₁₆th inch of the rivet in the chain. Remove the rivet-remover tool. Twist the chain to spread plates, pull the chain apart.

3. **Dip the chain in kerosene.** Don't use gasoline or any other highly flammable liquid. Not only are they fire hazards, but they penetrate too far into the chain and will remove the lubricant. Agitate the chain for a few minutes, lift it out, hold it up, wipe off excess kerosene, and lay it out flat on the floor, on a piece of newspaper.

4. **Lubricate the chain.** There are several lubricants that work well for me. One is molybdenum disulphide in a petroleum distillate base. One brand is called E.P. Liquid Grease, in a spray can, made by Dri-Slide, Inc. Be advised, however, that the Dri-Slide is black, sticky, and a mess if it get on your clothes. But it does keep the chain from wearing out fast. Another good lubricant is ordinary SAE 40-weight motor oil, containing graphite, which you can find at any automobile service station. A quart can should last you all year and is less expensive than the Dri-Slide. With the chain on paper on the floor, apply the lubricant of your choice on all four sides and let it soak in for a couple of hours, or overnight. Wipe off excess lubricant and reinstall the chain. Remember, you can't over-lube the chain. Wipe off accumulated dirt with a rag, and spray more lube onto it as often as possible.

5. **Reinstall the chain,** this time with the rivet you left in the chain facing toward the *left* side of the bike, so the chain rotates in the same direction it did before you removed it. Push the links together, and use the rivet tool to push the rivet back. Make sure the rivet is flush with the side plate. Look at other rivets for an example. Then grasp the chain in both hands, in front and behind where you fastened it, and twist the chain from side to side, to remove stiffness in that link.

*Fig. 180:* Chain rivet remover.

*Fig. 181:* Working parts of a chain. "A," roller; "B," sideplate; "C," sideplate; "D," spindle; "E," roller bearing.

6. **If the chain skips,** you probably need a new one. Remove the old chain, lay it out on your floor or workbench. Twist it so it forms a circle, not by the links, but by the side plates. Do the same with a new chain. If the old one has a lot more arc, can be bent more than the new one, toss it and install the new chain. But before you do, read the following section on freewheels and chainwheels, so you can check for worn teeth. It makes little sense to install a new chain on worn cogs.

7. **Check for correct chain length** if you install a new chain. Put the chain on the biggest front chainwheel and the smallest freewheel cog, as in Fig. 182. The chain is the correct length if, with the chain on these gears, the derailleur guide plates (Fig. 182, white arrow) are straight up and down, perpendicular to the ground, or slightly forward. If the new chain isn't long enough, try loosening the hub axle bolts and moving the rear wheel forward. If you still can't get the derailleur in the proper location, you'll have to add one or two links to the chain. For that you'll need to buy an extra chain and use links from it, as you replace old chains. It's better to have the chain slightly too long than too short. If, however, the chain bounces off the chainwheel when you hit a bump, it's probably too long.

*Fig. 182:* On an 18-speed ATB with wide ratio gears, say 34 teeth on the rear cog and 48 or 50 on the chainwheel, with the chain on both these gears the derailleur is going to be pretty well flat out, more or less parallel to the ground. On the same bike, when the chain is on the biggest chainwheel and smallest freewheel cog, the derailleur will be more or less perpendicular to the ground, as shown here. In extreme cases, with a 38-tooth rear cog, you probably won't be able to use the biggest chainwheel and biggest freewheel cog at the same time, but that's the price of super-low gears.

8. **A few cautionary notes:**

a. Never mix makes of chain links. If you add links, always take them from the same make and model of chain.

b. Never mix old and new chain links, except in an emergency.

c. Carry extra links on a trip so if you break one link, you can install another. Be sure to bring the rivet remover tool with you.

## Care of the Freewheel

**1. If the chain skips,** you probably need a new set of freewheel cogs. You don't have to discard the entire freewheel, its body should still be O.K. if you have cleaned and lubricated it as on p. 218. Check your freewheel cogs for wear on the teeth, especially on the "lands" of the teeth where the chain falls. Fig. 183 shows worn chainwheel teeth. The white arrow at the far right points to a burr on the tooth. The white arrow in the center points to where the lands of the teeth are worn down, as are most of the teeth in this freewheel. The arrow at the left, the black one, points to an indentation in the tooth. To replace worn cogs, follow the steps below.

**2. Remove the freewheel.** Fig. 158, on page 174, shows several types of tools. Buy the one that fits your freewheel (again, terrific standardization here, no? **No!** Why can't these people get together and make life easier for us home mechanics, I'll never know). Anyhow,

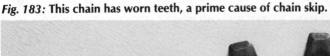

*Fig. 183:* **This chain has worn teeth, a prime cause of chain skip.**

insert the right size remover in the freewheel, after removing the axle nut on the freewheel side of the hub. When you buy a freewheel tool, make sure it not only fits your freewheel, but that its center hole is big enough to fit over the axle. Bicycle Research Products, Inc., makes a wide range of freewheel tools for most current freewheels that *will* fit over the axle. If your dealer can't supply one, write to this company at 1300 Galindo St., Concord, CA 94520, for their catalog or the name of a dealer near you.

O.K., now that the freewheel tool is in the freewheel, just screw on the axle nut to about a half-turn *above* the tool. Then turn the wheel over, put the wheel, tool side down, in a vise and grip the tool flats with the vise. Now twist the wheel counterclockwise (you'll need some muscle) and the freewheel should break loose. Once loose, you can remove the wheel from the vise, remove the axle nut over the tool, and twist the freewheel off by hand, using the tool.

3. **To change freewheel cogs,** grip the freewheel in a vise, with the teeth of the biggest or two biggest cogs held by wooden inserts in the vise. You will then need a cog remover (Fig. 184), to remove the cogs, starting with the smallest one. On most freewheels, only the first three or four cogs are threaded on. The rest slide off the freewheel body, just pull 'em off. When replacing, use same-make cogs; other makes won't fit.

4. **Adjustment.** Bearing surfaces inside the freewheel wear as do all bearings. On the SunTour freewheels you can adjust for bearing wear, but you will need special tools that you have to buy from the bike shop. SunTour has already prepared excellent instructions on this adjustment procedure, in their *Technical Manual No. 16.* Your bike shop should have a copy you can look at, maybe even borrow long enough to run out and Xerox page 5.

*Fig. 184:* To change freewheels, use a freewheel cog remover.

5. **Lubrication.** For years it was blasphemy to put any oil heavier than sewing machine oil in the freewheel, on the theory that the heavier oil would clog the pawls, which would then hang up. Then the freewheel would freewheel in both directions, which would get you nowhere, indeed. Now comes a radically different approach, the "freewheel grease injector" (Fig. 185). You have to remove the freewheel, screw the injector in the back (just as though the freewheel were being screwed onto a hub), and hold a tube of grease up to the fitting on the front. The injector also comes with a Zerk fitting so you can use a grease gun. What this thing does is fill the freewheel with grease, which is good for two reasons. First, it keeps dirt out. If you fill it up enough that grease comes out the other end of the freewheel, you will see that the grease forms a seal at both sides. Second, when filled with grease, the freewheel runs absolutely silently. For best results use Phil Wood grease. Don't use heavy mineral greases. There are different models of this injector to fit different makes of freewheels.

*Fig. 185:* **This grease injector fills up the freewheel with grease, seals out dirt, makes freewheel run noiselessly.**

*Fig. 186:* Freewheel disassembled. Arrow points to pawl (there are two) that dirt can cause to hang up so freewheel won't work. Note the jillion tiny loose balls at bottom, right. They are *very* easy to lose.

6. **Sometimes you will get a piece of dirt** in the freewheel that does hang up the pawls (see arrow in Fig. 186). Then you can pedal but nothing happens. The pedals turn but the rear wheel doesn't. The way out of this dilemma is to remove the wheel, pour a light solvent into the freewheel while you spin it rapidly, first in one direction, then in the other. Chances are good you'll be able to dislodge whatever is holding the freewheel pawls open, and you can be on your way. If you're in the wilds, and you have a gas cook stove, use some of the gas, but sparingly, and very, very carefully. Don't spill any on the tire, gasoline can eat rubber. When the freewheel is working again, drip in some light oil and spin it, before remounting the wheel.

## Chainwheel and Bottom-Bracket Maintenance

1. **You should wipe dirt, grease, mud, etc.** off the chainwheel as often as possible. Chainwheels are made of aluminum alloy, which is softer than steel. Abrasive materials on the chainwheels will wear it out much faster than if you keep it clean.

2. **To replace the chainwheel** (because its teeth are worn and cause chain skip or because you want to change gear ratios by installing a smaller or a larger chainwheel), follow these steps:

*a. First, remove the dust cap* (Fig. 187).

*b. With a 14, 15 or 16 mm wrench,* depending on crank binder bolt size, remove that bolt (Fig. 188).

*c. With a crank puller tool* (Fig. 189), remove the chainwheel/ crank assembly. The tool is in two sections. Before using it, hold it in your hand and make sure the front section is screwed counterclockwise, as far back toward the handle as possible. Then thread the front section into the chainwheel, into the same threads that held the dust cap. Make sure you have the tool *all the way* into the dust cap threads to avoid stripping them as you force the chainwheel off the bottom bracket spindle. Now turn the handle clockwise until the chainwheel is loose. The chainwheel may be wedged onto the beveled shank of the spindle so tightly that you can't force it loose without danger of stripping the soft aluminum threads of the chainwheel dust cap. In that case, tap the end of the tool with a ball peen hammer, turn the tool lever and repeat as necessary until the chainwheel and crank

*Fig. 187:* **Remove dustcap for access to chainwheel binder bolt.**

*Fig. 188:* Remove binder bolt with socket type wrench. (And tighten every 50 miles for first 200 miles, after removing and installing chainwheel.)

*Fig. 189:* Use chainwheel puller tool to force chainwheel or crank off bottom bracket spindle.

assembly is loose on the spindle. Then remove the tool from the crank.

*d. Disassemble chainwheels,* starting with the inner, small ring, using a 5 mm Allen wrench. Change to the desired chainring size, reassemble by repeating these steps. Make sure the new rings are compatible with the old chainset before buying, though.

**Caution!** After reassembly, be sure to check the tightness of the chainwheel binder bolts periodically (Fig. 190). They can work loose, even fall out, and cause the chainwheels to separate. Then the chain can drop between the rings and bind, causing you to lose control and possibly fall. Check these bolts on a new bike, or any ATB, periodically, whether or not you have disassembled the chainwheels!

**Caution!** After reinstalling the cranks, or on any new bike, retighten crank binder bolts every 50 miles for the first 200 miles, or after every 10 hours of trail use. If cranks loosen, it may be because the softer, aluminum tapered shank hole can be rounded off as the crank works against the harder steel of the bottom-bracket spindle. Torque spec on this bolt is 250 inch/lbs.

*Fig. 190:* Check tightness of chainwheel binder bolts every few weeks. If bolt works loose, chainwheel can spread, chain can drop down between chainwheels and cause an accident.

3. **Disassemble, clean, and relube bottom-bracket bearings** every month if you ride on dirt trails or in water a lot. For a nonsealed bearing set, after removing cranks, as above, do the following:

*a. Remove lockring* (Fig. 191), with wrench made for that ring. (Grrrr! again, no standardization.) You could use a cold chisel and hammer, but you'd gouge hell out of the lockring. The lockring is on the left side of the bike, turns counterclockwise to remove.

*b. With a pin wrench* (Fig. 192), remove adjustable cup, pull out bearings and spindle, clean, relube with water-resistant grease (such as Phil Wood's), and reassemble. Tighten adjustable cup clockwise till it stops, back off a half turn. Hold with pin wrench while you tighten lockring. Check adjustment by twirling spindle with fingers. It should turn easily, without binding. Move spindle from side to side. There should be no sideplay. Tighten or loosen adjustable cup and lockring till the spindle turns smoothly and has no sideplay.

*c. If the bearing is sealed,* remember there is really no such thing as a truly "sealed" bearing. Dirt and water can get in around the seal. So relube by prying off the bearing seal, *carefully,* with a thin bladed knife. Then force grease into bearing with your finger until you are sure it's loaded with grease. Replace the seal. To get at the seals, you should remove both cranks. Note: Phil Wood bearings are not user replaceable. You can replace most other makes.

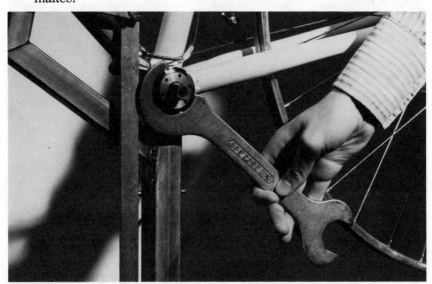

*Fig. 191:* To remove bottom bracket assembly, after removing crankset, use this notched tool that fits your lockring.

*Fig. 192:* After removing lockring, use pin tool to remove adjustable cup.

## Hub Maintenance

There are three designs of hub bearing seals. There are sealed bearings, such as those made by Phil Wood, with limited user service possibilities (Fig. 193). Sealed bearings on the Specialized and Sun-Tour bearings are replaceable. Another type is a conventional cone and cup, loose ball set, but with a labyrinth seal. A third type is the

*Fig. 193:* Phil Wood's sealed bearing hubs. Bottom shows how bearings are mounted on axle. Note also that axles are much thicker than other makes.

*Fig. 194:* Though this shows a non-sealed, conventional road hub, components are the same for ATB solid-axle hubs. "A" is locknut; "B" is spacer; "C," adjustable cone; "D," seal; "E," loose bearings; "F," spindle; "G," hub body.

conventional bearing set, without the labyrinth seal (Fig. 194). Sealed bearings need to be relubed almost as often as nonsealed bearings, particularly if you've ridden over sand or through water. Water in particular will wash out grease.

1. **Sealed bearing maintenance:** On Phil Wood hubs, remove wheel from dropouts and the freewheel from rear wheel. Carefully pry out seals, pack grease in, and replace everything. Fig. 195 shows a sealed bearing hub with bearing seal (arrow on right) removed. In Fig. 196, the arrows show pry points for removing the seal.

*Fig. 195:* Sealed bearing hub with seal removed. Seal is at right (arrow).

*Fig. 196:* Two makes of sealed bearings. Arrows point to where seals can be *care-fully* pried off with a thin blade knife, so you can stuff in fresh grease and push seals back in.

Remember, *these seals are extremely fragile.* If you bend them, you may not be able to get them back tightly. So be careful out there. SunTour's sealed hubs have adjusting nuts that require a special Sun-Tour wrench (here we go again) that fits nothing else in the bike world. Remove these nuts for access to the bearing seals.

2. **Conventional hub maintenance** on cone and cup bearings, with or without labyrinth seal, requires the following maintenance steps:

a. *Remove: wheels from bike,* axle nuts from axle, freewheel.
b. *Look at Fig. 194,* on page 230. This is a road hub with hollow axle, but the principle is the same for an ATB hub with solid axle. From left to right: A. adjustable cup locknut B. spacer washer C. adjustable cone D. seal E. loose bearings F. axle G. hub body.
c. *Remove the locknut (A),* washer and adjustable cup (C), pry out the seal (D). There is no standardization here. You will need either a pair of 13 and 14 mm, 15 and 16 mm, or 14 and 17 mm thin hub wrenches (Fig. 197). Hold the adjustable cup with one wrench (Fig. 198) and remove the locknut with the other. Be *very* careful when you remove these parts that you don't drop loose bearings on the floor. You may never find them. Your bike store has replacements.
d. *Remove all parts and clean.* Roll axle on a flat surface, check for alignment. If bent, replace it with a same make axle. Put a layer of grease inside hub-body cup and roll bearings around on the table, to cover with grease. Stuff bearings back, insert axle, cover bearings with more grease, replace seal, and adjust cone,

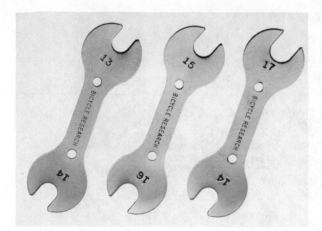

*Fig. 197:* You'll need a set of thin hub wrenches like these to work on your nonsealed bearing hubs.

*Fig. 198:* To take hubs apart or reassemble them and to adjust the cone, put one wrench on locknut and one on cone.

hand tight. Replace washer, screw down locknut. Check adjustment as described for bottom-bracket bearings above.

e. *On a bent sealed bearing axle*, if it's a Phil Wood, send it back
to him or have your bike shop do it. Phil Wood & Co., 153
W. Julian St., San Jose, CA 95110.

If it's a Specialized or SunTour sealed bearing axle, use their
excellent instructions for removing the axle. Send for instructions to Specialized at Specialized Bicycle Components, 1530 Concord Circle, Morgan Hill, CA 95037, or go to your bike shop, ask
them to open a hub box, and review the instructions in the box.
On SunTour bearings, write to SunTour, 10 Madison Road,
Fairfield, New Jersey 07006. Ask for *Technical Bulletin No. 2*, or
see a copy in your bike shop. It is important to replace a bent axle
as soon as possible, so you won't ruin the hub bearing cups. To
remove SunTour bearings, you will need a special tool, available
from your dealer for about $5. Replace wheel in dropouts.
Tighten per Torque Table on page 217. Tighten the front wheel
axle mounting nut to 264 inch/lbs. of torque. Tighten the rear
wheel axle mounting nut to 360 inch/lbs. of torque.

## Derailleur Adjustments

There are about six different models and at least three makes of
derailleurs used on ATBs that I know of, and I'm sure I haven't seen
all of them. Given the lack of standardization, the cable-fixing bolts on
front and rear derailleurs require different size wrenches, from 4 to 6
mm, including Allen wrenches. All of them do have at least one thing
in common: the low-gear adjusting screw is the one closest to the
derailleur mounting pivot-bolt, on both front and rear derailleurs, on
all makes and models. There are two kinds of derailleur adjustments
you will need to make from time to time. One is when shift cables
stretch and you can't get the rear derailleur to shift the chain onto the
biggest freewheel cog on the rear wheel, or the front derailleur to
shift the chain up to the biggest chainwheel. That's because you have
too much cable slack. The second adjustment is usually only made
once or twice, and that's when you install a new derailleur, and derailleur travel-limit stops have to be adjusted. Let's start with cable
slack.

1. **Derailleur cable slack take-up.** Shift so the chain is on the
smallest rear cog. Loosen the cable-fixing bolt at the derailleur ("C" in
Figs. 199 and 200), pull cable through, hold with a pair of needle-nose
pliers, and retighten. Check derailleur operation by shifting through

*Fig. 199:* Arrows point to "L," low gear adjuster; "H," high gear adjuster, "C," cable fixing bolt, and "S," cable stop.

*Fig. 200:* Another popular ATB derailleur. "L" and "H" are low and high speed adjusters, "C," cable fixing bolt.

all gears. If necessary, readjust derailleur, as specified below. Put the chain on the small front chainwheel, repeat this process with the front derailleur.

2. **Rear derailleur adjustment.** There's a high and a low gear stop or set screw on all derailleurs, "H" and "L" in Figs. 199 and 200. Shift so the chain is on the small cog. Adjust the "H" stop, as in Fig. 201, to limit derailleur travel. View the derailleur cage from the rear, to make sure jockey and idler wheels are lined up with the cog. Shift to the big cog and do the same. Then rotate the pedals by hand while you shift to the big and small cogs. The chain should not jump off the big cog toward the spokes, or off the small cog toward the chainstay. If you do this right, even when installing a new derailleur, you should be able to get accurate low and high gear adjustments the first time.

3. **Front derailleur adjustment.** Put the chain on the large front chainwheel. The chain should be about in the middle of the derailleur cage. If not, adjust the high gear stop (Figs. 202 and 203) to limit derailleur cage travel so the chain does not jump off the big, outer chainwheel. Fig. 202 shows the high gear stop limiting derailleur travel, to the right. Put the chain on the smaller, inner chainwheel,

*Fig. 201:* Here the high speed adjuster, "H," limits derailleur travel to the right, so chain won't jump off small rear cog. Low speed adjuster, "L," limits derailleur travel to the left, so chain won't jump off big rear cog and bind between cog and spokes.

*Fig. 202:* Two popular makes of ATB front derailleurs, showing "H," high speed adjuster and "L," low speed adjuster. Adjusters limit left and right derailleur travel.

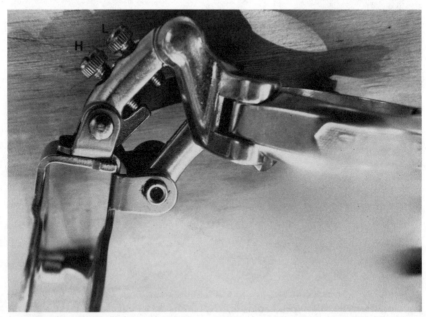

*Fig. 203:* Close-up of front derailleur, showing where high speed adjuster, "H," limits derailleur travel to right. "L" is low speed (small chainwheel) adjuster.

and repeat the process for the low, front gear. Fig. 203 shows both low and high gear adjusters. When you're through, the chain should shift to the low gear without jumping off toward the frame, and to the high gear without jumping off to the right. Note: A riding tip—if you've just climbed a hill and the chain is on the small front chainwheel, shift to the big chainwheel for maximum chain tension. That way there will be less chance of the chain jumping off the chainwheel as you hit bumps going downhill. That's most important in a race, when a stop to put the chain back on the chainwheel, manually, can lose precious seconds.

4. **Shift lever location:** For ease of reach, locate shift levers (Fig. 204) so the lever itself is parallel to the handlebars and the shift mechanism is as close as possible to the brake levers, without interfering with brake-lever travel. That way you can hold onto the bars, reach over with your forefinger, or thumb and forefinger and shift. Note: On top of levers there's a shift lever tension bolt. Sometimes the bike will shift by itself, which is a bit disconcerting, particularly when the shift is to an unwanted gear, such as a higher gear when you're going uphill. This is usually because the shift lever is loose. Twist the shift lever bolt clockwise to tighten. Some makes may have a small handle you flip up to twist to tighten the shift lever.

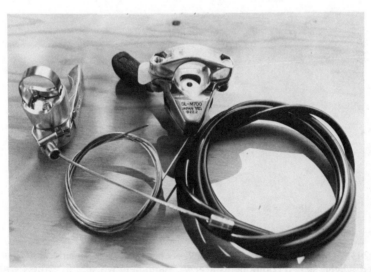

*Fig. 204:* Two types of derailleur shift levers. One on the right looks better, has covered shift lever for better grip. On either type, check tightness of mounting bolts from time to time.

5. **Clean derailleurs.** Every time you clean the chain, clean off dirt, mud, and abrasive laden grease from the derailleur mechanism, front and rear. Note: The front derailleur cage should be located no more than ¼ of an inch above the big chainwheel and the cage sideplates should be parallel to the chainwheels, to insure accurate shifting. Note also that as you shift up or down on the rear cogs, the chain assumes more of an angle, depending on which chainwheel it's on. As you shift through the gears, be aware of this changing angle and listen for chain rub on front derailleur cage sides. If this occurs, shift the front derailleur slightly one way or the other to keep the chain centered. This isn't as much of a problem on the new, wide-cage front derailleurs as it is on older models, with narrower cages. Also listen for chain rub on freewheel cogs and adjust the rear shift lever so this annoying, noisy chain- and cog-eating situation does not exist. Note: Front derailleur shift lever is on the left of the handlebars, rear derailleur shift lever is on the right.

*Sealed jockey wheels* are shown at the top in Fig. 205 and conventional nonsealed rear-derailleur jockey wheels are shown at the bottom. The sealed units do keep dirt and mud and water out better, and because they have bearings, they cut friction a tad. They're made by SunTour and are available in your bike store.

*Fig. 205:* Sealed bearing derailleur jockey wheel works more smoothly than non-sealed wheel. Sealed components are, "A," complete wheel; "B," wheel with seal pried off; "C," seal. Nonsealed bearing parts at bottom are "D," spacers; "E," plastic jockey wheel. "F," binder bolt and "G," shaft, are also used with sealed wheels.

## Wheels

The beating that wheels absorb during off-road riding can throw rims out of alignment, usually laterally (from side to side). If alignment is too far off, the rim will rub, in spots, on the brake shoes. This will make pedaling harder because of brake drag and it will also make accurate steering a bit more difficult. Besides, corkscrew wheels look so terrible. Another problem with wheels, not as severe as with road bikes because of the stronger rims on ATBs and because fat tires absorb shock better, is spoke breakage. However, if a spoke breaks on the freewheel side, replacing it is difficult, to say the least, because you have to remove the freewheel to do it. In the field, without a good machinist's vise, that is not easy or even, in some cases, possible.

1. **It's easy to straighten out-of-line wheels** at home or on the trail. All you need is a spoke wrench and to know which spoke to tighten or loosen. A finger alongside the rim will tell you where it's out of line, if you can't see it. Fig. 206 shows that if you tighten a spoke on the left side of the rim, you pull the rim to that side; loosen that spoke, and the rim moves to the right. To move the rim to the right, tighten a spoke on the right side of the rim. If you have trouble deciding which spoke is on which side of the rim, look at Fig. 207. A

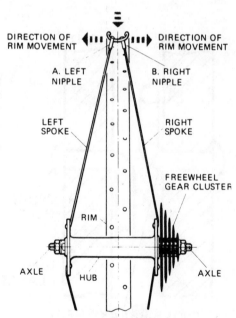

*Fig. 206:* Direction of rim movement related to spoke tightening. To move rim to left, tighten a left spoke nipple. To move rim to right, tighten right spoke nipple. If you can't tighten a nipple, loosen a nipple on the opposite side.

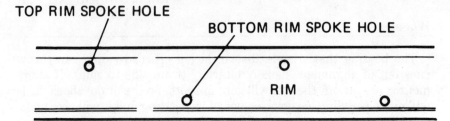

TOP RIM SPOKE HOLE

BOTTOM RIM SPOKE HOLE

RIM

*Fig. 207:* **Exaggerated rim drawing, showing that there are spokes on each side of rim, though that may not be apparent from casual look at rim.**

bit exaggerated, to be sure, but this illustration does show that spoke holes in the rim are staggered so that every other spoke is on an opposite side of the rim. The idea is to locate where the rim is too far to one side or the other, and tighten the spoke nipple or spoke nipples that will pull the rim back into alignment. You won't do a perfect job in the field, without a wheel truing stand, but you can get close, with a little practice. Turn spoke nipples no more than ¼ turn, check alignment, and use these steps until the rim is reasonably straight. Finish the job when you get home, on your truing stand, or take the wheel to the bike shop.

2. **Spoke replacement:** If you do break a spoke, remove the tire, tube, and rim strip; pull out the remains of the spoke from the rim and

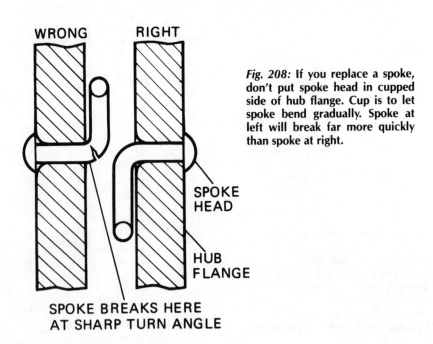

WRONG     RIGHT

*Fig. 208:* If you replace a spoke, don't put spoke head in cupped side of hub flange. Cup is to let spoke bend gradually. Spoke at left will break far more quickly than spoke at right.

SPOKE HEAD

HUB FLANGE

SPOKE BREAKS HERE AT SHARP TURN ANGLE

from the hub; insert a new spoke; and retrue the wheel. If the wheel is badly bent or dented, you should be able to get it back straight enough to get home. If you have to replace the rim, once you're home, please refer to my book on bicycle maintenance for instructions on wheel building with a new rim and spokes (see Appendix). If you break a spoke on the freewheel side, and you are far from a bike shop, you have a real problem. However, you may be able to readjust spokes enough for a truing job that will let you finish the trip, or get home. When you replace a spoke (I hope you have some spares along or else this discussion is academic) be sure the spoke head is in the hub flange as in Fig. 208. I know it's a temptation to put the spoke head in the cupped contour of the hub spoke-hole. But the contour is to spread stress where the spoke turns up out of the flange hole.

## Headsets

When I first began to ride test current makes of ATBs as part of my research for this book, I noticed that on some bikes, after the first 4 hours or so of riding, the headset (see Fig. 209) became loose. This was evidenced by a sloppy, loose feeling in the handlebars, as road shock hit my hands. I would stop, straddle the top tube with both feet on the ground, and pull the handlebars up and down to check for headset adjustment. Invariably I found that the adjustable cup (C, in

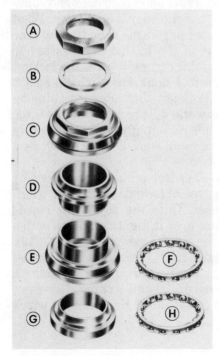

*Fig. 209:* If you replace your aluminum body headset with an all-steel one, this is the sequence the pieces go on. "G" goes on bottom of steering tube, on the fork. "E" goes in bottom of headtube (bike frame). "D" goes into top of head-tube. "C," adjustable cup, screws on fork steering tube and "B" and "A" on top, in that order. Bearings "F" and "H," of course, go in fixed cup "E" and adjustable cup "C."

Fig. 209) could be turned by hand. This meant that for some reason, the locknut (A, in Fig. 209) either was not tight enough, or the jolts of off-road riding on rough terrain had loosened it. What worried me was the two negative effects of such looseness. One was the damage being done to the headset bearings (F and H, in Fig. 209). When the adjustable cup is properly adjusted there is no up and down play or looseness in the headset, and so road shock is evenly distributed through all components. But when the headset is loose, bearings get a double whammy as cones and cups slam into them on rough terrain. Further, such pounding can also damage the precisely machined bearing surfaces of the cone and cup. What concerned me more than physical damage to the headset was the possibility of front-end shimmy because of headset looseness. This isn't as serious a problem on ATBs as it is on road bikes, because ATBs aren't tearing down paved hillside roads at 40 mph or more. However, ATBs can get up enough speed on some downhill trails or fire roads for any front end shimmy to cause loss of control and an accident. I was able to tighten the adjustable cup, and the locknut on top of it, well enough by hand to take out most of the free play. This served as a stopgap until I got back to my tool kit in the car. But still, headsets should not bounce loose on the trail.

What caused the headset to loosen? I doubt very much that it was careless work at the factory, or poor make-ready by the dealer. I found that all steel headsets stayed adjusted. Only headsets with aluminum cups and cones came loose. True, aluminum cups and cones had steel inserts as bearing surfaces, but the body is aluminum. What I believe happens is that the aluminum components compress just the few thousandths of an inch, under road shock, that is necessary to leave free play in the bearings. When this occurs, it gives the locknut and adjustable cup a chance to loosen. I don't know whether such deformation is permanent or not. I do know that after retightening the adjustable cup and locknut, they worked loose again two or three more times before staying put. For this reason, if you have this problem, I recommend changing over to an all-steel headset, such as a Campagnolo.

One possible solution to the loose headset problem is offered by SunTour. They have a head lock-up type of locknut (Fig. 210), which replaces the locknut on your headset. Once the adjustable cup is properly adjusted, you screw this unit over it, tighten it down with a 32 mm wrench, and tighten down the Allen screws (3, in Fig. 210). These screws push nylon plugs (2) into a ring (4), which is held against steering-head threads. SunTour has a new version of this unit, a sample or photo of which was not available at this writing. However, the brochure shows a photo of a unit called an XC Head Binder, which

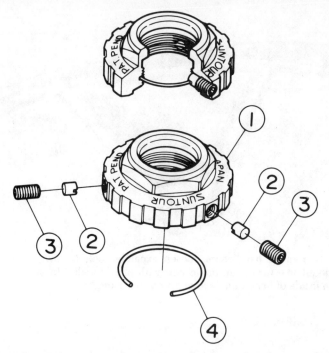

*Fig. 210:* One solution to loosening headsets is this SunTour clamp locknut. Allen bolts tighten down on plastic inserts and hold them against steering head threads. An improved version is in the works at this writing.

is sleeker and better looking than the old one. It replaces your old headset locknut and looks very functional.

Another reason for loosening headsets is out-of-parallel facing of the headtube and/or steering tube, just above the fork crown, where the bottom headset cone rests. This causes misaligned bearings. The only solution to this problem is to take the bike to the shop and have the headtube ends and the steering tube accurately machined. A well equipped bike shop will have the tools and the know-how for this procedure.

*Sealed bearings* on a headset do keep out some dirt and grit, and some water. But the headtube and steering head of the fork will deform (for a millisecond, not permanently) just enough on bumpy terrain to permit abrasives and water to enter headset bearings. For that reason, you should clean and relube any type of headset-bearing system every few months, if you bike a lot off-road, and after *every* trip involving going through water. Here are the steps to take in sealed bearing headset maintenance.

1. **Remove the handlebars,** using a 6 mm Allen wrench (you may need a different size. Again, no standardization). Unscrew the bolt

*Fig. 211:* **To remove handlebars, loosen expander bolt (arrow), with an Allen wrench, about five turns; tap down bolt with plastic mallet to break wedge nut loose from inside of head tube below; lift out stem and bars as a unit.**

just enough that it comes out about ¼-inch (Fig. 211). Don't unscrew it all the way. Then tap it with a plastic mallet. The handlebars should be loose and you should be able to lift them out. If you disconnect the front brake crossover wire there will be enough slack to put the handlebars on the top tube, out of the way.

2. **Remove the front wheel.**

3. **With a 32 mm wrench** (a monkey wrench will do, but there's less chance of rounding the flats with a precisely fitting 32 mm wrench), loosen the locknut. You will probably have to use a 2″ × 4″ or other piece of wood in the fork blades to hold the fork.

4. **Remove the washer under the locknut** and unscrew the adjustable cup, which may be hand loose.

5. **Remove the top bearing and pull out the fork.** The bottom bearing will be on the fork.

6. **Pry open bearing seals carefully** with a sharp blade, press grease in by hand, reinsert seals, and reassemble the fork, reversing steps above. Tighten top cup by hand. You will need *two* 32 mm wrenches. Hold the cup with one wrench, tighten the locknut with the other wrench. Rotate fork. There should be no tightness, fork should turn freely. Grasp the fork near the dropouts, push and pull the fork back and forth. There should be no slack or free play in the bearings. Loosen the locknut and readjust bearings as necessary.

## Nonsealed Bearings

1. **Remove handlebars, front wheel, locknut, and adjustable cup as above.**

2. **Remove fork and bearings.** Bearings will be in a retainer. Replace upper and lower bearings if you have been riding a lot for several months. Otherwise, clean, regrease, and reassemble.

NOTE: If you have a Shimano headset, use the special Shimano tools (Fig. 212). They grip a lot better than a 32 mm wrench, although any 32 mm wrench will work on a Shimano headset.

*Installing a new headset.* This requires special tools, so I recommend you let the bike shop do it. That way the shop can also check the machining on the headtube and steering head, and remachine if necessary. If you do want to do this job yourself, you can knock out the upper cone and lower retainer with a hammer and long screwdriver, and remove the cone from the steering head in the same way. But you *must* have an exact size replacement headset. Use a piece of pipe that is just big enough to slide over the steering head to seat the cone on the steering head (fork). Use a plastic mallet to insert cone and cup in the headtube. *Make sure all cups and cones are accurately seated.* Otherwise the first time you hit a bump, these parts will seat themselves and you'll have a very loose headset.

*Seal it yourself.* From Gary Fisher of Fisher MountainBikes comes this tip. Use a piece of old bike inner tube around the bottom of the headset, as a seal. Use heavy wheel bearing grease that resists being washed away by water.

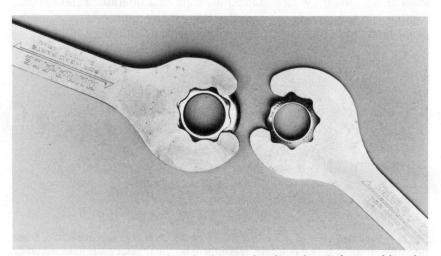

*Fig. 212:* Special wrenches to fit only Shimano headsets do grip better, although a 32 mm wrench will also work, and it will fit other makes of headsets.

## Pedal Maintenance

Keeping pedals spinning is a pretty straightforward proposition. Please refer to Fig. 213 and follow these steps:

1. **Remove pedal from crank.** Remember, pedal always unscrews in the opposite direction of pedaling and tightens in direction of pedaling. Remove dust cap, 8.

2. **Unscrew locknut, 7, remove washer, 6, and unscrew adjustable cone, 5.**

3. **Caution: Bearings are loose. Disassemble over a rag to catch bearings.**

4. **Pull out spindle, 2, dust seal, 3, and remove all ball bearings.**

5. **Clean all parts.** Put a layer of grease in both bearing cups. Lay bearings in inner cup first, cover with more grease. Insert seal, 3.

6. **Insert spindle, 2, and bearings in outer cup, put more grease on bearings.**

7. **Thread adjustable cone, 5, down hand tight.**

8. **Insert washer and locknut. Tighten locknut.**

9. **Twirl spindle between thumb and index finger.** Spindle should turn freely, with no binding or side play. If it binds, loosen locknut, loosen adjustable cone ¼ turn, tighten locknut, and repeat check. If spindle has side play, loosen locknut, tighten adjustable cone ¼ turn, tighten locknut, and check spindle. Repeat the appropriate adjusting procedure until spindle turns smoothly, with no side play.

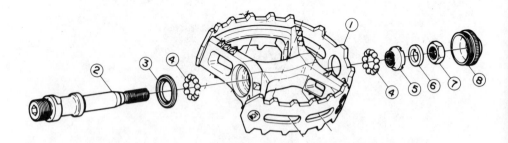

*Fig. 213:* Exploded view of a SunTour XC-11 pedal. Oval cage is removeable. Some riders file down fangs on one side, leave them on the other. Pedals have excellent seals, which are removeable, as are bearings and spindle. Toe clips and straps can be added.

## *Tire Care*

Most of the time the fat, knobby tires you use for off-road riding are more immune to puncture than skinny road tires. However, the inevitable will happen, and sooner or later you'll have a puncture and a flat tire. Here's what to do when your tire goes flatter than yesterday's beer:

1. **Look at the tread.** You may see a thorn, a tack, or some other foreign object sticking out of it. That's most likely where the tube is punctured. You could just use a tire iron to remove the tire at that point, without removing the wheel. Pull out the tube there and pump it up to make sure that's where the leak is. Try putting some liquid on the tube at that spot. Bubbles reveal the puncture. Dry off the liquid. Using the roughing tool in your patch kit to roughen the tube around the puncture.

2. **Apply rubber cement,** let it dry. Peel off backing from patch, put patch over puncture, pump up the tube a bit. Force the tire back on the rim with both thumbs, pump it up and pray a lot. If you did a good job on the patch, great. If not, you'll know soon enough.

3. **Alternatively, remove the wheel and remove the tire with a tire lever.** Fat tires are a lot easier to remove and reinstall than skinny road tires. Pull out the tube. Look inside the tire, check carefully for any foreign object that might have caused the puncture and remove it. Do the same for the exterior of the tire. Check tire sidewalls for cuts and slits. If the tire is cut or slit anywhere, follow step 5, below. Install a new tube. Put the tube in the tire, and put the tire, one side at a time, back on the rim. You should be able to get the tire on using only your hands. If not, use a tire iron, *carefully* so you don't puncture the tube against the rim. Get the tire seated. Repair the old tube later.

4. **Make sure the tire is seated in the rim** (Fig. 214). Before pumping up, push the valve down a bit, make sure the tire bead is seated in the rim at this point, a critical area. Pump up five strokes of the pump, check for bead seating. Pump ten strokes, check again. If bead is not seated in the rim, you will have a blow-out as tube pushes the sidewall out, as in Fig. 215.

5. **Fat tires have skinwalls** (hold a tire up to a light and you'll see) that can be cut on a sharp rock. You should bring along a roll of duct tape to make an emergency patch on the inside of the tire. Put duct tape at least two inches on all sides of the cut. If it's a bad cut, put two or even three layers of duct tape over it. Put tire and tube back on

*Fig. 214:* Arrows point to where the bead of the fat tire fits into rim. Full bead seating is vital when replacing the tire. Otherwise tube can pop out here and you'll have a nice loud blow-out.

*Fig. 215:* Here's a blow-out waiting to happen. Tire is being forced off rim because bead was not properly seated in rim.

rim, pump up and take off. Duct tape is aluminum colored and thin, but tough enough to be used on furnace vent pipes as a joint seal. Get it at any hardware store.

**Caution:** A 2.125 tire can be used on a 1.50 or 1.75 rim, but a 1.50 or 1.75 tire cannot be used on a 2.125 rim. I'd also use same size tube as your tire.

### A Word About Saddles

There are many saddles on the market, made out of a variety of plastics and of natural leather. I vastly prefer the leather saddles, even though they are butt-busters until broken in. Once broken in,

*Fig. 216:* This is one of the most comfortable saddles you can buy. It's the Brooks B-66, with springs. It's all leather so it shapes to you. However, the four wires (arrows) are 1-mm thinner than two-wire saddles, so you might have to file down seatpost so it grips saddle wire. Breeze makes an adapter so all four wires will be gripped. See text.

however, they will fit your tuckus like a glove, and will be superbly comfortable because the fit is so great. Plastic saddles, no matter how well padded, will always retain their original contours and will never shape to fit your natural curves.

You can break in a real leather saddle, such as the Brooks B-66 (Fig. 216) and the Brooks B-72. These are superbly made saddles that cost no more, or even less, than plastic ones. These saddles also are spring mounted. I use them on my ATB. They are just great in terms of comfort, and the saddle springs absorb road shock beautifully. To break in a new leather saddle, use neat's-foot or some other leather lubricant, liberally, soaking it overnight. After you have put about 24 hours of time on it, you'll have a saddle that's contoured to fit just you.

There is just one problem with the Brooks saddles. They have four wires, two on each side, as shown by the arrows in Fig. 216. These wires are 6 mm thick. If you try to mount this saddle in a seat post, as in Fig. 217, you can only use two of the wires. You may have to file down the mounting area of the seat post because it's designed for the conventional two-wire road bike saddle, which is 7 mm thick (A, in Fig. 218). The filing is necessary so it will grip the thinner 6-mm wires of the Brooks 4-wire saddles. I have been riding with just the two wires gripped in a filed-down LaPrade seat post (see Fig. 217), for a couple of months, and it seems to hold up.

I weigh 155 lbs. But the saddle may not hold up for a heavier rider, for whom I have good news. Joe Breeze has designed and sells an adapter, so all four wires of these Brooks saddles can be held by

*Fig. 217:* The Brooks B-66 saddle in a filed-down LaPrade seatpost. So far the two-wire mounting is holding up.

Campagnolo, Sugino, La Prade, and other seat posts. The adapter costs $16.95. Tell Joe what make seat post you have when you order from him at Breeze and Angell Development Co., 28 Country Club Dr., Mill Valley, CA 94941. Joe also makes the Hite-Rite quick-adjust seat locator, mentioned earlier in this book.

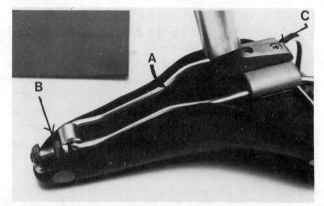

*Fig. 218:* Brooks Professional two-wire "A" saddle, like all leather saddles, will stretch. Stretch can be removed at adjuster, "B." "C" shows where seat tilt is set.

When you mount any saddle in a good seat post, you have the option of tilting the saddle to suit yourself. I prefer my saddle tilted slightly downward so I can put a bit more weight on the bars and less on my bottom. To alter saddle tilt, there are adjustments under the saddle. Some seat posts have a one-bolt adjustment, others two bolts (C, in Fig. 218).

Leather saddles will eventually stretch, and unless you like a sway-back saddle that sags in the middle, you should take out the stretch by tightening the adjuster nut (B, in Fig. 218). The saddle in this illustration is also leather, by the way, but without springs and used on my road bike.

## How to Make Your Own ATB from a Junk Frame

The following section on building your own ATB was contributed by Jeffrey L. Fleming of Modesto, California. He has made a number of these machines.

"You can make your own fat tire ATB from an old coaster brake bike, for about $150 worth of parts and some mechanical ingenuity. Here's how:

"1. **Find the frame:** Best for conversion to an ATB are mild-steel, lugged, three- or ten-speed frames. Chrome-moly frames don't heat uniformly, tend to kink when bent. Lugged frames are stronger. You can find suitable frames in bike shops, at garage sales and swap meets. Look for a bike with quality cranksets, stems, seatposts, and gear trains that can be reused on your to-be-built ATB. Before you buy the bike, measure the width between seat stays to make sure they will clear a fat tire. That way you only have to bend chainstays. Bending seat stays is a hassle that I don't recommend.

"Look for a frame with shallow, 70-degree angles and a long wheelbase, ideally about 41 inches or more. That kind of frame will be better at soaking up road shock than a more upright frame. The longer wheelbase assures fat tire clearance at the chainstay bridge or kickstand mount, and clearance for the front derailleur and the tire. You also need a frame a couple of inches shorter (measured by seat tube length) than your street bike. You can use street-bike brakes (center-pull or side-pull) if the seat stay bridge and fork-brake mounting holes will accept the brake-mounting bolt. However, it's easier to remove wheels when cantilever brakes are used. Clamp-on cantilever mounts are available from Moots Cycles (see section on brakes, on page 215), or braze on mounting bosses that come with the cantilever brake set.

"Even if the frame has been crashed so it has a slightly bent down-tube, you can still use it. See the March 1981 issue of *Bicycling* magazine for an excellent article on frame straightening. Install a gusset at the weak spot where the frame was bent (a gusset is a triangular steel reinforcement).

"2. **Equipment you will need:** Here's what you'll need for this job:

    *a. An outside concrete paved area.*
    *b. Water hose availability.*
    *c. A propane torch.*
    *d. Bicycle frame.*
    *e. Crowbar.*
    *f. Pencil, measuring tape, and a large carpenter's square.*

"You might need a brazing torch (propane alone isn't hot enough) to do brazing if the seat stays spring loose from the brake bridge as you bend the chainstays. It's handy for installing gussets and mounting cantilever brake bosses. I like the little Mapp gas/oxygen brazing unit you can buy at the hardware store for around $40. You'll also need a scraper and sandpaper for removing paint around areas to be heated, so you don't get blown away by the obnoxious odor of heated paint. A quart or so of fine sand, inside the tubes, makes bending easier because the sand helps distribute heat more evenly, with less kinking.

"*3.* **Make a pattern:** First, strip the frame of parts and of paint in the areas to be bent. Set the frame down on the pavement and scribe an outline, on the pavement, on both sides of the chainstays (Figs. 219 to 223). Draw the new chainstay outlet you wish to create right over the old outline, so you can see both outlines at the same time. The new outline should show enough chainstay spread to clear the fat tire, yet bend back in enough to clear the ends of the pedal cranks. If you're not sure, reinstall the bottom bracket assembly and cranks and mark their locations on the concrete, then remove these parts again. In drawing your new outline, also make an allowance for nondished rear wheels, or 6-speed axles, if you will be using them. Draw bends as gradual as possible yet still clear tire and cranks. Avoid sharp bends.

"4. **Turn on water hose.** Light up the torch, heat the chainstays near the kickstand bridge for an outward bend (Fig. 224). With the metal red hot, lay the frame on its side, with the hot stay up. Grasp the rear stays where they come together, at the rear wheel (Fig. 225). Gradually bend the stay toward you, checking with your pattern until the stay matches the pattern. Quench with the hose. Repeat for the other stay.

"5. **Check alignment:** Set the frame on your pattern on the con-

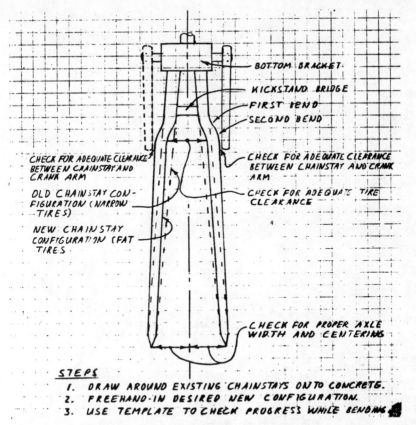

BOTTOM BRACKET

KICKSTAND BRIDGE
FIRST BEND
SECOND BEND

CHECK FOR ADEQUATE CLEARANCE
BETWEEN CHAINSTAY AND
CRANK ARM

OLD CHAINSTAY CON-
FIGURATION (NARROW
TIRES)

NEW CHAINSTAY
CONFIGURATION (FAT
TIRES·

CHECK FOR ADEQUATE CLEARANCE
BETWEEN CHAINSTAY AND CRANK
ARM

CHECK FOR ADEQUATE TIRE
CLEARANCE

CHECK FOR PROPER AXLE
WIDTH AND CENTERING

STEPS
1. DRAW AROUND EXISTING CHAINSTAYS ONTO CONCRETE.
2. FREEHAND-IN DESIRED NEW CONFIGURATION.
3. USE TEMPLATE TO CHECK PROGRESS WHILE BENDING.

**Fig. 219:** Pattern you can draw on concrete when converting an old bike to an ATB.

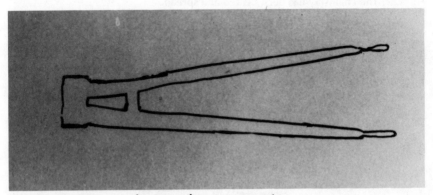

**Fig. 220:** Here's an actual pattern, drawn on cement.

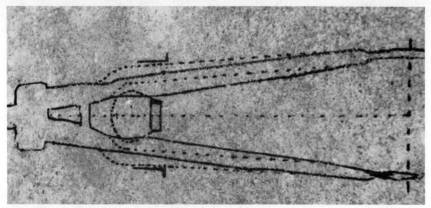

*Fig. 221:* Another pattern, showing stay spread.

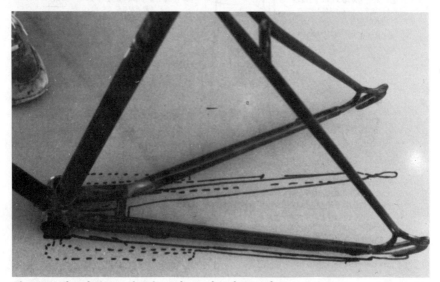

*Fig. 222:* The chainstay has been heated and spread.

*Fig. 223:* Making pattern on concrete.

*Fig. 224:* **Heating chainstay with propane torch till it glows red, prior to bending stay.**

*Fig. 225:* **Bending heated stay.**

crete. Stretch a string from rear stays to and around headtube and back to the stays. Bring the two ends of the string together so their midpoints just touch the seat tube without bending. The two ends of the string should be equidistant from the center point of the axle line. If not, the frame is out of alignment and needs to be bent straight. If you look down at the frame, from above, you should be able to see which side is bent in and which side is bent out. Carefully bend the two stays as needed, without heating (Fig. 226) to straighten the frame. Be sure to maintain the same distance between the stays as shown on the template. See Figs. 219 (on page 253) and 227 through 230 (pages 256–58) for more details.

*Fig. 226:* After bending stay for tire clearance, stay is bent back to the correct clearance, usually 130 mm, between dropouts for 6-speed freewheel.

*Fig. 227:* Here stays are bent. Note deeper bend in right chainstay for crank clearance.

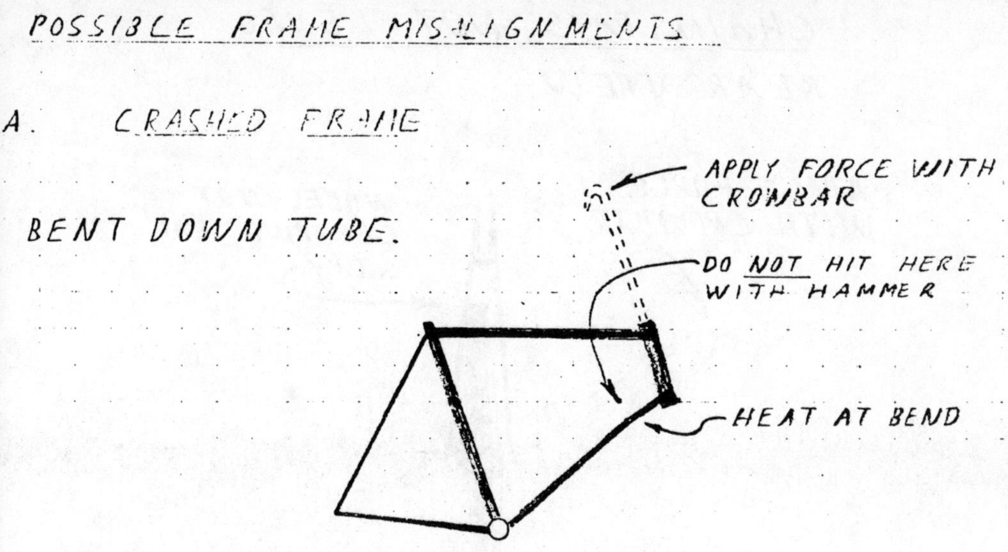

POSSIBLE FRAME MISALIGNMENTS
A. CRASHED FRAME
BENT DOWN TUBE.
APPLY FORCE WITH CROWBAR
DO NOT HIT HERE WITH HAMMER
HEAT AT BEND

**Fig. 228:** Straightening a bent downtube with crowbar.

FRAME OUT OF LINE
(TOP VIEW)
REAR TIRE NOT IN LINE WITH TOP TUBE.
PUSH HERE
PULL HERE
HEATING NOT NECESSARY

**Fig. 229:** Straightening out-of-line frame.

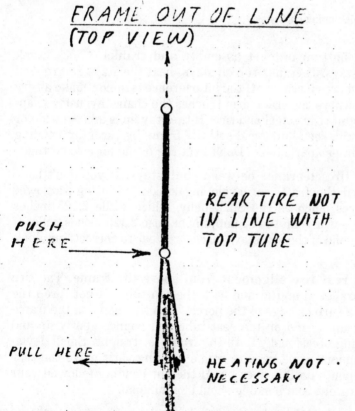

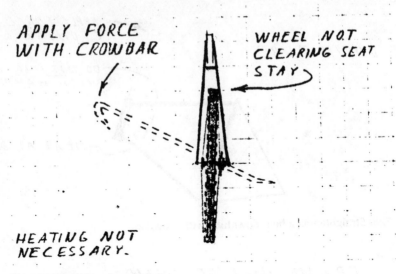

CHAINSTAYS NOT LEVEL

REAR VIEW

APPLY FORCE
WITH CROWBAR

WHEEL NOT
CLEARING SEAT
STAY

HEATING NOT
NECESSARY.

**Fig. 230: Straightening chainstays.**

"6. **Install bottom bracket assembly and cranks.** Check crank clearance of stays. If cranks rub on stays, heat the stays and rebend them to give more clearance. If the interference is minor, make a *very* slight indent where the crank arm touches the chainstay, using channel locks. Install rear wheel and tire. If the stay ends are too wide or too close for the rear hub, 'cold-set' the frame by carefully bending stays together, or apart, to fit. Don't heat the frame for cold setting.

"7. **Check tire clearance between chainstays.** If you don't have clearance, and the frame is developing kinks, try using narrower profile fat tires, such as the Snakebelly, which while 2.125 inches wide, are narrower than the Stumpjumper, also 2.125 inches wide. If a tire touches one of the seatstays, use a crowbar to correct, but don't dent the stay.

"8. **Check rear tire alignment from above the frame.** The tire should be parallel to and in line with the top tube. If not, prop the frame up on a curb or edge of the porch, with the 'bend' in the frame line pointing up. Stand on the seat tube and bounce gently up and down, checking occasionally until the frame is straight. Small deviations in alignment won't require frame bending. Just move the rear wheel in dropouts until it lines up. If the hot bending followed your pattern accurately, cold bending should be minimal.

"9. **If the brake bridge has broken loose** from seat stays, rebraze it. Or better yet, braze on cantilever brake bosses. While the brazing equipment is out, you might also consider brazing on reinforcing gussets, as mentioned earlier. If you do braze, be sure to clean off the paint around the brazing area. And when you're through, wire brush and sand any brazing flux from around the brazed area, otherwise new paint won't adhere.

"10. **Repaint,** using the same color as the rest of the frame. Sand down brazed areas to bare metal, hang frame up. Use a rust resisting primer first. Then use a spray can that matches the old paint and touch up the brazed area. Or sand the entire frame, not necessarily down to the metal, but enough to give the new paint a "bite" for adhesion, and spray the entire frame with the color of your choice.

"11. **Install components.** Bottom-bracket width permitting, install a good quality triple chainwheel and bottom-bracket set if possible. Use 1.75″ × 26″ aluminum rims and good hubs, such as made by Shimano, SunTour, or Specialized. Replace old dropped or flat bars and stem with ATB components. Specialized offers a good selection of bars and slingshot alloy stems. If you bought cantilever brakes you will also have the correct brake levers for the new bars.

"Now you will have built yourself a decent ATB (Fig. 231), for around $150 in parts. I've never broken one of these home-built ATBs, so I don't know what their weak points are. I would guess that the headset and the chainstays would be the first to die in any radical stunting."

If you're interested in the ATB racing scene, you'll find a quick review of racing basics in the next chapter.

*Fig. 231:* **The final product, an old 10-speed converted to an ATB. Total cost, for complete bike, about $150.**

# 6

# Racing the Fat-Tire Bicycle by Todd Sloane

 Even if you have never raced a road bicycle or been on an off-road bike, the exciting new sport of all-terrain racing could be for you.

Unlike its highway cousin, all-terrain bike racing doesn't mean having to keep up with a fast-moving pack of riders, with nothing but the road or the next biker's wheels for company.

Instead, fat-tire racing is a stew of solitary struggles with the course, tough technical riding of rock or tree-limbed obstacle courses (Fig. 232) and breath-taking downhill descents, hot on the trail of another rider (Fig. 233). Instead of just road, the surfaces crossed vary from rocks to streams (Fig. 234) to sand to logs (Fig. 235). Riding with a pack is difficult, so riders can be content to travel at their own pace, sometimes even winning age and sex group categories when they have never ridden in a race of any kind before. That alone could explain why so many all-terrain bike owners find themselves sooner or later in a race or organized tour, many more, percentage wise, than ever show up at a road race. Being involved in such a new sport naturally brings people together, and where many riders gather, there is the valuable exchange of information on equipment, clothing, riding techniques, and where the hottest new trail may be found.

ATBs have shown up at traditional cyclo-cross races, and in some cases have come close to winning those events against the lighter machines because of superior ability to get through the mud and to handle obstacles. A cyclo-cross bicycle is a modified road bike, designed for rough terrain but not as well suited to all-terrain surfaces as an ATB. Where cyclo-cross riders must run, ATB riders are still on

*Fig. 232:* An ATB rider's path may not always be smooth. The agility and ridesmanship needed to negotiate this sort of terrain is part of the fun, and the challenge, of off-road riding.

*Fig. 233:* Going full blast down a mountain trail in the Sierra Mountains of northern California is part of the ATB racing scene. This rider is airborne as he jumps over a drop in the trail.

*Fig. 234:* Racing through water at top speed, this rider stays upright as he pushes toward the finish line.

*Fig. 235:* Skilled observed-trials riders literally claw their way over logs, as this rider is doing. Note the single chainwheel, which is sometimes used to grip the log momentarily as the rider pushes up, over and down the other side.

their machines, spinning like nobody's business. Where there is snow, the ATB reigns supreme.

The sport is still so new it is evolving by the month rather than by the year. While it has been largely confined to California and Colorado in the past, it has now spread to the East Coast and to Europe, where it is seen as a natural extension of the cyclo-cross racing tradition (Fig. 236). Here in the States, a national series of closed-circuit races held across the country in 1984 and scheduled on an on-going basis for future years is sure to spread interest in the sport.

## Racing Categories

The National Off-Road Bicycle Association is the governing body of off-road racing. NORBA categories, in terms of the rider, are:

    a. Novice, essentially a beginner of any age.
    b. Expert, a good quality racer with off-road racing experience.

*Fig. 236:* Champion all-terrain cyclist Gary Fisher demonstrates that the fun of ATB racing is an international sport, as he competes in a tough downhill challenge in France. Gary now makes Fisher Mountain Bikes and operates the first ATB-only bikeshop in the U.S.A.

   c. Pro/AM, a professional team racer sponsored by a manufacturer.
   d. Veteran, anyone over 35.

Here is a summary of the types of off-road racing:

**Downhill:** Just as in skiing, the idea of the downhill race is to follow the course and get to the finish line first in your category. Downhill racing is especially popular in the East and West. Probably the oldest and best known downhill race is the Repack of Marin County, California, so called because before there were multispeed ATBs, racers rode down on coaster brake bikes. The heat of braking on the fast downhill runs would melt the grease right out of the coaster brake hub, hence they had to be repacked after every race. Basic to this competition is staying out of trouble; that is, staying in control and on the bike and avoiding losing time through falls, skids, braking for turns and so on. The rider who remains calm while hurtling through space at speeds as high as 40 miles per hour is likely to be the type who will win events such as these. Gary Fisher, a pioneer in this sport, has won the now famous Repack downhill in Marin County by flying down a long mountain descent from around 2,500 feet to near sea level, in four and a half minutes.

**Uphill:** The uphill race is also popular on both coasts and in the Rocky Mountain area. This can be an extremely challenging and difficult race, not for the out-of-shape rider.

In many cases, an uphill precedes the swift downhill, and some races award prizes for first one up, fastest one down and overall fastest finisher. These races are often massed start, though some larger races are now time trials, with the overall fastest finisher winning. This can be a dangerous sport, because of its hell-for-leather tactics, and injuries can crop up when less-skilled riders try to do battle with the experts. The uphill/downhill races, however, quickly see the lesser riders separated from the strong riders on the uphill.

**Closed course:** A race over a marked circuit, usually a dirt road or fire trail, which mixes sharp turns, jumps, streams, and up and downhill all in one race.

In all of these races, the first rider to the finish line in his or her racing category is the winner in that category.

**Observed Trials:** This type of race involves riding over an obstacle course under the watchful eyes of judges. Penalties are assessed for each time the rider has to put a foot down on the ground. Fig. 237 shows such a course, in Issaquah, Washington. This is the newest

*Fig. 237:* Hopping over obstacles is part of the fun of all-terrain cycling, but a skill that takes a bit of practice.

sport, a challenge for anyone's riding skills. It is not an endurance event as such, but is so technically difficult as to be a workout. When I say technically difficult, read crash-city. Think of a fifty-yard section involving a 15-percent grade, then over into a rocky downhill, with a quick bunny hop over a section of log, then a sudden left turn, then over a 36-inch-high fallen tree, and you begin to get the idea.

Borrowed from moto-cross events, the courses are laid out in sections, with a different challenge awaiting on each section. The object is to ride through each section without touching a foot to the ground, which is known as a "dab." Each dab counts a point, with a three being the worst possible score per section as long as the rider completes the section without coming to a halt or refusing to complete the section. If the section is not completed, it is scored a five. Thus, the event is scored like golf, with the lowest score being the winning score.

There are often ten sections in the trials on which to score. To ride a section without dabbing once is to "clean" that section, something akin to a hole-in-one, though not quite that difficult. The best trials courses are those that offer variety. One section might be a climb of a steep trail, going over a section of loose rock and then up a series of steps. Another might be a quick downhill, with a quick turn and then uphill again. Still another might be a tricky climb of a very large object, such as the 36-inch-high log mentioned above. Riders will seriously discuss throwing their bike into an almost vertical position to get the front wheel over, then using the chainring to grind into the tree, and then flinging the back wheel over the rest of the tree.

Rider categories for observed trials races are:

a. Junior: Anyone under age 18.
b. Novice: Must be an experienced off-road racer but new at observed trials.
c. Intermediate: Some observed trials experience.
d. Expert.
e. Advanced.

## Self-Sufficiency Required

NORBA rules specify that in all races, riders must be totally self-sufficient. If anything goes wrong with the bike, the rider must fix it right then and there. Team mechanics, toting spare parts, extra wheels and tools, are not allowed. If the chain falls off, you stop and put it back on yourself. If you get a flat, you fix it as the race goes on. If the seat post breaks, you finish the ride on the pedals. These rules are designed to promote preride preparation. The bike must be in top-notch mechanical condition and self-sufficiency is the byword. NORBA feels that this is good preparation for all off-road riding.

There are already stage races, or a series of races where the winner is the one who has the lowest overall time. The National Off-Road Racing Championships, sponsored by NORBA, are held over two days. There was also talk, in 1984, of a week-long set of races like the famed Tour de France road race, only this one taking place in forest area and the riders fending for themselves enroute.

A popular tour that is more like a road race is the Pearl Pass excursion, held each year. Pearl Pass just happens to be a nearly impassable (except to ATBers) trail from Crested Butte, Colorado, to Aspen. Talk about a workout.

The most exciting thing about this sport is just getting started. The number and type of events seems limitless. Already, major bike makers are sponsoring teams that are really full-time bikies, making a name for themselves in a new sport. At the 1983 National Championships, such big names in road racing as Olympic gold medalist Alexi Grewal and Ironman Triathlon winner John Howard took part. The event was won by Steve Tilford, a Raleigh team member and off-road specialist.

## A Word About Racing Equipment

First, there is the pure-bred racing ATB. These bikes sacrifice some of the sturdiness of conventional ATBs for lightness. They also have 1.75-inch tires and the very best of components. They are designed for high performance. They weigh 25 pounds, as compared with the 28 to 30 pounds of a fine ATB designed for general purpose riding. Conventional design ATBs may, and indeed are used in racing events. In fact the racing model ATB, costing upwards of $1,500 to $1,600 for the complete machine, is in the minority at these races, which anybody can enter who subscribes to NORBA rules. Excellent examples of hand-built, high-quality ATBs are the *Competition* model made by Fisher Mountain Bikes and the *Team Comp* made by Ritchey, U.S.A. (see chapter 2).

While this book has gone into equipment needs in earlier chapters, racing brings up a few special problems and equipment requirements. I think toe-clips are essential to most off-road racing, with the exception of observed trials. The clips give you optimum efficiency throughout the turn of the cranks. When you are racing for your life up a steep embankment, you don't want your foot to slip off the pedals and find it lodged in a crevice as other riders whizz past.

While I am at it, many riders are now eschewing the widest 2.125-inch fat tires for the faster, thinner 1.75 or even 1.5 inches, with less aggressively knobbed tires. The reduced control you get from these tires is compensated for by less weight and rolling resistance, and by the expertise of the rider.

Some racers are also changing to shorter handlebars and even using dropped handlebars in distance events. The idea is to get a better position for downhills. Where maximum control is important, the standard 27- or 28-inch-wide bars are better, but where pure speed is of the essence, use your own judgment.

Now that you are interested in trying this off-road racing thing, how do you get involved? In the case of California residents, that should be no problem. There are chapters and area NORBA representatives in many areas of the state. For the rest of the country, there may be a bit more trouble finding a NORBA-sanctioned event, but that is rapidly changing. There were NORBA reps in Colorado, Georgia, Connecticut, Indiana, Maryland, Massachusetts, Michigan, Montana, New Hampshire, New Mexico, New York, North Carolina, Texas, Vermont, and Maryland as of late 1984. For information about a local contact or about national and local races, contact NORBA at 2175 Holly Lane, Solvang, CA 93463 or phone (805) 688-2325.

Local bike stores, particularly those with knowledge of and a good stock of ATBs, should also be a good source of information.

## NORBA Regulations

NORBA sanctions most off-road events, and in the absence of another sponsoring body, racers should participate only in NORBA-sanctioned events. The NORBA rules govern the way an event ought to be run. For example, NORBA prescribes that a preliminary race meeting be held to inform riders of the course, of the rules, and about safety. NORBA specifies that riders must wear helmets, a major point in its favor, given the danger of a crash. In off-road racing, a crash isn't a possibility during a racer's career, it is a probability.

For example, NORBA rules specify that riders must finish the race on the same bike they started on and riders riding their bikes have right of way over riders walking their machines. It is this kind of control that makes for safer races. While there may be organizers who chafe under NORBA's insistence on promoting itself through racing, it is the only game in town as of today, and so events should be sanctioned by NORBA.

Also on this subject, NORBA can provide access to low cost insurance, which is a valuable protection for organizers and racers alike.

So join NORBA, perhaps in time for the fall National Championships, where skills and conditioning can be tested against the best the nation has to offer. It is one of the few sports in which a new rider can start off in the same event as a national champion, though the champion will likely disappear over the next hill. No matter. Part of the real fun of the sport is that it is man or woman and their ATB against the hills, the prairies, the streams, and time. See if you can be a winner too.

And if you don't want to race, I know you will enjoy this new sport of all-terrain bicycling, and I do mean ALL-TERRAIN (Figs. 238 and 239).

*Fig. 238:* This scene is what the term "all-terrain" is all about. One moment the rider is on flat gravel, the next he's going down a breathtakingly steep hill, the next negotiating a narrow trail through a dry gulch.

*Fig. 239:* Seems impassable, even to an ATB, doesn't it? Not so, demonstrates this rider. A skilled rider can go almost anyplace, and, what's more, have fun doing it.

# Appendix

## Bicycle Catalogs

There are a number of excellent bicycle and bicycle parts and components mail order firms in the U.S. If you can't find a particular part or component, you will most likely find it in one of the catalogs listed below.

*Bikecology:* 1515 Wilshire, Santa Monica, CA 90403. In California, 213/394-7059. Outside California, 1-800/233-BIKE. Catalog, $2.

*Bike Nashbar:* 215 Main St., Box 290, New Middletown, OH 44442. Catalog, $1.50.

*Lickton's Cycle City:* 310 Lake St., Oak Park, IL 60302. 1-800/323-4083. In IL 312/383-2130. Catalog: $1.

*Palo Alto Bicycles:* P.O. Box 1276, Palo Alto, CA 94302. 1-800/227-8900. In California, 415/328-0128. Four-color catalog, free.

*Pedal Pushers:* 1130 Rogero Road, Jacksonville, FL 32211-5895. 1-800/342-BIKE. In Florida, 1-800/342-7320. Color catalog, $3 in U.S., $4, Canada.

*Performance Bicycle Shop:* 1126 Sourwood Dr., P.O. Box 1741, Chapel Hill, NC 27514. 1-800/334-5471. Color catalog, free.

*PS&S:* P.O. Box 82, Horsham, PA 19044. 1-800/523-7576. 1-215/672-0202. Catalog is free.

## Camping and Other Outdoor Catalogs

*L. L. Bean:* The old standby. Everything you ever wanted for the outdoors and more. Free. L. L. Bean, Inc., Freeport, ME 04033. 207/865-3111.

*Campmor:* Discount camping gear. Quite reasonable prices, wide selection. Includes survival equipment, such as Skyblazer, a self-contained launcher and flare that shoots a 20,000 candlepower signal 400 feet up, weighs one ounce, costs $12.50, and a 10-mile signal mirror, costs $6, as well as tents, bags, etc. Campmor, Paramus, Box 999, Paramus, NJ 07653-0999. Outside NJ, 1-800/526-4784, in NJ, 201/445-5000. Free.

*Early Winters:* Very wide selection of very high-quality camping gear, made by or for people who camp and bike. A pleasure to look at. Free. Early Winters, Ltd., 110 Prefontaine Place So., Seattle, WA 98104. 204/624-5599.

*Moss Brown:* Good collection of active-wear clothing for all seasons. Free. Moss Brown & Co., Inc. 5210 Eisenhower Drive, Alexandria, VA 22304. 1-800/424-2774. In VA, 703/823-4600.

*Robert Edmunds:* Not a camping catalog, but lots of hi-tech health related equipment. Free. Robert Edmunds, 101 E. Gloucester Pike, Barrington, NJ 08007. 1-800/257-6173. In NJ, 1-800/232-6677.

*Norm Thompson:* Mostly clothing, some high fashion outdoor wear. Free. Norm Thompson, P.O. Box 3999, Portland, OR 97208. 1-800/547-1160. In OR, 1-800/772-7226. In Alaska and Hawaii, 503/644-2666.

*Ramsey:* Camping gear, clothing. Prices seem good. Free. Ramsey Outdoor, 226 Route 17, Paramus, NJ 07652. 201/261-5000.

*Recreational Equipment, Inc. (REI):* Very good selection of high-quality camping gear. If you join their benefits program (fee $5) you receive a membership card which, when used with orders, gives you a quite substantial discount. Catalog is free. Recreational Equipment, Inc., P.O. Box C-88125, Seattle, WA 98188. 1-800/426-4840. In WA, 1-800/562-4894. For Canada, Hawaii and Alaska, 1-206/575-3287.

*Sierra Club:* Not much camping gear, but excellent collection of outdoor books on survival, naturalist's guides, guides to recreation areas of the U.S., totebooks you can take on the trail about cookery, field photography, guides to wilderness trails, and more. Free, and a valuable guide I urge you to get. Sierra Club, 205 South McKemy, Chandler, AZ 85224. 602/961-0333. (I also urge you to join the Sierra Club, P.O. Box 7959, San Francisco, CA 94120.)

*Wear-Guard Weekend Editions:* Outdoor clothing. Free. Wear-Guard Weekend Editions, Norwell, MA 02061. 1-800/343-4406.

## Publications

*Bicycling:* Broad selection of articles each month on all aspects of bicycling. $14.87/yr. or $2 a copy at newsstands. Rodale Press, Inc., 33 E. Minor St., Emmaus, PA 18049. 215/967-5171.

*Bicycle Guide:* A new publication. First issue October, 1984. The magazine will cover all aspects of cycling, according to the publisher. $14.97 a year, nine issues, or $2.50 a copy. Bicycle Guide, 128 N. 11th St., Allentown, PA 18102. 215/435-7570.

*Bicycle Sport:* Carries informative articles on touring, race results, equipment and repair. $16.50/yr. or $2.50 a copy at the newsstand. Wizard Publications, Inc., 3162 Kashiwa St., Torrance, CA 90505. 213/539-9213.

*Bicycle USA:* Official publication of the League of American Wheelmen. Free with membership in the L.A.W. at $18/yr. At newsstands, $1.50 a copy. News of bike club activity, articles on cycling. A nonprofit oriented, refreshingly frank look at the entire bicycling scene in the U.S. League of American Wheelmen, Inc., 10 East Read St., Baltimore, MD 21202. 301/727-2022.

*Cycling:* A new (in 1984) publication, which so far seems more oriented to the racing scene, but with some touring information in the U.S. and abroad. $11.87/yr. or $2/copy. Cyclist, 20916 Higgins Court, Torrance, CA 90501.

*Fat Tire Flyer* As I said earlier in this book, this is one publication you should be reading because it's devoted to the interests of the all-terrain bicyclist. It's not slick, but you will enjoy the down-to-earth and often humorous articles on ATBs, most from the pen of editor Charles Kelly, a pioneer off-road racing and touring cyclist. You won't find this magazine on the newsstands, at least not for awhile. Published bimonthly (at this writing). Annual subscription is $10 and worth it. Fat Tire Flyer, P.O. Box 757, Fairfax, CA 94930.

*Sierra:* Bimonthly bulletin of the Sierra Club. Lots of fine articles on how to select camping gear, as well as on the out-of-doors. Free to Sierra Club members, or $10 a year. Sierra Club, 530 Bush St., San Francisco, CA 94108. 415/981-8634.

*Tri-Athlete:* Strictly for the racing cyclist/runner/swimmer crowd. $15.87/yr or $2 per issue. Tri-Athlete, 6660 Banning Drive, Oakland, CA 94611. 415/530-4580.

## Books

White, Frank R., & Wilson, David G. *Bicycling Science.* Boston, MIT Press, 1982. In chapter 2 of this book I said I did not want to get into the math and the physics of bicycle design. If you are interested in this subject, this book will give it to you, and how!

Bunnelle, Hasse & Sarvis, Shirley. *Cooking for Camp and Trail.* San Francisco, The Sierra Club, 1984. An appetizing guide to energy sustaining foods for the trail.

Sloane, Eugene A. *The All New Complete Book of Bicycling.* New York, Simon & Schuster, Inc., 1981. Modesty forbids me to say anything more about this book than that if you don't have it, you should.

*The Complete Guide to America's National Parks.* Washington, D.C., The National Park Foundation, 1984. Comprehensive data on all 360 U.S. National Parks, including maps, mailing addresses, phone numbers, directions, permits, fees, facilities, regulations, weather, points of interest, and more. At $10 a copy, a real bargain. Cost is tax deductible as a contribution to the nonprofit chartered National Park Foundation, P.O. Box 57473, Washington, D.C. 20037. 1-202/785-4500.

Gatty, Harold. *Finding Your Way on Land or Sea, Reading Nature's Maps.* Brattleboro, Vermont, The Stephen Greene Press, 1983. Some good info on keeping from getting lost, but a lot of this book has to do with the oceans.

Bunnelle, Hasse & Thomas, Winnie. *Food for Knapsackers (and Other Trail Travelers).* San Francisco, The Sierra Club, 1971. A totebook, with lots of excellent data on nutrition, meals planning, equipment, and recipes. You can get hungry just browsing through this book.

Kals, W. S. *Land Navigation Handbook.* San Francisco, The Sierra Club, 1983. A book on the use of map and compass. Tells you how to decide where you are, which way to go, how far you have to travel to get there. It's a step-by-step manual for the novice. Covers basics of altimeter navigation, navigation by the sun and stars (any place in the world), and how to read metric-based maps.

Kellstrom, Bjorn. *Map & Compass.* New York, Charles Scribner's Sons, 1973. This is the book that seems to be preferred by people who teach orienteering and the use of map and compass. It's an easy-to-use self-teaching guide as well. The author is a former

Swedish orienteering champion and a founder of the U.S. Orienteering Federation. You can get lost without it.

Bengtsson, Hans & Atkinson, George. *Orienteering.* Brattleboro, Vermont, The Stephen Greene Press, 1977. Strictly for the hiker (so it will be fine for the biker). Covers use of map and compass, gets into orienteering as a sport (afraid the sport would lose me, though, I just want to be able to get where I'm going and get back).

Higley, Donn C. *Pocketwise Tips On Use of the Compass, Man-made and Natural.* Seattle, Washington, Self-published, 1981. This booklet is as short as its title is long, but it does cover the basics, in simplified form, of the use of the compass. Covers topo map reading and some star sighting.

Fleming, June. *Staying Found.* New York, Random House, 1982. Another simplified approach to orienteering, map reading, and compass use.

Lobeck, Armin K. *Things Maps Don't Tell Us.* New York, The Macmillan Company, 1956. Kind of a fun book on map reading and interpretation. Not for finding your way about, but an explanation of why land, lake, and other natural formations are the way they are. Sort of a phrenological approach to the way the world is shaped today.

Sloane, Eugene A. *Eugene A. Sloane's Book of Bicycle Maintenance.* New York, Simon & Schuster, Inc., 1982.

Watts, Alan. *Instant Weather Forecasting.* New York, Dodd Mead & Company, 1968. A really great little guide, with color photos of how to interpret local weather phenomena, such as clouds, wind direction, and velocity, to predict the weather you'll likely face each day. A practical approach to being your own weather forecaster, wherever you are.

# Index

Page numbers in *italics* refer to illustrations.